Strategic International Human Resource Management

MORE PRAISE FOR
STRATEGIC INTERNATIONAL HUMAN RESOURCE MANAGEMENT

"This must be one of the best researched and referenced books on international human resource management that has been written in a long time. The research is both academic and practical... [and] deals with the subject at a very high level looking at the choices and consequences that organizations face when operating in an international market.
The balance between the practical and academic is a strong feature of the book and one of the few I have found that crosses both streams satisfactorily. Also, it not only covers all aspects of HR management but details the interactions and interdependencies of each aspect in an international context.
It really is a 'must have' text for anyone researching or operating in international human resource management."
Clive Wright, Chair, Reward Forum, CIPD and European Partner, Mercer Human Resource Consulting, Chartered FCIPD

"Students taking Masters programmes and MBAs will find this book particularly suitable. It is lively and well-informed, and aims to combine discussion of strategic choices in international HRM with an analysis of their consequences for real people – employees and managers."
Michael Gold, School of Management, Royal Holloway University of London

"Perkins and Shortland have produced an invaluable volume for both students and practitioners alike. Uniquely, they link the theory and practice of international HRM in a clear and understandable way. They also raise key issues, both in the text and in relevant and thought-provoking questionnaires, which can form the basis of further enquiry and activity by both students (and their tutors) in academic discourse and by practitioners in facing new and/or difficult business issues."
Alan Chesters, International HR Consultant and Accredited CIPD Examiner

"At last! – in the growing literature on international human resource management (IHRM) a book which focuses on the strategic choices and decisions faced by individuals and groups in multinational management and the consequences flowing from these. Stephen Perkins and Susan Shortland's book is especially valuable in describing and evaluating strategic IHRM in practice whilst at the same time engaging with different theoretical approaches to the subject."
Professor Linda Clarke, Westminster Business School, University of Westminster

Strategic International Human Resource Management

Choices and Consequences in Multinational People Management

Second edition

Stephen J Perkins & Susan M Shortland

KOGAN
PAGE

London and Philadelphia

Publisher's note

Every possible effort has been made to ensure that the information contained in this book is accurate at the time of going to press, and the publishers and authors cannot accept responsibility for any errors or omissions, however caused. No responsibility for loss or damage occasioned to any person acting, or refraining from action, as a result of the material in this publication can be accepted by the editor, the publisher or any of the authors.

First published in Great Britain and the United States in 1999 by Kogan Page Limited as *Globalization: the people dimension*

Second edition published in 2006

120 Pentonville Road	525 South 4th Street, #241
London N1 9JN	Philadelphia PA 19147
United Kingdom	USA
www.kogan-page.co.uk	

© Stephen J Perkins and Susan M Shortland, 2006

The right of Stephen Perkins and Sue Shortland to be identified as the authors of this work has been asserted by them in accordance with the Copyright, Designs and Patents Act 1988.

ISBN 0 7494 4357 X

British Library Cataloguing-in-Publication Data

A CIP record for this book is available from the British Library.

Library of Congress Cataloging-in-Publication Data

Perkins, Stephen J.
  Strategic international human resource management: choices and consequences in multinational people management / Stephen Perkins and Sue Shortland.– 2nd ed.
    p. cm.
  Rev. ed. of: Globalization : the people dimension : human resource strategies for global expansion 1999.
  Includes index.
  ISBN 0-7494-4357-X
  1. International business enterprises–Personal management. 2. International business enterprises–Employees. 3. Employees–Recruiting. 4. Employment in foreign countries. I. Shortland, Sue. II. Perkins, Stephen J. Globalization. III. Title.
HF5549.5.E45P428 2006
658.3–dc22

                              2006001623

Typeset by Digital Publishing Solutions
Printed and bound in the United States by Thomson-Shore, Inc

Contents

Figures and tables   *viii*
Preface   *ix*
Acknowledgements   *xiii*

**Part One   Theorizing strategic international human resource   1
              management**

Introduction: SIHRM choices and consequences   3
Introduction 4; Defining choice and consequence(s) in SIHRM 6;
Choices in the context of competing international managerial
streams 9; Conceptualizing strategic choice making and its
consequences 12; Material influences on SIHRM choices 16;
Summary reflections 17; Outline of subsequent chapters 18

**1 Globalization and international HRM orientations: choices and   25
    consequences**
Theorizing globalization and its corporate consequences 29;
Governance and SIHRM implications 32; Inexorable or 'bargained'
globalization? 35; Globalization and 'The Jones Corporation' 36;
Devil in the detail? 40; Concluding remarks 41

Part Two   Applying strategic international human resource   49
management in practice

2   Culture, welfare and international mobility: choices and   51
consequences
The influence of culture 53; Culture shock 64; Managing
international assignment stress 66; Repatriation and reverse culture
shock 72; International mobility and implications for the
psychological contract 74; Concluding remarks 75

3   Choices and consequences in resourcing global business   79
operations
Introduction 80; The increasing pace of organizational resource
internationalization 81; The process of organization and employee
resource internationalization 81; Managing strategic international
investments 83; International leadership resourcing: the
international cadre 87; International executive recruitment 90;
Identifying international executive capabilities 92; Specifying
international competencies 92; Psychological research on international
adaptation 95; The selection process for internationally mobile
employment 96; Women and international assignments 99;
Repatriation of internationally assigned employees 100; Expatriate
employee localization 102; Concluding remarks 103

4   Training and development in the global environment: choices   107
and consequences
Introduction 108; International training 108; International
development 122; Strategic HRD: local training and development
interventions 131; Concluding remarks 133

5   Choices and consequences in international employee   137
compensation
Introduction 138; Definitions: substance and process in reward
management 140; Culture and beyond: national, industry and
corporate contexts 143; Thinking through choices and consequences
in international reward systems 145; Defining 'multinational'
employees for reward management purposes 147; Strategic choices:
organizational formations and leadership profiles – imperial
governors, expatriate ghetto residents, global champions? 147;
Reward strategies for internationally mobile executives 155; Intra-
region mobility and diversity: 'third-country national' rewards 165;
Managing the effort–reward bargain for non-headquarters-
sourced employees 166; Evaluating normative commentary: theory
and practice 170; Observable transnational practices 173;

Designing rewards for the internationalizing business unit 176; Concluding remarks 178; Technical appendix Part 1: Guiding principles for expatriation: the 10-stage journey 182; Technical appendix Part 2: International assignee remuneration approaches 185; Technical appendix Part 3: International contracts and the global employment company 196

6   **Choices and consequences in international employment   201
       relations**
Introduction 202; Regulating employment relations 203; Managerial strategies: global rules – multi-local processes? 206; Extra-managerial roles in regulating employment relations systems 211; The dependent state and diversity in employment relations consequences 216; Regulatory norms under pressure? 219; Giving voice to human resources and resourceful humans? 222; Experimentation: the (new) norm in employment relations practice? 224; Concluding remarks 227

7   **Choices and consequences: SIHRM trends and priorities?**   235
Global consensus on top HR issues 235; Change management 238; Leadership development 240; Measuring HR effectiveness 243; Concluding remarks 244

Index   *249*

Figures and tables

FIGURES

0.1 Framing material influences on strategic international HRM 17
5.1 Excess cost versus excess value of using expatriates 162
6.1 State and trade union interactions in employment systems 213

TABLES

1.1 Stylized phases of globalization 30
1.2 The impact of alternative governance drivers 35
3.1 Matching capabilities to strategic business requirements, retaining core capabilities which differentiate the business to win, and outsourcing non-core activities 85
5.1 Multinational structures and international employee reward principles 149
5.2 The 'expat-flexible-pot' approach 164
5.3 Paying people right? 169
6.1 Indicators for a two-system comparison 205
6.2 Influences and viewpoints on employment relations strategies 208
6.3 Trends in employment relations 226

Preface

The major theme of this book is the need for careful attention to the choices individuals and groups face as people management is approached as a strategic and international phenomenon, and the consequences that flow from those choices. We are both English Europeans; our education and experience have taken place within western human resource management (HRM) traditions. Our interpretation of the cases and stories that illustrate our arguments reflects in some way the people we are, and the preparation we have had to write a book such as this over the course of our professional careers to date. We cannot alter those characteristics now, even though for many years we both have been engaged in, and exposed to, the substantive and ideological fabric of organizational life in a globalizing world.

As practitioners, and as university lecturers supervising our students' developing education and research profiles, we interact with people associated with the people management field from diverse geographies, cultures and institutional settings. We continue to draw strength from their diversity, but our experiences and how we remember and interpret them inevitably reflect our subjective experience. We have tried, however, to challenge and provoke one another to think about and comment on that experience.

We have tried to be systematic, as a minimum, and objective as far as possible in weighing the multiple knowledge claims and forms of evidence that we present. But we do not attempt to offer our views as though they hold universal significance; and we do not try to avoid the fact that we do not think or interpret evidence exactly as Africans or Asians, Americans or Antipodeans might do.

The book is directed largely at people who are part of an organization's efforts to internationalize, either as part of the 'home' outward-bound team, or accountable for supporting initiatives in host countries. It should be of interest to both practitioners and students. We begin by considering the problems encountered in managing western (probably Anglo-American) enterprises, for profit or motivated otherwise, across the world's countries and continents.

However, we hope that what we have to say will be of equal interest to those on the receiving end of western investment and transnational policy (which includes the initiatives of the International Monetary Fund (IMF), the World Bank, and other supranational non-governmental organizations, as well as regional entities such as the European Union). Those in both developed and developing countries who are directly or indirectly associated with Anglo-American forms of organization are likely to encounter normative HRM commentary that has largely emerged from English-speaking countries: in particular the United Kingdom and the United States, but there are increasingly significant Australasian contributions to the literature. Sometimes there is a nod in the direction of Japanese past practice.

Students from a multiplicity of locations worldwide enrol at Anglo-American business schools. We hope to have something of interest to say to all of them, whether their backgrounds mirror ours or differ greatly from them. However, we want you to be clear about our credentials: we may be cosmopolitan in outlook and experience, but the prism of our formative years still shapes our experience in both personal and work situations. Although inwardly this book is a result of reflection on our experiences as practising specialists in the arenas of strategic international HRM, outwardly it is intended to encourage reflection on the part of our readers.

Throughout the book, we comment reflexively on two issues. The first concerns the strategic HRM dilemmas facing choice-takers who aim to build and sustain transnational enterprises. They need to find ways to synthesize organizational know-how and revenue-stream diversity, in a world where events over the past half-decade have severely destabilized interpersonal trust and commitment. The second involves the ways in which emergent conceptual frameworks, and new theoretical insights relevant to international HRM, may be harnessed to underpin an analysis of the events and ideas that have a strategic impact on the people dimension of global business management. In so doing, we draw and build on Stephen's earlier work in *Globalization: The people dimension* (1999).

Reflecting these two points, we have divided the book into two sections. In Part One, we engage with the theoretical approaches. There are several approaches that may be used as frameworks for the HRM aspects of international business development, and we consider how they might be selected, and how they shape the specification and interpretation of choices and consequences, as multinational managements and their advisers attempt to organize and manage their staff.

In Part Two, we move beyond the theory to describe and evaluate strategic international human resource management (SIHRM) in practice. Our aim is to demonstrate and assess the merits of applying SIHRM and related theory in support of corporate strategies and diverse business systems. We also take account of how individual employees perceive their interactions with multinational organizations. We consider the usefulness of competing theories, but our emphasis is on applied analysis of real-world situations. We analyse the strategic challenges faced by general and specialist managers reflexively overseeing organizational behaviour in pursuit of transnational competitive advantage and value creation.

References are given at the end of each chapter, rather than in a complete bibliography at the end of the book. We felt on balance that this would make sources of further reading more easily accessible for those who wish to follow up on the detail.

We hope the text will come to be regarded as essential reading for MBA and related business management students, and practising managers alike, as they encounter the trials and tribulations, as well as the joys of interaction and discovery, involved with strategic international HRM.

REFERENCE

Perkins, S J (1999) *Globalization: The people dimension*, Kogan Page, London

Acknowledgements

There are a number of people whom we would like to acknowledge as having supported this project. We would like to thank in particular Helen Kogan for having commissioned the work, as well as all the staff at Kogan Page who have helped in the technicalities of its production. We would also like to thank our correspondents for sharing their stories with us, without which our 'picture postcards' could not have been brought to life. Thanks are due also to our professional colleagues who have reviewed the text – your comments have been invaluable. Finally, as with any project, there are choices and consequences. It was our choice to write this book; Erica, George and Laura have had less of our attention as a consequence. We therefore dedicate this book to them.

Part One

Theorizing strategic international human resource management

Introduction: SIHRM choices and consequences

CHAPTER AIMS

This chapter sets out to do the following:

▌ introduce you to the notion of 'choice and consequence' interactions that are relevant to strategic international human resource management (SIHRM) approaches;

▌ explore the alternative conceptualizations of strategy that influence organization and associated approaches to people management internationally;

▌ outline a contextual model for evaluating interactions between organizational strategy, transnational business systems and human capital perspectives;

▌ summarize the chapters that follow this introduction.

INTRODUCTION

What are the choices faced in approaching strategic international human resource management (SIHRM)? Are the parties to SIHRM a homogeneous social entity? How can the strategy that informs choices be conceptualized? And what are the influences (via knowledge claims) on this conceptualization? How do settings inform agency from the perspective of organizational strategy? This can be seen in two senses: there are alternative contexts for business systems, and different perceptions of the views of the targets of HRM strategy. In what ways do logic, on the one hand, and reported empirical research findings, on the other, help us to predict what will happen if we make particular choices in this context?

Silverman (1993: viii) observes:

> A textbook writer has two options. The first option is to write a general survey of the field, covering the territory in a fairly dispassionate manner. This has the advantage of conveying to the student many competing positions without imposing the author's view. The second option is to structure the book around a central argument. This is likely to produce a more lively and integrated text – but at the cost of fairness and range.

As our opening set of pointed questions should make clear, on the whole we have chosen the second option. We hope this book has a fairly clear argument. However, although there are various models derived from political economy that can be used to govern the choices made by those involved in SIHRM, we have tried to avoid the temptation to assert that particular models are 'right' or 'wrong'. We have also tried not to take sides on issues where views are particularly polarized: for instance on HRM convergence versus divergence, and individualism versus collectivism.

So what is our central argument? Many textbooks introduce this 'rapidly developing field' (Scullion, 2005: 3), which can be considered as a subfield within applied management science, by outlining the 'challenges' faced by organizations in an 'internationalizing' (Harzing and Van Ruysseveldt, 2004; Ozbilgin, 2005) or even 'globalizing' (Evans, Pucik and Barsoux, 2002) context. They look at the implications of this context for human resource management, and the interplay between organization and people management strategies (Scullion, 2005). Sometimes they try to outline a specifically culturally focused, comparative or 'multinational' approach to the topic. The latter approach tends to emphasize the firm as the unit of analysis (Jackson, 2002; Harris, Brewster and Sparrow, 2003; Dowling and Welch, 2004). This range of emphases reflects the complexities of international HRM. However, common to all of these approaches is a widespread view that HRM should be regarded as 'strategic to business success' (Boxall and Purcell, 2003).

Each of these viewpoints merits consideration. However, our approach is cautious. We feel there is a risk of reifying institutions and/or practices. As we see it, it is rather that institutions and practices form the spaces within which the purposeful organizing and management of people is influenced and takes place (Watson, 2005). Organizations do not act: it is people in them with the authority and power to make choices who act.

Agency is based on an assessment by individuals and groups of their accountabilities and options. Not least, it reflects their own interests when they reproduce their relations with others in economic, political, social and technological contexts.

A second cautionary note needs sounding here. It is a precarious endeavour to approach international HRM as though 'strategic' courses of action may be read off some form of template. This is so whether the template emphasizes norms or 'best practices', or the need to match managerial agency to the circumstances in which operations are to be located. It is entirely possible to choose to do either of these things, as a blanket approach or case by case, or even to set out to blend the two extremes into hybrid forms of employment coordination. Our purpose, though, is to highlight the merits of informed premeditation.

Management students and practitioners alike may benefit in their interpretations and decision taking from reflecting on the choices that individuals and groups associated with international organization might make. They also benefit from weighing carefully the complex network of consequences that might arise from these choices, drawing either on rational abstraction or empirical data sources. This should save them from entering into what could prove to be uninformed (or ideologically misdirected) commitments. It is easy to fall prey to ideological misdirection if you read literature uncritically (including that on offer from a range of commercially focused agencies), or try to follow unitary forms of corporate governance imperatives in too doctrinaire a way.

Our argument is that there is merit in exploring the relationship between the various strategic choices organizational actors may make in pursuit of international activities. We draw attention to the assumptions underlying alternative choices available in framing 'people management' interventions, and the potential consequences that flow from them. In some cases, it may be necessary to explore the consequences by theorizing the logical implications. In others, it is possible to draw on empirical research, and we do this as far as possible in this book. 'Stories' of practice can also be used to summarize and learn lessons from a wide range of interventions. Such 'storytelling' provides coherence and helps us to make sense of a chaotic world.

We have of course had to make choices ourselves in deciding how best to illustrate our argument. We have chosen to draw upon 'picture postcards' (case vignettes, offering a transnational set of practical viewpoints). We hope their illustrations of SIHRM actions will be of benefit to you. Of course, we recognize that our choices have consequences for your understanding and interpretation of a complex and constructed social world.

The next part of this chapter will cover three principal aspects, derived from the outline proposition we have just put forward. First, if the notions of choice and consequences are significant in approaching SIHRM, what do these terms imply? We explore possible definitions to address this question. Second, we position SIHRM choice making in the context of heterogeneity in socio-political relations around the organizational control frontier (Edwards, 1990). Here 'streams' of management may be perceived as 'competing' (Teulings, 1986). Third, we reflect on the range of influences that may be drawn on to consider and evaluate the consequences arising from choice making.

Ideological influences flow from a variety of ways in which students and managers approaching the international organization and management of people consciously (or implicitly) draw on readings of the business strategy literature (Wright *et al*, 2005). At a more substantive level, we outline a model to help frame the dimensions on which competing managerial streams may engage with a series of interacting phenomena, centred on the goal of securing purposefully organized performance outcomes. We recommend you to give holistic consideration to the interactions between strategic principles, transnational business system settings, and employees' perceptions of their own interests. All this is done under the SIHRM rubric (Perkins and Hendry, 1999, 2001).

DEFINING CHOICE AND CONSEQUENCE(S) IN SIHRM

Human beings continuously exercise choices in both their private and organizational lives. We are concerned in this book with the latter, of course, although private lives may well spill over into the ways people act in employment settings. Sometimes this is something that is overtly sanctioned, depending on the nature of the organization (for example, it could be a small family-owned firm) and the geocultural location. Indeed, when it comes to moving people around the world, it is almost inevitable that their private lives will spill over into organizational decision making. This happens to a greater extent in this context than in almost every other aspect of HRM.

A theoretical vein within neoclassical economics contends that the organizational actor merely acts instinctively in pursuit of maximum material gain for minimum expenditure of effort (Watson, 2005). This deterministic view has influenced at least one strand of the strategy literature we explore (the strand of agency theory). However, in a rationally organized enterprise, it is possible to argue that choices about how to organize – including the organization of people in interaction with other forces of production and consumption – are made consciously. Our intention here is to explore the alternative ways in which managers weigh the alternative choices about how to organize and manage employees in an international context, and how they bear in mind the possible consequences of their decisions before the choice is made.

To some extent this can be seen as a logical exercise: if this is done, what will be the consequences? It can also be seen in the context of empirical research: similar decisions will have been made before, and the choices made and the outcomes have been observed and recorded. But what do the terms 'choice' and 'consequence' mean?

The noun 'choice' may be defined in a variety of ways, and several of them might be seen as relevant in a SIHRM context. Choice is first an 'act of choosing', involving 'preferential determination between things proposed' (Oxford English Dictionary (OED)). This conscious human act (or form of agency) involves making selections between possibilities, electing for one thing over one or more alternatives. The dictionary definition does not explore whether or not the act of choosing implicitly or explicitly involves taking likely outcomes into account.

An alternative definition sees choice as a positive-value word. Something is deemed to be 'choice' if it is 'picked' (for example, a 'choice companion' would be a desirable companion). It is excellent or even elite: 'the pick' (OED) of what is on offer, chosen as 'the preferential part of anything' (OED). It may reflect esteem conferred on the object of the choice – someone or something worthy of being chosen, having 'special value' (OED) to the chooser. Being without choice, by contrast, implies selecting something 'without distinction, indiscriminately' (OED). Of course, there is the well-known phrase 'Hobson's choice', used to indicate that the choice taker is faced with the option of what is on offer or nothing.[1]

Having choice may be indicative of power – the one who has options, reflecting a dispositional advantage relative to others, conferring a right to choose – a privileged (socially located) situation, where one is 'at choice' or 'at pleasure', enjoying the right or privilege of choosing (OED). This situation may also imply someone who enjoys an abundance and/or variety (of choices), providing scope to choose from among a range of alternatives. The choice may be the person or thing chosen; acting with choice may also be defined as decision taking that reflects judgement or circumspection.

Choice, as defined here, thus has an active disposition. It locates decision takers socially relative to others, and it implies, among other things, the exercise of discrimination and judgement to secure the most favourable (or fit-for-purpose) outcome. The aim is to attain something that is worthy of being chosen, that has special value relative to other available options.

But how do we make choices? How do we weigh options, and shoulder the responsibility of selecting the best one? One way of addressing this question is by reference to knowledge. As we mentioned above, this might involve either logical analysis or empirical evidence, to help us select the preferred outcome (that is, one that is anticipated and accords with the project being pursued by the chooser).

Once again, we turn to the OED for definitions of the noun 'consequence'. At its simplest, consequence may be defined as 'a thing or circumstance which follows as an effect or result from something preceding' (OED). As a second definition, consequence is 'the action or condition of following as a result upon something antecedent; the relation of a result or effect to its cause or antecedent' (OED). In this second definition, there is a suggestion that the consequence of a particular choice is predetermined (part of a cause and effect relationship). But is the matter so clear-cut? Arguably it is not, especially where social relations are involved, as in the case of choosing between international human resource management strategies.

Consequences can form a logical sequence, starting with a specific choice; and in some circumstances it is possible for them to be deduced logically from premises – 'a logical inference' (OED). But clearly this is not always so. Sometimes judgement is necessary in predicting or inferring consequences, and there is no absolute certainty what the consequences will be. In these contexts, it is useful to draw on empirical knowledge. When no past knowledge is available, another option is scenario building: using logic to accumulate 'virtual experience' (de Geus, 1997). Here, it is impossible to know in advance what the actual consequence of a choice will be, but it is possible to predict or simulate possible sequences of events for the benefit of 'organizational learning'.

Empirical reports themselves, of course, need to be viewed critically. Any historical or analytical 'discourse' may be constructed in a variety of ways to suit the purpose of the analyst or patron.

The 'sequel' (OED) to the act of choosing may take a variety of forms. The 'round game' of consequences, in which a narrative of the meeting between two persons, their conversation, and the ensuing 'consequences', is 'concocted by the contribution of a name or fact by each of the players, in ignorance of what has been contributed by the others' (OED), may form a useful analogy here.

A range of scenarios and reported observations may usefully be weighed before making judgements about the likely consequences flowing from choices in SIHRM, therefore. However, to move on to an alternative definition, choices may lead to outcomes that are 'of consequence': that is, they are endowed with 'importance, moment, weight' or 'assumed consequentiality' (OED). They have an impact (positive or negative) on the people and circumstances in which the choice plays out. The corollary of this assertion is that students and managers alike will benefit from consideration of the possible or likely (inferred) consequences of their choices. This will enrich their stock of knowledge in attempting to make sense of issues surrounding the field of SIHRM.

CHOICES IN THE CONTEXT OF COMPETING INTERNATIONAL MANAGERIAL STREAMS

SIHRM choices should not be considered in isolation. Instead, analytical attention should be paid to how one set of interested choices interacts with the choices exercised by others – other groups of managers (in particular those who are accountable for applying policy), organizational partners, investors and customers/consumers, as well as the wider community. Choices thus give rise to relations, and these may lead to forms of negotiation. At the very least there is a need for effective dialogue (not just one-way communication) between parties whose material and ideological positions are not necessarily consistent with those of the policy maker.

If this is taken to be so, it follows that organizational actors should not be regarded as a homogeneous mass. Rather, they form dynamically competing streams of interest (Teulings, 1986; Perkins, 2004). If we are to avoid reifying organizations, and treating them as though they were independent socio-economic actors, we need to pay attention to the ways in which choices and consequences result from competition and contestation between the different actors within the organization. This is true both at micro level (the spaces created within organizations) and at macro level (in markets, in which dominant organizational actors also compete to sustain their capacity for independent action).

We would argue that both material circumstances and ideological positions have become more polarized over the last few years. This has led to a variety of alternative cultural and world views. In the context of purposeful efforts to organize and manage people internationally, we need to be aware of these differences, and to reflect carefully on the possible consequences of choices which might lead either to cooperation, or to conflict and confusion, before we go on to act on those choices.

Following this line of reasoning, managers and their representatives inside and outside multinational organizations may perceive the options available differently. On the basis of these perceptions, they then compete to impose the interested logic of productive organization on the enterprise. Given indeterminacy in systems of employment (Marsden, 1999), this involves taking advantage not only of dispositional factors (who has the greater material control over organizational resources) but also of ideological factors (Perkins, 2004). There is a battle for ideas surrounding organizations, and this becomes increasingly complex, the greater the scale of the organization and the more geographically and culturally dispersed it is.

Individuals entering the firm, either as managers or at other levels, will have been socialized by their prior experience in both their public and private lives. This might lead them to adopt varying views of the bases on which organization and employment relations can be effected and legitimated.

The issue is particularly significant for dominant interests: for example, foreign direct investors (FDI) and their managerial representatives. When they enter a new business environment, they face choices about the degree to which they can, and should, use organizational resources to socialize others to a particular project. For example, this might involve the system of governance and its implications for members of the organization. Take the example of empowering local staff to act in the corporate interest. Managerial representatives of foreign capital, probably coming from the neo-liberal tradition, might perceive that the local staff tend to adopt a different view on the political economy of organizations. Perhaps their tradition places equal or greater emphasis on securing a social contract, using economic resources to provide social welfare rather than individual wealth accumulation. To what extent should they empower the local staff in these circumstances?

There might well be perceived to be a disconnect in this situation, and it could be argued that only the expatriate overseer from the parent country is in a position to manage the potential contradictions in the company's best interests. On the other hand, there is a cost to making this choice. There are many arguments for using local staff to the greatest degree possible, including issues of morale and the need to use them to secure 'insider' status in consumer markets. In these circumstances those allocating corporate resources might conclude that it is necessary to make significant efforts to socialize the local staff into the firm's way of thinking. If this is not fully achievable, given their different background and orientation, at least this should be done to a sufficient degree to appease the financial backers, since corporate management's legitimacy rests on their approval.

If this socialization is not achieved, in this context there could clearly be negative repercussions. The financial investment could be transferred elsewhere, either through sales of stock, or through a hostile corporate takeover. The perceived 'errant' managerial regime might be neutralized by loss of autonomy, or even removed from office.

These differences of perception are not only found in managerial streams: lower-level employees too have different perceptions and values. Employees might be socialized to a 'habitual' perception (Veblen, cited by Watson, 2005), in which they are resigned to a status as an atomized, hired labour commodity. Alternatively, their prior experience might lead them to expect to take a more proactive role in the organization. They might be used to collective action. They might have, or perceive themselves to have, the actual or latent power to influence effort–wage bargaining, and an awareness of how this can be used to provide collectively created value for private financial investors. Domestic institutions (the state, employer federations and the like) might sanction this kind of dynamic relationship bargaining around employment; or again, they might not.

As another alternative, employees might perceive themselves primarily as citizens engaged in communally dependent economic projects, but for communal rather than private benefit. Again, the issue is whether dominant inward-investing interests in the multinational corporation have the power (and inclination) to enforce a different world view, and how they might set about doing so. They might, for example, call on supranational institutions such as the International Monetary Fund (IMF) and the World Bank to reconfigure the economic context along neo-liberal lines through 'structural adjustment' programmes. Alternatively, they could call upon local state representatives to enforce their world view (Bhopal and Todd, 2000). Yet another option is to invest in socialization initiatives to persuade employees to adapt to the corporate norm. These might be reinforced with material resources, for example individualized cash incentive schemes for those who display the 'appropriate' traits.

People's individual subjectivities are complex and multiple. Which one should the firm appeal to: employee/commodity labourer, citizen, parent/homemaker? And in what ways might the subjects be expected to respond? They are independent, albeit habituated, choice makers in their own right.

Other key questions follow for corporate initiatives. Is it legitimate to use SIHRM policy making and its practical application in order to enforce a dominant view of what constitutes 'effective' international organization and its people dimension? Is its role to try to homogenize the members of specific corporate entities? Should they be expected to accommodate their own interests, and the ways in which they behave (through either habit or conviction), to an externally imposed diktat? What credence should be given to a dispositionally advantaged (Edwards, 1986, 2003) culturally specific (or ethnocentric) form of governing ethos, and what impact should it have on the division and application of labour?

The power of SIHRM actors is socially constructed, and hence provisional and subject to cooperation on the part of other affected social actors. What are the implications for the choices multinational corporate choice takers might exercise in framing, delegating to operational overseers, and thus implementing people strategies across the various constituent parts of the enterprise? And to adopt a holistic orientation to SIHRM, how does this impact on the diverse functional elements of the HRM portfolio (hiring and firing, socialization, deploying, resourcing and appraising, rewarding, developing staff and so on)?

CONCEPTUALIZING STRATEGIC CHOICE MAKING AND ITS CONSEQUENCES

Considering issues associated with the notion of choice in the international organization and management of people leads us to make linkages with propositions in the literature on strategy. The world-renowned Harvard economist Michael Porter has argued that, at its most basic, strategy 'is about making tough choices' (quoted in Hammonds, 2001: 150). That is to say, it revolves around the weighing of alternative courses of action which are accompanied by the need to invest scarce organizational resources. We have argued that adopting a strategic approach to international human resource management involves exercising choice, accompanied by consequences. The search is then for the means to evaluate the consequences that flow from choosing to follow specific paths in international people management policy and practice.

But what is 'strategy' in this picture? Are there different interpretations of what is, at first glance, a singular term (Whittington, 2001)? How can interested parties decide which they are working with, and the implications of embarking on a course of action that follows? What is the impact, for example, of adopting a normatively informed HRM approach? What does the literature have to say about the experience of organizations operating in countries around the world depending on their adoption of particular approaches (for example, based on what they have traditionally done in the country of origin, as opposed to doing what they think they need to do to fit in with the indigenous operational environment (Anakwe, 2002))? Of course there are many variations between these two themes, not only across countries but, it has been argued (Brewster, 2001; Bloom, Milkovich and

Mitra, 2003), on an intra-national basis too, depending on what organization managers feel disposed to do, or think they can attempt to get away with.

Where are the ideas influencing policy choices coming from? Whose view will prevail, assuming there is a debate within the organization over the most effective ideas to draw on? What are the mechanisms to weigh ideas on their merits? And will the ideas be subjected to scrutiny based on a particular view of corporate strategy, or cultural assumptions across the operating regions and countries, or the views of individuals themselves? What choices are actors in multinational entities being exhorted to take? What stated or implicit assumptions underlie the normative prescriptions, taking account of business strategy, business systems and human capital perceptions and their interactions? What choices are being taken according to empirical research, and again, what underlying assumptions appear to be involved? And what consequences are being mapped?

Four major perspectives in the strategy literature may be helpful in interpreting the ways in which international organization managers conceptualize and weigh the choices they are faced with in approaching the employment and coordination of people in pursuit of organizational objectives (Wright et al, 2005). These are (in no particular order) transactional cost theory, agency theory, resource-based theory (sometimes developed under a 'core competencies' rubric), and institutional theory.

Transactional cost theory (eg Williamson, 1975) focuses on which form of transaction cost management – market, hierarchy or hybrid – is the most appropriate in governing an organization. Agency theory (eg Jensen and Meckling, 1976) emphasizes attention to ways in which the organization can be governed so that managers' (agents') and shareholders' (principals') interests are aligned. Resource-based theory (eg Barney, 1991) puts the spotlight on the internal resources of the organization as the basis for explaining the differences between firms and the ways they secure sustainable competitive advantage in internationally open product markets. Institutional theory (eg March and Olsen, 1989) draws attention to the ways in which organizational behaviour may be shaped by the economic, political and social systems that form the environment in which commercial and productive activity takes place.

Thus, transactional cost theory-oriented HRM choice making will place stress on the cost of getting things done where, for example, stable versus unstable political structures and/or well-developed or inadequate infrastructural features (such as the general levels of education and skills available to employers) feature highly in the assumptions underpinning policy and practice. To some extent the same may apply to agency theory, where the scope for corrupt practice and/or commercial capabilities of indigenous managers are likely to feature in the assumptions regarding the potential of local recruits to act as agents, with the primacy of the firm's owners at the forefront of considerations. Resource-based theory-influenced assumptions will lead decision makers to factor in the ways that accumulated core competences in the organization of production will impact on the fortunes of the organization. For example, in a transforming or emerging economy, there could be a devaluation of the net worth of organizational resources that were valuable under a previous regime, when subjected to 'market liberalization' initiatives.

A core question for resource-based theory-influenced SIHRM is how organizational actors and associated interest groups may overcome barriers to the acquisition of capabilities and resources necessary to succeed in more internationally 'open' operating conditions. In the case of developed economies, exposed to 'globalization' market pressures, the quest becomes one of shaking off apparent rigidities that once-valuable corporate resources might be perceived as imposing (for example, stable employment relations structures).

Institutional theory influences on HRM choice makers' assumptions are likely to lay particular stress on the speed of institutional adaptation to the continuously changing organizational environment (for example, 'globalization' pressures, to be discussed in Chapter 1). As will be evident from the preceding comments, institutional theory-informed decision taking involves consideration of the ways in which institutional theory interacts with the other theories, and the ways in which it retains or diminishes in importance as changes in the organizational and wider environment that enable and constrain productive operations bring other theoretically derived issues to the fore. So an enhanced institutional basis for managing the cost of transactions, or aligning managerial and shareholder interests, or the sedimentation of resources that are rare, valuable, non-substitutable and inimitable (Barney, 1991), might lessen the need for attention to the comparative nature of the institutional environment in which HRM policy and practice is formed and enacted.

There are choices (with consequences) to be made around specifying the resource base for productive activity in international operations: for example, the degree of care and prior consideration given to how potential employees can be identified, attracted, screened/evaluated and socialized into the organization. One of the key choices is the purpose – explicit or otherwise – of making a hiring decision. Multinational organization leaders must consider this in their dealings with international sources of labour to support the application of business strategies. This choice is made in the context of choices about the division of labour across the organization. Is the aim simply to achieve the most performance from people at the least cost (and what does 'cost' mean in this context?), and to find employees who will fulfil this? Questions like this might be articulated as the result of transaction cost theory and/or agency theory-influenced thinking. Alternatively, reflecting the influence of resource-based theory and institutional theory, is the general aim founded on the view that sustainable productive endeavour in contemporary competitive exchange markets is founded on the knowledge and skills of the people with whom the organization builds a relationship? Is this relationship a generic one, or is there a distinction made between people in certain roles, levels and/or locations?

There are choices and consequences too around the basis and level of investment to be made subsequent to hiring: in nurturing, training and developing the various components of the international workforce. This is true both of individual employees and of groups or work teams. There are choices about the ways in which the (indeterminate) relationship may be developed, and the institutional arrangements surrounding that development, as well as the substance of relationship maintenance. There are choices around how people are to be instructed in what is expected of them, how they will be supported in performing their roles, and the basis of appraisal and evaluation of the contribution they make to the organization in their local, regional and global places in the organizational network. And there are choices to be made around how the workforce in its various forms is to be rewarded and recognized for its contribution to local and corporate success.

A lot of assumptions will be built in to the way these choices are exercised. These assumptions necessarily reflect the theoretical underpinnings of the organization and governance strategy selected by corporate managements. Those making the decisions, as well as those advising them, would be well advised to have the means systematically to reflect openly and transparently on what the assumptions are, and the implications for applying them to inform policy and practice. What immediate and wider influences impact on the assumptions and attendant choices? What does this imply for the interpretation of the organization, business and governance context, for the wider business systems around the world, and for the views and needs of the individuals and groups of employees targeted with the chosen policies and practices?

Multinational managers might choose to treat labour as a cost of production, or to regard the people the organization employs as 'human capital', a source of value to be invested in. In what ways does the organization regard its people as a whole, and in what ways does the international and functional division of labour appear to characterize such decision taking? Following on from these considerations, in what ways does the organization choose to account for its workforce – explicitly? And does it have a measurement system in place, capable of capturing benefits as well as costs of employment in different localities, and evaluating these phenomena holistically (Franklin, Mackie and Rigby, 2005)?

MATERIAL INFLUENCES ON SIHRM CHOICES

What are the assumptions that underlie the ways human resource management is understood and implemented, taking account of alternative contexts – for strategy, for business systems and for the people involved? (Those involved in this context include both the targets of the strategic choices and those accountable for managing the choices and consequences.) Drawing on systems theory, Hendry (2003) highlights a series of characteristic 'boundary tensions', around which change in employment practices takes place. He contends that these change processes may be seen all over the world, driven by economic and institutional influences. 'By focusing on these boundary tensions, we can see how changes in the external environment act as a lever to change approaches to employment' (Hendry, 2003: 1430).

The model outlined in Figure 0.1 is offered as a holistic, systemic basis for capturing and interpreting organizational agency to design and operate a performance-based employment relationship between multinational enterprises and their workforces. The influences on SIHRM outcomes are framed in terms of three sets of forces. First, there are the organizational and HRM priorities multinational managements set as they expand international operations. Second, there are the 'varieties of capitalism' characterizing particular 'business systems' (Whitley, 2000), combining cultural and institutional factors at national and regional levels. These impinge on individual and organizational orientations toward business and employment. These factors include corporate governance models and attitudes towards equity in the distribution of rewards from commercial undertaking and employment. Third, the framework takes into account human capital choices: 'the motivations and aspirations of people whom international businesses seek to attract, retain and motivate; the way they view the alternative career paths open to them; and the social and economic forces that shape their attitudes and opportunities' (Perkins and Hendry, 1999: 4).

The model offers an impression of spaces within which choices are affected by actors in the corporate strategy setting, in business systems contexts and on the part of targets of policy, all centred around the focus of a performance-based employment relationship. The meaning of 'performance-based' here could be subject to varying constructions depending on the parties to the contested terrain at the frontier of organizational control. Human capital

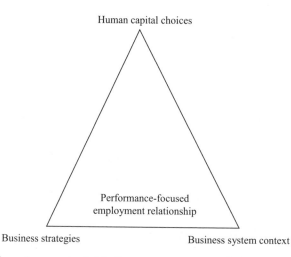

Human capital choices

Performance-focused
employment relationship

Business strategies   Business system context

Figure 0.1   Framing material influences on strategic international HRM

perspectives (these are far from homogeneous, of course – hence the plural-
ization) are also subject to the interpretations of the various categories of
corporate choice takers (different levels of line management, specialists
and so on) as well as of the individuals themselves. Consequences may be
weighed or emergent; anticipated or otherwise.

These considerations generate a triangular model, each element of which
remains in continuous dialectical interaction with the others. It has been assumed that there will be tensions between the elements, out of which specific
outcomes may emerge. The model may be used to orient empirical research
to explore the ways multinationals make choices about SIHRM systems. This
could be as a strategic conduit between organizational aims and objectives,
and managerial efforts to release the potential inherent in the workforce employed in various operations transnationally and in specific geographical
locations. Alternatively there could be a corporate order of strategy that
overshadows consideration of HRM subsystems (Purcell, 1992). This could,
for example, be a function of corporate governance preoccupations to satisfy
the demands of nominally footloose 'global' sources of finance capital.

SUMMARY REFLECTIONS

In this Introduction, so far, we have presented the argument that 'organization' is the product of decisions taken by human actors. Organizations and
institutional influences are not imbued with the capacity for independent
action. It is people who make choices that give rise to consequences – for

their corporate projects and for those affected by their choices. The character of corporate projects in particular times and spaces is subject to debate and contestation between competing streams of 'management' interests.

The ideological influences on decision takers and the choices they make as reflexive actors may be found in the various conceptualizations of corporate strategy – a concept that itself may be regarded essentially as a process of choosing where to locate scarce resources. At a more material level, the space within which the influences on competing managerial streams may be explored can be represented as a dynamic model which frames consideration of the material form of corporate strategy, the varying business systems contexts for its development and application, and the perspectives of different categories of human capital on whom SIHRM is targeted.

When we follow through the logic of multifaceted but holistically considered material influences, and alternative ideological prisms for interpreting the governance project and the resultant human relations through which it is mediated, we can discern possible consequences, either theoretically or empirically. In doing so we must be cognisant of the competing nature of the relations involving streams of management. Working through the process in this way may assist the student and practitioner of SIHRM in laying foundations on which to identify and evaluate the range of approaches to organizing and managing people internationally. These alternatives are then subject to the social act of choosing as a basis for purposeful corporate initiatives.

To conclude the Introduction we outline the coverage of the remainder of the book, which reflects this overarching conceptual stance.

OUTLINE OF SUBSEQUENT CHAPTERS

While we follow convention in the ensuing chapters of this book, and discuss the various elements that together make up the international human resource management (IHRM) portfolio, we do so in the knowledge that a strategic and holistically inclined approach demands attention throughout to the ways in which decisions and activity in one specialist domain (say, reward management) have consequences for other aspects (say, development and career management). At all times we strive to keep in mind the dynamic and interactive nature of the 'HR bundle' (Purcell, 1999), drawing attention to the interconnectedness of choices and consequences across the elements, whether these are contextual (globalization debates), or functional (resourcing, managing employment relations, training and developing, managing and rewarding performance and so on).

In Chapter 1, we engage with debates surrounding the 'globalization' phenomenon. This sets a macro context for consideration of approaches to SIHRM. We consider alternative ways in which commentators define and interpret globalization (as an economic, political and social phenomenon), and attempt to theorize its progress over the past three decades.

In this context SIHRM decision takers, interacting with discussions of the varieties of capitalism championed among others by Hall and Soskice (2001), have choices to make. What are the consequences in HRM terms of following 'neo-liberal' or 'social market' corporate governance prescriptions in organizing productive activity? These consequences are material for the multinational business project, since the decisions may involve the employment of individuals in countries whose traditions of political economy vary from those of multinational managers subject to the discipline of a particular variant of capitalism.

In Chapter 2, we consider the consequences of culture on international mobility and employee welfare. We provide a theoretical context, discussing societal culture, culture shock and the role of the psychological contract on employee performance, commitment, and business and individual success. These 'soft' issues are frequently passed over in strategic decision making in an international context. This chapter explores the potential folly of such a strategic choice by using theoretical and practical examples to demonstrate the impact of cultural and well-being issues in the global arena.

In Chapter 3, we consider the choices and consequences of employee resourcing in a rapidly internationalizing business environment. The issues explored include how business growth can be developed via strategies ranging from new start-ups to joint ventures. The recruitment and selection implications of various approaches, ranging from the use of local staff to international assignees from home or third-country locations, are explored both in practical terms and via theory. The chapter goes on to examine the implications of diversity in resourcing, and sets recruitment and selection of expatriates within a cycle including preparation and support, repatriation and localization. Drawing upon cultural and well-being issues examined in the previous chapter, it provides examples from the real world of choices and consequences in international resourcing.

In Chapter 4, we consider training and development in an international environment. Rather than focus solely on the traditional approach to these topics as examined in the expatriate literature, we consider them within the theoretical framework of learning. We therefore apply theories and models of learning and development to the training and development programmes typically used by international organizations. This might be seen as an unusual choice, but we believe that the consequences of understanding the role of learning theory in international training and development can be immensely beneficial, both in the design of the programmes themselves and in the investment decisions made when deciding their role, place and value within international assignment strategy. Training and development should not be viewed in isolation, so in addition we consider training and development interventions in the light of models of global growth. This relates this chapter to the previous one on resourcing. The cultural and employee well-being aspects associated with the need for training and development of international assignees are also addressed.

In Chapter 5, we turn our attention to the complexities surrounding the reward–effort bargain, which has been described as the symbolic and practical nexus – the point at which employee and employer interests interact most significantly. Given the extensive literature on the terms and conditions applicable to expatriation, as well as the literature on the contested issue of convergence around 'world's best practice' versus cross-national divergence, we have segmented the units of analysis. We distinguish multinational reward management practice directed towards an internationally mobile cadre, and that directed to the remaining 90 per cent of core payroll constituents. In the interests of holism we have chosen to make this a single chapter (incorporating a technical appendix), with the consequence that it is longer than the other chapters.

In Chapter 6, we build on the ideas developed in theorizing globalization and HRM, as well as the convergence line of reasoning, to explore the implications of privileging the notion of 'flexibility' at the centre of employment relations. Drawing on comparative literature on employment relations and employment systems, we identify the ways multinational organization managements appear to be experimenting in an era when 'deregulation' has been a dominant theme influencing policy makers around the world.

To conclude the book, in Chapter 7 we look briefly at perceived trends and managerial priorities that may influence choice making in SIHRM over the decade ahead.

YOUR TURN

To round off the introduction, there follow a series of questions that readers may wish to reflect on. These could also form the basis for seminar discussions in boardrooms or classrooms. We offer similar opportunities for reflection at the end of each subsequent chapter.

▌ What is the source of the organization leaders' conceptualization of strategy?

▌ How does this impact on the view of the relationship between people employed and the corporate governing objective of the organization?

▌ Is the managerial orientation towards the workforce universal, or does it vary between different categories, levels and locations of people employed to work in the organization?

▌ What is the view of human nature as this features in work and employment relationships? And how is this understanding translated into how employees' priorities and aspirations are perceived?

▌ What are the markets the organization wishes to operate in?

▌ What is the view of the business system in which the organization operates?

▌ Is it the view that strategies and practices may be transplanted from HQ to locations, or is adaptation required? Or is a transnational solution deemed desirable and/or possible?

▌ Is the point of comparison inter-country or some other measure on an intra-locational basis?

▌ What are the logical or empirically recorded consequences of the choices that these questions frame?

▌ What methodological basis have the key organizational actors chosen for assembling data to evaluate these strategic choices?

NOTE

1 'Hobson's choice' is a term named from Tobias Hobson, the Cambridge carrier (commemorated by Milton in two epitaphs), who let out horses, and is said to have compelled customers to take the horse which happened to be next to the stable door, or go without (OED).

REFERENCES

Anakwe, O P (2002) Human resource management practices in Nigeria: challenges and insights, *International Journal of Human Resource Management*, **13**(7), pp 1042–59

Barney, J (1991) Firm resources and sustained competitive advantage, *Journal of Management*, **17**(1), pp 99–120

Bhopal, M and Todd, P (2000) Multinational corporations and trade union development in Malaysia, *Asia Pacific Business Review*, **6**(3 & 4), pp 193–213

Bloom, M, Milkovich, G T and Mitra, A (2003) International compensation: learning from how managers respond to variation in local host contexts, *International Journal of Human Resource Management*, 14(8), pp 1350–67

Boxall, P and Purcell, J (2003) *Strategy and Human Resource Management*, Palgrave Macmillan, Basingstoke

Brewster, C (2001) HRM: the comparative dimension, in *Human Resource Management: A critical text*, ed J Storey, pp 255–71, Thomson, London

de Geus, A (1997) *The Living Company*, Nicholas Brealey, London

Dowling, P J and Welch, D E (2004) *International Human Resource Management: Managing people in a multinational context*, 4th edn, Thomson Learning, London

Edwards, P K (1986) *Conflict at Work: A materialist analysis*, Blackwell, Oxford

Edwards, P K (1990) Understanding conflict in the labour process: the logic and autonomy of struggle, in *Labour Process Theory*, ed D Knights and H Willmott, pp 125–52, Macmillan, Basingstoke

Edwards, P K (2003) *Industrial Relations: Theory and practice*, 2nd edn, Blackwell, Oxford

Evans, P, Pucik, V and Barsoux, J (2002) *The Global Challenge: Frameworks for international human resource management*, McGraw-Hill, London

Franklin, T, Mackie, B and Rigby, S (2005) Barriers to effective human resource measurement in New Zealand, *New Zealand Journal of Human Resource Management*, **5** (unpaged) [Online] http://www.humanresources.co.nz/articles/2005_articles/HRINZ_Barriers_Revised_1_Apr.doc, accessed 7 July 2005

Hall, P A and Soskice, D (2001) *Varieties of Capitalism: The institutional foundations of comparative advantage*, Oxford University Press, Oxford

Hammonds, K H (2001) Michael Porter's big ideas, *Fast Company*, 44, p 150

Harris, H, Brewster, C and Sparrow, P (2003) *International Human Resource Management*, Chartered Institute of Personnel and Development (CIPD), London

Harzing, A and Van Ruysseveldt, J (eds) (2004) *International Human Resource Management*, Sage, London

Hendry, C (2003) Applying employment systems theory to the analysis of national models of HRM, *International Journal of Human Resource Management*, **14**(8), pp 1430–42

Jackson, T (2002) *International Human Resource Management: A cross-cultural approach*, Sage, London

Jensen, M C and Meckling, W H (1976) Theory of the firm: managerial behavior, agency costs and ownership structure, *Journal of Financial Economics*, 3(4), pp 305–60

March, J G and Olsen, J P (1989) *Rediscovering Institutions: The organizational basis of politics*, Free Press, New York

Marsden, D (1999) *A Theory of Employment Systems*, Oxford University Press, Oxford

Oxford English Dictionary, Oxford University Press, Oxford

Ozbilgin, M (2005) *International Human Resource Management: Theory and practice*, Macmillan, Basingstoke

Perkins, S J (2004) A warranted manager's identity: leadership imperatives for shareholder value?, paper presented at 64th Annual Meeting of the Academy of Management, New Orleans, 6–11 August

Perkins, S J and Hendry, C (1999) *Guide to International Reward and Recognition*, Institute of Personnel and Development (IPD), London

Perkins, S J and Hendry, C (2001) Global champions: Who's paying attention?, *Thunderbird International Business Review*, **43**(1), pp 53–75

Purcell, J (1992) The impact of corporate strategy on human resource management, in *Human Resource Strategies*, ed G Salaman, pp 60–81, Sage, London

Purcell, J (1999) Best practice and best fit: chimera or cul-de-sac?, *Human Resource Management Journal*, **9** (3), pp 26–41

Scullion, H (2005) International HRM: an introduction, in *International Human Resource Management: A critical text*, ed H Scullion and M Linehan, pp 3–21, Palgrave Macmillan, Basingstoke

Silverman, D (1993) *Interpreting Qualitative Data: Methods for analysing talk, text and interaction*, Sage, London

Teulings, A (1986) Managerial labour process in organizational capitalism: the power of corporate management and the powerlessness of the manager, in *Labour Process Theory*, ed D Knights and H Wilmott, pp 142–65, Macmillan, Basingstoke

Watson, M (2005) *Foundations of International Political Economy*, Palgrave Macmillan, Basingstoke

Whitley, R (2000) *Divergent Capitalisms*, Oxford University Press, Oxford

Whittington, R (2001) *What is Strategy – and Does it Matter?* Thomson, London

Williamson, O E (1975) *Markets and Hierarchies*, Free Press, New York

Wright, M, Filatotchev, I, Hoskisson, R E and Peng, M W (2005) Strategy research in emerging economies: challenging the conventional wisdom, *Journal of Management Studies*, **42**(1), pp 1–33

1

Globalization and international HRM orientations: choices and consequences

---

CHAPTER AIMS

This chapter sets out to do the following:

▮ introduce you to the debates among academics and other commentators surrounding the notion of globalization and its impact;

▮ develop a theoretically informed view of how economic globalization has emerged historically and the consequences for decision taking related to organizing employment transnationally

▮ examine the proposition that the ideology of 'globalization' and the ideology associated with normative HRM may be joined in some way.

On the cusp of the present millennium, influential social commentators were unequivocal: the phenomenon of 'globalization' was reshaping our lives (Giddens, 1999), regardless of the human consequences (Bauman, 1998). Simultaneously, managers of commercial and not-for-profit organizations were on the receiving end of 'extravagant claims' for the 'universal applicability' of a best practice model of HRM, 'implying one recipe for successful HR activity' (Purcell, 1999: 26). Such claims prompt the questions to which this chapter is addressed. Can HRM be perceived as globalization's junior partner? Is there a discernible linkage between the ideas of 'globalization' and 'HRM', when HRM is considered in its paradigmatic form (that is, as a specific prescription for people management policy and practice)? And what are the implications for SIHRM choice making of the answers to these questions,? The problem sets the meta-level context for our enquiries, in subsequent chapters, into the choices and consequences for the range of activities that combine to make up the SIHRM portfolio.

Every organization is faced with the problem of utilizing human resources, and hence managing them in some way, from which it may be inferred that 'human resource management (HRM) is universal' (Brewster, 2001: 255). Do 'globalizing' trends imply the likely convergence of practice around a specific ideology of HRM, therefore? Alternatively, in spite of universalizing 'rhetorics' of HRM (Legge, 1995), is the presence of contextually embedded tendencies (Cheng and Cooper, 2003; Schuler, Budhwar and Florkowski, 2002) likely to sustain a 'local' character in how multinational managements apply HRM thinking, even where the organizational thrust is towards a common set of corporate governance norms? Do 'effective global HR strategies' ultimately depend on 'the ability to judge the extent to which an organization should implement similar practices across the world or adapt them to suit local conditions' (Brewster, Harris and Sparrow, 2002: 7)?

This chapter focuses initially on scoping the topic: it is easy to forget that the alternative definitions of globalization are grounded in specific perspectives with competing agendas. Comparative variation in the ways academic commentators choose to approach 'globalization', and the consequences for organization and people management, may profitably be evaluated heuristically. Comparative analysis facilitates attempts 'to distinguish the essential from the accidental, the simple from the complex, the primary from the derived' (Thomas and Znaniecki, 1974: 17, cited by Guth and Schrecker, 2002: 292). A heuristic evaluation may be defined as a method for discovering the extent to which an abstract concept might be useful, and this is linked by Nielsen (1994) to an iterative design process. Here our goal is to design a lens through which to look for possible associations between the abstractions of globalization and HRM.

Perspectives are presented below to compare and contrast the ways in which scholars are interpreting the concept of globalization and its consequences for people and employment, in theory and in practice. While not claiming to be exhaustive, the discussion attempts to shed some light on the underlying meaning with which key terms are imbued, before moving on to attempts to theorize socio-political interaction and its consequences among groups in the arena of global economic relations (Watson, 2005). In brief, our argument is that, at the macro-level, corporate governance norms evolving over the early years of the 21st century are being institutionalized in a tendency among mainstream western commentators to homogenize ways of thinking about organization, and the consequential substance and process of people management internationally. Observable practice among multinational managements, by contrast, is tempered at the micro-level by contestation and experimentation.

The topic of 'globalization' may be looked at from several angles, including its implicit grounding in unitarist and neo-liberal ideology, its status in relation to socially embedded institutions, and its assumed universalism and 'runaway' power (Giddens, 1999; Rowley, 2000).

The optimist

One definition of globalization is 'attracting foreign investment, while increasing exports and developing international alliances to penetrate new markets'. It is also 'a worldwide pressure for change' (Granell, 2000: 89). The same author argues that 'Globalization does not mean eliminating differences, imitating others, or allowing more developed nations to impose their models' (2000: 89). In place of what could be regarded as a negative judgement, Granell (a professor at a Venezuelan institution) adopts an optimistic view of the concept: 'It means integrating differences, putting together our strengths, building from the differences and being able to join efforts for a win-win process' (2000: 89). She presented evidence to the Australian Human Resource Institute Annual Convention of perceptions among respondents in academia, corporate business and consulting, surveyed across seven regions of the world, that globalization is one of the most important and frequent external trends and a pressure for organizational change. This 'globalization factor' (42 per cent) was followed closely by technology advances (40 per cent), skill shortages (36 per cent) and competition (33 per cent). Notwithstanding these general findings, the rank order of importance of globalization differed between the regions canvassed. Europeans, Japanese, American and Australian respondents put globalization as one of the strongest trends.[1] By comparison, Asia-Pacific (excluding Australia), Canadian and Venezuelan respondents gave top ranking to other trends such as domestic and global instability, technology and competition, suggesting the need to seek out contrasting perspectives.

The critic

Another definition of globalization is offered by the Australian Department of Foreign Affairs and Trade in a document cited by McKenna (2000: 75), as a phenomenon 'driven by many factors, of which technology, the related mobility of people, goods and ideas, and a liberal trading environment are perhaps the most obvious'. McKenna draws on this definition to argue that the term 'globalization' is 'inextricably linked with neo-liberal ideology and technophilic hyperbole to produce questionable "mantras"' (2000: 74). While on the surface based on an objective assessment of the 'facts', this techno-cratic discourse may have a hegemonic function (that is, it adopts the moral high ground to sanctify a politically interested position, by extension deni-grating alternative perspectives as irrational). Globalization sits alongside other such 'mantric notions' as enterprise, efficiency, productivity, interna-tional competitiveness, trade liberalization and the information economy (2000: 75). For McKenna they are (over)used to the point of meaninglessness, but as part of a discursive construction of reality that reinforces and natu-ralizes the overarching rationality of a neo-liberal political-economic system. Thus they become a touchstone for gaining closure over what is deemed legitimate in policy debate (and what is not). Discursive connections are made so that terms such as 'enterprise' (as in 'free' enterprise, uncontami-nated by non-market interventions – a neo-liberal political economic con-cept) become unquestioningly associated with 'flexibility' (for instance, to refer to a market for waged labour not 'burdened' with legal restrictions on employers, or interventions by third parties such as trade unions). The im-pression is created and embedded over time that enterprise (good, associated with freedom of self-expression) automatically interfaces with flexibility. Any challenge to the suppression of wage demands (or of workers' claims over the distribution of wealth creation) is branded inflexible (bad, associ-ated with 'anti-progressive' thought).

Disciplinary definitions and the 'regionalization' tendency

Attributed meanings can usefully be compared in commentaries on global-ization from four alternative disciplines: economics, strategy, marketing and organization studies (Floyd, 2001). Economists emphasize the 'freeing up of labour and capital flows'. Business strategy writers define globalization as applicable to an industry 'when it can achieve a competitive advantage from being global', although Floyd points out that there is a continuum from the economists' theorizing, concerned with the trade advantages associated with 'efficiency and low cost labour' (Floyd, 2001: 111).

Rather than a sole focus on the freeing up of capital and labour flows internationally, a management issue arises in this connection, given the emphasis on multinational managements' requirement to make increasing use of global networks, and to manage operations worldwide to supply various regions of the world with global products. Business/marketing commentators are cited by Floyd (2001) as suggesting that globalization arises from the interaction of modern technology and consumerism. The first of these (in the form of transport and information and communications technology (ICT)) extends global reach through an increased capacity to disseminate information and to deliver larger quantities of goods and services profitably across national borders. The latter is concerned with the convergence of national cultures, making 'products' saleable as 'desired'. Floyd alleges an Americanization in marketing activity to this end.

Organization theorists are cited by Floyd (2001: 112) as arguing that the globalization concept is weakly specified. By surfacing some of the prerequisites for true globalization, these commentators illustrate the barriers to the allegedly inexorable tendency. 'A truly global economy would be one in which national processes are subsumed in and transformed by international markets and conditions of production... the nation state is very much a key component in this definition' (Hirst, 1997, cited by Floyd, 2001: 112). Rather than speak of globalization, 'regionalization' may thus be more appropriate. 'Fully global companies are few and far between in addition to the fact that the formation of trading blocs supports trade within the bloc rather than outside' (2001: 112).[2] As an alternative in the same field, Ohmae is cited by Floyd as explaining globalization as the result of attempts by firms to insure against currency exchange rate volatility: they 'need to be in regions in order to neutralize these effects' (2001: 113).

THEORIZING GLOBALIZATION AND ITS CORPORATE CONSEQUENCES

Globalization is represented as a very 'current' phenomenon, viewed from a number of disciplinary and institutional vantage points (eg Hughes, 2002; Kaldor, 2000; OECD, 2002). Alternatively, globalization may be theorized as the outcome of a cumulative political economic trend-line that may be traced back at least three decades, having emerged in three distinct phases. Grahl (2002) has developed a stylized framework to catalogue the globalization of the international capital finance system, which brings to the surface implications for corporate organization and employment. Employers are subjected to pressures to change the substance and process of their relationship with the workforce. An important consequence of the phased, emergent nature of economic globalization is that it has encouraged policy makers and commentators alike to downplay the existence and to understate the social consequences of a 'globalization effect', Grahl argues.

Following Grahl (2002), we summarize the phases of globalization (in Table 1.1) to guide theoretical reflection on the macro context in which alternative approaches to SIHRM decision making and the likely outcomes may be evaluated. Later in the chapter we present a case vignette that illustrates the ways multinational managements may interpret and act on globalization in practice.

Table 1.1 Stylized phases of globalization

Phase one (1970s)	Phase two (1980s)	Phase three (1990s–)
Post-Bretton Woods development of world currency markets.	International bond market growth in state debt.	Competition for debt between states and (privatized) corporations.
Fiscal pressure on states.	Extraneous influences on 'social contract' framework.	Dispersion of corporatist consensus.

Source: after Grahl (2002).

First phase (1970s)

During this period, a world market in currencies developed. The abandonment of controls under what had been known as the Bretton Woods system, which controlled the exchange value of traded currencies, leaving only 'market controls' (in other words, no politically oriented controls) put national economies and their governments under pressure to reduce inflation. Thus, the Keynesian-inspired willingness on the part of governments to accommodate the inflationary consequences of maintaining 'full employment' was placed under threat, once currencies were being bought and sold on the international foreign exchange markets around the clock.

Second phase (1980s)

Early in this period, public finance globalization began with the growth of international bond markets for state debt. This development increasingly constrained national-level economic growth policies. Under these conditions, external influence is exerted implicitly on the basis that developed countries are anxious not to lose their access to state debt financing at preferred rates, which might be threatened by market perceptions of relatively higher risks of capital gains distribution passing to labour in 'inflationary' wage levels and social benefits, rather than to capital interests. For the developing world, in these circumstances, 'dependency' pressures are likely to be experienced even more severely than before, as we discuss later.

Third phase (1990s–)

For a decade and a half, the globalization of public finance has been extended to corporate finance. While the impact may be an indirect one, a line may be traced linking the current stage of development of financial globalization to the earlier phases, enabled by their cumulative effect – free-floating currencies, and the increasing dependency of state legislators and administrators on non-democratically accountable interest groups. Bauman (1998) has argued that global financial interests constitute no more than 'tourists and vagabonds'. Unlike the spatially bound working populations around the world, finance capital exists in the abstract, enabled by technology. Its owners have no interest other than capital accumulation. National governments must cope with the consequences – but with reduced capacity to raise the means to do so through taxation of the wealthy (who may not be tax-paying residents of the country from which they draw economic rents on their investments).

Debt has been running from governments to corporate debt markets, with consequential effects for equity markets (the alternative option to debt financing). With the increased propensity of industrial enterprises to shift from debt-based financing of growth (bank borrowing), where firms are competing with governments for access to investment funds, managements have tended to increase their dependency on equity funding. The gathering momentum of 'privatization projects' worldwide, where instead of being state underwritten large utilities must compete with other trading entities for funds, has exacerbated the situation. The result has been increasingly active trading in corporate stocks, with an increasingly dispersed shareholding. McKenna (2000) emphasizes the pressures implicit in technocratic discourse to accept 'market logic' as self-evident for these developments. The macro-economic trends carry with them a momentum for transforming the governance rationale underpinning corporate organization.

It is tempting to characterize the emerging scene as the expression of American imperialism: 'an unholy alliance between state powers and the predatory aspects of finance capital' (Harvey, 2003: 136). However, retaining a balanced perspective, Hutton (2002a, 2002b) argues:

globalization has progressed so fast and so thoroughly because it has *not* been imposed by the US. It has developed as it has due to a framework of trade treaties, international accounting and legal standards and a willingness by all players to submit to the judgements of the World Trade Organization or IMF.

(Hutton, 2002b: 26, emphasis added)

Hutton argues that question marks have arisen regarding the ongoing march of globalization, as a result of the uncertainties around America's unilateralism under the Bush administration, which is having a depressing effect on the collective judgements of international stock markets. In his words:

Once a new rule is in place – that the US can and will do what it wants when it wants – one of the pillars of globalization falls. We are then moving into a new world in which the law of the jungle holds, and the markets don't like what they see.

(Hutton, 2002b)

Harvey (2003) acknowledges that to imply a premeditated US global economic takeover would probably be an overstatement. But the roots of the ideology that rationalizes 'free-market fundamentalism' (Hobsbawm, 2000: 69), may be identified as having developed originally in the United States. The 'American hegemony' may be taken as seeking to present as universally applicable a value set rationalizing corporate governance practices that emerged in a particular geography, under exceptional historical circumstances.[3]

GOVERNANCE AND SIHRM IMPLICATIONS

Given the competing range of conceptualizations, extending the comparison with heuristic intent brings to the surface a variety of potential interpretations of the practical consequences of globalization for corporate regulation and IHRM. Does 'going global' imply harmonization of HR systems internationally (IDS, 2000)?

Proponents of the globalization thesis argue that pressures of globalization have set in motion a convergence process of employment relations patterns in MNCs towards the individualistic Anglo-Saxon approach, regardless of MNCs country-of-origin (eg Reich, 1991). Yet another strand of the debate argues that the nation state and different models of capitalism continue to be the basis of economic actors engaged in the world economy (eg Hirst and Thompson, 1996; Lane, 1995).

(Tüselmann, McDonald and Heise, 2000: 27)

Normatively, 'a deep analysis of the set of values, beliefs and behaviour patterns that govern day-to-day organizational performance' is called for (Granell, 2000: 90). Globalization makes culture 'an increasingly strategic issue that has to be faced and properly managed' (2000: 90). The implication is that, at the organizational level, embedded social institutions, norms and practices can potentially support or inhibit change. How SIHRM analysts determine whether culture represents an opportunity, a challenge or a threat becomes a significant empirical issue, therefore.

If we frame the range of elements of this theoretical debate using the model outlined in the Introduction, the arena for policy choice making may be focused as follows. Strategic choices surrounding management of employment relationships may be influenced primarily by 'home country' values and practices. But those managing operations in one or a range of host country environments face the challenge of transplanting 'ethnocentric' principles (Perlmutter, 1969), justifying the consequential policies and practices in their interactions with local managers, other employees and external representatives.

The alternative is 'polycentric' adaptation (Perlmutter, 1969) to a multiplicity of 'business system' conditions, which managers located in particular host countries will in turn need to justify to dominant interest groups: corporate management streams and/or investors. It may be that certain segments of the workforce in the host country are open to aligning 'local' aspirations with the alien modus operandi, provided the individuals and groups perceive material benefits in internalizing Granell's (2000) 'win–win' philosophy. Such 'adapters' may be particularly open to embracing hybrid organizing practice – interpreting corporate ideology in ways that may be seen to reflect reciprocal organizational adaptation.

For example, to take one of the world's fastest developing economies, it may be possible to chart the emergence in some joint ventures of what has been described as 'western informed management with Chinese characteristics' (Warner, 1996, 2002, cited by Ng and Siu, 2004: 879). A willingness to embrace transplanted or even 'regiocentric' or 'geocentric' hybrids (Perlmutter, 1969) may not follow in the case of all organization members: their socialization or perceived interests may militate against it.

Despite perceptions of recent checks on the globalization trend-line, because of world political events in the opening years of the 21st century, it is worth assessing the prospects for the continued diffusion of a normative HRM associated with the management of people employed in multinational organizations. Two links may be hypothesized between the neo-liberal advance and consequences for employment systems. First, sacrificing full control over economic levers to global finance markets, with the consequences for suppressing inflationary forces, has a consequence for social security systems. The safety net for labour to fall back on when in struggle with capital interests is thus threatened. Second, the globalization of corporate finance leads to hegemonic corporate governance norms, which in turn prompt demands for labour market deregulation. (This undermines the advances in the redistribution of wealth between capital and labour in advanced industrial economies, won over decades through labour mobilization at the parochial and strategic political levels.)

The key factor arising from the corporate finance change dynamic that impacts on employment and people management internationally appears to be the demand for a unitarist determination of the corporate governing objective. This is linked to 'flexibilization' as the received wisdom informing and legitimating approaches to employment. The 'Americanization' of the constitution of the corporate enterprise changes conceptions of the firm, overturning antecedent governance models with deep social meaning (Grahl, 2002). The employment model changes as the governance model shifts from being 'voice' based, premised on reproducing the socio-economic order grounded in a bargained contract, underscored by national regulation, to being 'exit' based. Under the latter conditions, finance capital interests discipline firms, their management and workforces, by the potential threat of liquidating their shareholding, exposing firms to hostile takeover bids, or at least the loss of investment funds to finance growth. The operational indicators in Table 1.2 illustrate the position.

Under the voice-based system, for example, the firm is a vehicle for integrating a variety of interest groups (for example, customers, employees, finance and suppliers), whereas under an exit-based system the firm is strictly designated the property of shareholding 'owners' (Parkinson, 2003). These differences are translated into the basis on which the firm's activities are monitored. In voice-based firms, stakeholders participate in day-to-day governance; under the exit model, scrutiny is restricted to financial performance indicators. The danger inherent in voice-based governance is that 'group-think' blinds insiders to under-performing assets; under exit governance, wider stakeholder interests are subordinated to idiosyncratic and short-term speculator behaviour. Socially embedding corporate stakeholding, subject to voice-based governance, may act to constrain expansion, whereas an exit-based system offers more efficient access to investment capital. Such benefits are offset by the dilution of 'situated' control, however.

Table 1.2 The impact of alternative governance drivers

Voice-based	Exit-based
Coalition of interests	Property of owners
Scrutiny based on day-to-day owner/ managers (including banks and other long-term sources of credit)	Scrutiny based on financial data
Cronyism risk	Speculation risk
Socially embedded (expansion constrained?)	Disembedded – access to market finance, but loss of control to abstract interests (money abstraction)

Source: after Grahl (2002).

Voice- or exit-based, the rationality of organization depends on the perspective adopted by the observer. With the cross-border flows of financial investment, there is evidence that home-based criteria are abandoned to the common denominator of ruthless speculator capitalism. The case of BMW in its UK Midlands experiment (Rover Group) offers a practical example. The most significant IHRM issue may be the tendency of technocratic discourse 'to remove people from sentences' that underlie policy development (McKenna, 2000: 76). In the Australian Department of Foreign Affairs and Trade definition of globalization cited earlier (McKenna, 2000: 75), while there is a reference to humans in the sentence quoted, 'it is an economic concept' (2000: 75).

INEXORABLE OR 'BARGAINED' GLOBALIZATION?

Qualifying his stylized globalization trajectory, Grahl (2002) advocates caution before arguing deterministically. In particular, national differences may be observed in the speed with which economies transfer to a primary reliance on market equity. For example, France is moving quite quickly, while in Germany the pace is slower. In the United Kingdom the market equity system has been embedded over the longer term (Hutton, 1996), although the 1980s 'big bang' deregulation may be seen as having paved the way to a situation in which domestically owned finance institutions have been emaciated in favour of particularly American- and German-owned corporate finance lenders. A stock market downturn has seen companies moderating their enthusiasm to issue equity stocks. In some cases, there has been a return to banks, the state and individual investors with 'deep pockets'. There are opportunities for manoeuvre on the part of interests other than mobile global finance, therefore. And a balanced appraisal should also avoid overlooking the power of the US system of corporate governance in its capacity to reallocate resources (Harvey, 2003).

Embedded social institutions, such as co-determination arrangements in parts of mainland Europe, representing the legitimate means of ordering relations between capital, labour and state, act as another potential check on homogenizing forces impacting on the global employment and governance paradigm. There are variations in the manner in which flexible realignment of a consensus-based social contract may be applied to categories of workers. There are groups who enjoy an episodic advantage (Edwards, 1986) through their possession of skills that are in short supply but critical to the production of surplus value (and thus profits and dividend streams). These workers may be able to exact a price for cooperation with employers (which is frequently administered through elaborate systems and processes).

This segmented position of advantage remains provisional, however. 'Scientific' management represents an unending search for new processes associated with further divisions of labour, to enable work to be specified in ever-greater detail as part of the profit seeking at minimum cost to capital. The latest variant is 'knowledge management' (Hull, 2000). Contingent employment systems also offer scope to inhibit the accumulation of social capital on the part of groups of high-discretion, advantaged workers. This is done by manufacturing competition between individuals for zero sum rewards and even 'self-competition', and persuading individuals to sacrifice seniority rewards in favour of non-guaranteed performance pay (developments discussed in more detail in Chapter 5). Variable pay systems transfer the risk of ensuring sustained high productivity to labour. In what Manuel Castells (2000) terms 'generic labour', instead of securing collectively bargained premiums, these increasingly peripheral and atomized workers are placed in solidarity-destroying competition. This may be extended on an international basis as capital encourages firms to relocate non-core activities purely on the basis of the cheapest available labour.

GLOBALIZATION AND 'THE JONES CORPORATION'

To exemplify how organizations might grapple with the practical implications emerging from the globalization debate, let us consider developments in 'The Jones Corporation' (a hypothetical enterprise, representing an amalgam of several multinationals known to us). A health-care company, headquartered in the United Kingdom, Jones Corp manufactures and sells pharmacy and cosmetics products across several continents. It employs

80,000 people worldwide and is currently highly profitable, with excellent investment returns for shareholders. The firm's operations are structured regionally, divided into three main geographical areas: Europe, the Middle East and Africa; North America; and Asia-Pacific. Jones Corp has research and development (R&D) facilities in the United Kingdom and the United States. It has manufacturing and distribution operations in both of these countries currently, as well as in Germany and Australia. Its retail operations are based in a range of countries such as South Africa, Australia, Japan, Thailand, Canada, the Middle East, the United States, and across the European Union. Jones Corp's management view the firm as a multinational, but are acutely aware of 'gaps' in its retail operations: for example, it is not present in China, India and key markets in Latin America.

International knowledge and skills transfer – organization and HRM recalibration

Jones Corp senior management have traditionally addressed the problem of transferring knowledge and skills through the medium of international mobility. Expatriates have most typically been drawn from the UK headquarters when required, to oversee the setting up of new operations and to train local employees, with the prospect that the latter might run subsidiary/country businesses in the longer term. However, in practice, long-serving top management have remained a little wary of entrusting commercial governance to local managers. Their socialization is suspected to have ingrained ways of thinking about business and its primary goals that are different from those accepted as a given in the Anglo-American environment from which Jones Corp has emerged, despite its multinational pretensions.

Expatriation has not only been used to control overseas subsidiary activities; it has also been used to provide career development for high-potential managers, in support of corporate senior and top management succession. Until recently, the notion of a non-UK board membership appointment has not even been considered a remote possibility – even if the candidate came from another English-speaking country.

In pursuit of organic growth, the board of directors has determined that the time is right for Jones Corp to take steps to become a major global player in its sector by entering the remaining key target retail markets: China, India, Brazil and Argentina.

This strategic choice has added to difficulties in aligning business demands with Jones Corp's traditional approach to people management. Already, within the past three years, the pool of leadership talent has been extended. Now, for example, an Australian heads up the American manufacturing operation long-term, and two German nationals are working on expatriate assignment terms at senior management level in R&D, in the United Kingdom and the United States, for career development reasons. Career development has also been initiated for senior managers in R&D and manufacturing, via a series of international short-term assignments, typically around six months to one year's duration. In some instances, such assignments are arranged on a reciprocal basis: for example, a manager in Germany undertakes an assignment in the United Kingdom while his/her UK counterpart works in Germany. Traditionally, Jones Corp retail operations have tended to be managed at local level (after initial training and knowledge/skills transfer from the corporate centre), albeit with 'localized' parent country expatriates. Recently, however, a series of short-term training assignments have been initiated across retail operations, enabling retail managers with senior leadership potential, identified among the locally sourced workforce, to experience Jones Corp's approach to retailing in other countries within their regional grouping. For instance, a Japanese retail manager is currently undertaking a month's assignment to Australia while her counterpart from Australia works in Japan.

Jones Corp's preference has always been for a 'greenfield', new start-up approach to expansion, but opportunities to grow the business internationally via mergers and/or joint ventures have been raised in a management consultant's report. These are seen as something to which the board of directors should give serious consideration. The consultants have recommended that a review be undertaken of Jones Corp's existing R&D and manufacturing bases of operation. In addition, the consultants argue, restructuring should be considered to determine whether the current geographical approach remains relevant to Jones Corp's planned future as a major global player in the sector.

A new group personnel director has recently been recruited on the retirement of her predecessor. She is based in the United Kingdom at Group HQ, and was recruited in part because of her experience of guiding companies through progression to a more networked form of transcontinental HR management. Now she has been charged by the board with reviewing the current international HR strategy. The stated intention is to explore the ways in which globally situated leadership and workforce resources can be drawn on to support Jones Corp's international growth aspirations. Among the range of policies for cross-border mobilization of corporate knowledge and skills, the international assignment policy has been identified as a suitable candidate for recalibration.

Jones Corp management appear to be adopting an optimistic view of globalization, while responding to prevailing corporate governance demands. However, experience indicates that strains are emerging in coping with the demands of knowledge exchange and operational oversight of new business formations, forcing a rethink of where senior managerial talent may be sourced from and deployed to. And the 'exit based' approach to employment management, derived from Jones Corp's corporate governance orientation, implies that some of the more imaginative ideas for matching organization needs with human capital across a multiplicity of business contexts might result in outcomes that are unexpected and possibly unwelcome to corporate top management and their finance capital investment principals.

Like HRM policy makers generally, the new HR functional regime at Jones Corp is likely to be focused on identifying institutional barriers to enacting the strategy desired to serve the corporate governance objective, and then finding ways to navigate around these. Alternatively, if the transnational growth plans are central to corporate sustainability, the management team might accept the need to moderate the degree of flexibility demanded of local labour, and accommodate the higher 'entry costs' to operate in particular countries.[4] Depending on the degree of dependency at national economy level, the large multinational corporation might be able to put state regulators under pressure to lessen the negative impact of institutional factors, as perceived by foreign direct investment (FDI) sources, possibly ushering in a two-tier system as a transition to full flexibilization.[5]

At normative level, the focus 'on integrating differences, putting together our strengths, building from the differences and being able to join efforts for a win–win process' (Granell, 2000) appears generally positive, as nominally embraced by Jones Corp's management. However, taking a more cautious approach, we can identify a number of emergent questions for analysis under the SIHRM rubric:

▮ 'Who sets the criteria for evaluating 'win–win' outcomes?'

▮ What count as 'rational' measures of organizational success?

▮ Is the implied objectivity suspect, where 'abstract technical rationality' is in practice 'interested rationality'?

▮ What does an employment 'partnership' discourse, juxtaposed with that of globalization, imply for state regulators and the representatives of organized labour – the traditional basis of their authority, their resources, and their capacity to mobilize workforce members?

▮ How fragile are developments in new institution building, and how sensitive to market shocks?

▮ What price 'partnership' in the face of a major slump?

DEVIL IN THE DETAIL?

We shall be taking up questions such as those listed above as they interface with issues of employee resourcing, human capital development and mobilization, reward and recognition, and employment relations regulation (including 'employee voice') in subsequent chapters. However, initial insights may be gained by reference to recent empirical research conducted in the Netherlands (Kleinknecht, 2002). The findings bring out some negative consequences of neo-liberal-influenced market capital allocation – efficient at the macro economic level, but inefficient at the micro level. The data also connect with questions arising from the parallel trends of calls for greater employment system flexibility.

The researchers assembled data to assist in evaluating an alleged 'job creation miracle' in the Netherlands. Two issues were placed in the foreground: first, wage restraint on the part of labour, and second, flexibilization of labour markets. The latter was measured both externally – for example, in the casualization of contracts – and internally – for example, cross-posting and contingent pay (De Haan *et al*, 1994: 57, cited by Kleinknecht, 2002). Kleinknecht (2002) investigated the question: 'Does flexibility lead to higher performance?' His conclusion is that there is no clear evidence that it does. The reasons are a complex amalgam of factors, explored through testing the following hypotheses:

1   Through achieving savings in wages costs, employers will hire more people, reducing unemployment (the traditional rationale behind comparisons of 'inflexible' European countries against the 'high job creation' United States); but

2   The increased mobility of labour will undermine traditional institutions of trust between the parties to the employment relationship, reducing commitment, and leading to the loss of social capital ('corporate memory' – or cumulative, institutionally embedded, workforce knowledge); and hence

3   The combined outcome will be equilibrium in terms of macro-economic performance levels.

Kleinknecht (2002) gathered data to facilitate comparative multivariate analysis between 'innovative' and 'non-innovative' firms, defined as (innovative) firms with R&D facilities and (non-innovative) firms with no R&D facilities. Operational indicators of firm performance were wages levels, profit as a percentage of sales, increases in sales, and increases in number of employees.[6]

The findings indicated that while lower wage rates may facilitate increases in the number of employees, firms tend to innovate less (possibly because they no longer have the capability to do so), retaining 'older vintages' of products for longer. Raising some important implications for training and capability development (Chapter 4), this 'innovation gap' may be perceived as the reason behind a decade of wage moderation but reduced market share in the eight largest OECD countries, which together account for 75 per cent of foreign trade worldwide.[7] While the OECD average level of job mobility is 9 per cent of people changing jobs per annum, the figure in the Netherlands is 10 per cent.[8]

CONCLUDING REMARKS

In this chapter, we set out to discover the global context for SIHRM. Drawing together the strands, key questions may be posed and answered in summary.

What is globalization?

We have considered conceptual and operational definitions, with the qualification that there are numerous approaches commentators and policy makers seem to adopt, contingent on their perspective and/or disciplinary interests. The tests applied to evaluate the existence and potential extent of global and regional developments are similarly varied. An especially interesting proposition is that developments associated with international finance capital need to be interpreted over a long-run trajectory, advancing cumulatively (Grahl, 2002).

What impact is globalization having on organizations?

Again, we find that the answer depends on the commentator's perspective, ranging from the optimists who adopt a normative orientation, implying scope for the parties to exercise 'strategic choices' (Child, 1972) to pool capabilities and overcome the possible negative effects of diversity. More cautious commentators raise questions regarding the impact on the exercise of strategic choices of asynchronous material and ideological relations between the various institutional actors. Even the cautiously optimistic regarding the prospects for consensual globalization highlight the unknown impact on its future trajectory arising from recent evidence of American unilateralism in political economic affairs.

What are the implications for employment and IHRM?

Again, the messages are mixed and conditional. On the one hand, it might be argued at the macro level that the efficient manner in which American-style management facilitates the transfer of corporate capital to finance production internationally is a source of job creation. In return, the need for flexibility in the matching of labour resources to production requirements (internally and externally to the enterprise) may be regarded as a reasonable compromise. However, evidence can be marshalled to illustrate the potential inefficiencies of the neo-liberal-inspired governance form, when scrutinized through the lens of social capital (trust, commitment, innovation, and corporate memory transfers) over the longer term.

The choices for SIHRM policy makers and their advisers appear to focus, on the one hand, on finding ways instrumentally to make short-term deals with 'talent' which leverage 'episodic advantage' in the market, while exploiting cost minimization opportunities at the global periphery. Alternatively, corporate agents may seek to manage the global dynamic through institution (re)building, in spite of the countervailing pressures of 'dispersed portfolio-style' capitalist investment. As a 'third way', in place of the apparent dichotomy, some may be willing to accept the challenge of attempting to reconcile these tensions through 'social partnership' initiatives.[9] However, empirical evidence to date suggests that, at enterprise level, while the workforce may be 'empowered' and 'involved' at the point of production, such managerial initiatives will not only form part of a work intensification programme. They may also lead to trade union substitution strategies, muting the collective 'voice', limiting the scope for employees to defend their bargained 'gains' and 'privileges' at a time of economic downturn, while removing even those few locations in the global political economy where co-determination principles have offered labour interests legitimate access to strategic forums. Consideration of these factors, drawing on our provisional discoveries regarding the character and impact of globalization in this chapter, and using the dynamic three-node analytical model outlined in the Introduction, will inform further detailed discussion of strategic international HRM in its contemporary environmental context over the remainder of the book.

And finally: are globalization and HRM trends linked in some way?

The universal HRM mantra of 'commitment, flexibility, quality, and strategic alignment' (Guest, 1987) may be interpreted as one indicator of the hegemonic influences of American-style capitalism. And its diffusion may be perceived as associated with the neo-liberal-inspired corporate governance regime. However, a deterministic impulse should perhaps be resisted. As with many aspects of the contemporary political economy, diverse traditions and institutional factors appear to drive equally diverse interpretations on the ground. And recent large-scale surveys even in the Anglo-Saxon heartlands (such as WERS 98 in the UK and complementary studies in the United States) find only limited application of comprehensive 'HRM' in terms of workplace managerial practice.

While any conclusion needs careful qualification at this stage, an alternative to the notion of centre-driven homogenization of SIHRM is the countervailing diversity in experimentation surrounding regulation of the employment relationship, from the various sites of labour–management interaction. We return to the question of 'deregulation' and what Katz and Darbishire (2000) label 'converging divergences' when we consider international employment relations (in Chapter 6).

YOUR TURN

- What are the ways in which the debates surrounding notions of 'globalization' may be approached?

- Why might different actors in socio-economic relations across the world's countries and regional blocs choose one definition of globalization over the alternatives?

- How may globalization be situated as a historical phenomenon, with links to particular spaces that form the arena(s) for international political economy?

- What effect is the 'dispositional advantage' enjoyed by those who control the flow of foreign direct investment likely to have in terms of emphasizing 'voice' versus 'exit' in employment management practices?

- What are the choices HR specialists may encounter in supporting attempts by the organizations whose senior managements they advise to expand operations on a transnational or global scale?

- What are the consequences of different choices in governing multinational corporations according to 'globalization' criteria faced by employees – as individuals and groups – and their representative institutions?

- Why might trends towards diversity and experimentation among multinationals be as likely to be observed empirically as homogenization tendencies at this time?

ACKNOWLEDGEMENT

Some of the material for this chapter appeared as an article by Stephen published in the *European Industrial Training Journal*, **27**(9) (2003), pp 461–72.

NOTES

1 'Triadization' of the world's economies between the United States, western Europe and Japan has been juxtaposed to the 'straight' globalization thesis (Rugman, 2000), locating developing and transforming economies beyond the integrated network.

2 Examples of trading blocs are ASEAN countries, the European Union, and the North American Free Trade Association (NAFTA).

3 Hobsbawm adds that, to some extent, the United States is 'an ideological power which originated, just like the Soviet Union, from a revolution, and therefore feels the need to guide the world in accordance with its principles, as an essential part of its foreign policy' (2000: 17).

4 The incidence of high-level IT skills in India serving US 'silicon valley' enterprises suggests this is not universal, however.

5 The juxtaposition is between local employers and MNCs.

6 Kleinknecht (2002) counsels caution in interpreting the findings because of the possible situation of reverse causality – is employment growth driven by sales growth or vice versa?

7 Australia, Canada, France, Germany, Italy, Japan, the United States, the United Kingdom.

8 It is interesting to note that there are 7 million active in the Dutch workforce, with 1 million on permanent 'sick leave'. This is a well-known highly controversial system that the state is unable to overturn because of the likely outcry on the part of not only labour institutions, but also employers. It offers a most efficient (that is, cheap) way of dealing with workforce layoffs.

9 Arguably, this is an institution-building derivative informed by a neo-pluralist perspective on political-economy (Ackers, 2002).

REFERENCES

Ackers, P (2002) Reframing employment relations: the case for neo-pluralism, *Industrial Relations Journal*, **33**(1), pp 2–19

Bauman, Z (1998) *Globalization: The human consequences*, Polity Press, Cambridge

Béret, P, Mendez, A, Paraponaris, C and Richez-Battesti, N (2003) R&D personnel and human resource management in multinational companies: between homogenization and differentiation, *International Journal of Human Resource Management*, **14**(3), pp 449–68

Brewster, C (2001) HRM: the comparative dimension, in *Human Resource Management: A critical text*, ed J Storey, pp 256–71, Thompson Learning, London

Brewster, C, Harris, H and Sparrow, P (2002) *Globalising HR*, Chartered Institute of Personnel and Development (CIPD), London

Castells, M (2000) Materials for an exploratory theory of the network society, *British Journal of Sociology*, **51**(1), pp 5–24

Cheng, J L and Cooper, D (2003) A strategic context approach to international human resource management research: towards greater integration of theory and practice, in *Leadership in International Business Education and Research*, ed A M Rugman, Elsevier Science/JAI Press, London

Child, J (1972) Organizational structure, structure and performance: the role of strategic choice, *Sociology*, **6**(1), pp 1–22

Cully, M, Woodland, S, O'Reilly, A and Dix, G (1999) *Britain at Work: As depicted by the 1998 Workplace Employee Relations Survey*, Routledge, London

Edwards, P K (1986) *Conflict at Work: A materialist analysis*, Blackwell, Oxford

Floyd, D (2001) Globalisation or Europeanisation of business activity? Exploring the critical issues, *European Business Review*, **13**(2), pp 109–13

Ghoshal, S and Bartlett, C (1998) *Managing across Borders: The transnational solution*, Random House, London

Giddens, A (1999) *Runaway World: How globalisation is reshaping our lives*, Profile Books, London

Grahl, J (2002) Finance and flexibility: recent evidence, paper presented at Seminar on European Labour Markets, London Metropolitan University, 20 September

Granell, E (2000) Culture and globalisation: a Latin American challenge, *Industrial and Commercial Training*, **32**(3), pp 89–94

Guest, D E (1987) Human Resource Management and industrial relations, *Journal of Management Studies*, **24**(5), pp 503–21

Guest, D E (1999) Human resource management: the workers' verdict, *Human Resource Management Journal*, **9**(3), pp 5–25

Guth, S and Schrecker, C (2002) From the rules of sociological, method to the Polish peasant: a comparative view of two foundational texts, *Journal of Classical Sociology*, **2**(3), pp 281–98

Harvey, D (2003) *The New Imperialism*, Oxford University Press, Oxford

Hobsbawm, E (2000) *The New Century*, Abacus, London

Hughes, C W (2002) Reflections on globalisation, security and 9/11, *Cambridge Review of International Affairs*, **15**(3), pp 421–33

Hull, R (2000) Knowledge management and the conduct of expert labour, in *Managing Knowledge: Critical investigations of work and learning*, ed C Pritchard, R Hull, M Chumner and H Willmott, St Martin's Press, New York

Hutton, W (1996) *The State We're In*, Vintage/Random House, London

Hutton, W (2002a) *The World We're In*, Little Brown, London

Hutton, W (2002b) The future of globalisation, *Personnel Today*, 10 September

IDS (2000) *IDS Focus: Going global*, Incomes Data Services, London

Jackson, T and Bak, M (1998) Foreign companies and Chinese workers: employee motivation in the People's Republic of China, *Journal of Organizational Change Management*, **11**(4), pp 282–300

Kaldor, M (2000) 'Civilising' globalisation? The implications of the 'Battle in Seattle', *Millennium*, **29**(1), pp 105–14

Katz, H C and Darbishire, O (2000) *Converging Divergences: Worldwide changes in employment systems*, Cornell University Press, Ithaca

Keep, E (1992) Corporate training strategies: the vital component?' in *Human Resource Strategies*, ed G Salaman, Sage, London

Kleinknecht, A (2002) Labour market flexibility and innovation, paper presented at Seminar on European Labour Markets, London Metropolitan University, 20 September

Legge, K (1995) *Human Resource Management: Rhetorics and realities*, Macmillan, Basingstoke

Mabey, C (2002) Mapping management development practice, *Journal of Management Studies*, **39**(8), pp 1139–60

Martinelli, A (2003) Global order or divided world? *Current Sociology*, **51**(2), pp 95–100

McKenna, B (2000) Labour responses to globalization: the Australian experience, *Asia Pacific Business Review*, **7**(1), pp 71–104

Nielsen, J (1994) Heuristic evaluation, in *Usability Inspection Methods*, ed J Nielsen and RL Mack, Wiley, New York

Ng, C Y and Siu, N Y M (2004) Training and enterprise performance in transition: evidence from China, *International Journal of Human Resource Management*, **15**(5), pp 878–94

O'Keeffe, T (2003) Preparing expatriate managers of multinational organisations for cultural and learning imperatives of their job in dynamic knowledge-based environments, *Journal of European Industrial Training*, **17**(5), pp 233–43

Organization for Economic Co-operation and Development (2002) *Measuring Globalisation: The role of multinationals in OECD economies, Vols I & II: Manufacturing Sector 2001 Edition*, OECD, Paris

Parkinson, J (2003) Models of the company and the employment relationship, *British Journal of Industrial Relations*, **41**(3), pp 481–509

Perlmutter, H V (1969) The tortuous evolution of the multinational corporation, *Columbia Journal of World Business*, **4**(1), pp 9–18

Purcell, J (1992) The impact of corporate strategy on human resource management', in *Human Resource Strategies*, ed G Salaman, pp 60–81, Sage, London

Purcell, J (1999) Best practice and best fit: chimera or cul-da-sac?, *Human Resource Management Journal*, **9**(3), pp 26–41

Ramirez, M and Mabey, C (2003) Comparing national approaches to management training and development in Europe: an institutional perspective, *Proceedings of the 7th International Human Resource Management Conference*, University of Limerick 4–6 June

Rowley, C (2000) Review symposium: labour and management going global? *International Journal of Human Resource Management*, **11**(5), pp 1008–13

Rugman, A (2000) *The End of Globalisation*, Oxford University Press, Oxford

Schuler, R S, Budhwar, P S and Florkowski, G W (2002) International human resource management: review and critique, *International Journal of Management Reviews*, **4**(1), pp 41–70

Streeck, W (1997) German capitalism: does it exist? Can it survive?, in *Political Economy of Modern Capitalism: Mapping convergence and diversity*, ed C Crouch and W Streeck pp 33–54, Sage, London

Taylor, P J (2000) Izations of the world: Americanization, modernization and globalization, in *Demystifying Globalization*, ed C Hay and D Marsh, pp 49–70, Palgrave, London

Teague, P (2002) Financial integration and employment relations in the EU, paper presented at Seminar on European Labour Markets, London Metropolitan University, 20 September

Thompson, P (2003) Disconnected capitalism: or why employers can't keep their side of the bargain, *Work, Employment and Society*, **17**(2), pp 359–78

Tüselmann, H-J, McDonald, F and Heise, A (2000) Globalisation, nationality of ownership and employee relations German multinationals in the UK, *Personnel Review*, **31**(1), pp 27–43

Visser, J (2002) Why fewer workers join unions in Europe, *British Journal of Industrial Relations*, **40**(3), pp 403–30

Watson, M (2005) *Foundations of International Political Economy*, Palgrave Macmillan, Basingstoke

Part Two

Applying strategic international human resource management in practice

2

Culture, welfare and international mobility: choices and consequences

CHAPTER AIMS

This chapter sets out to do the following:

- introduce you to the notion of societal culture and the influences of culture upon making choices in SIHRM; outline the stages of culture shock and highlight its consequences in terms of business issues and employee welfare;

- examine the concept of stress and examine its consequences on business performance and employee well-being, particularly in an international environment;

- explore the choices concerning welfare issues in repatriation of internationally mobile personnel;

- discuss the concept of the 'psychological contract' and explore how SIHRM choices can have (unintended) consequences in this respect.

In a period such as we are experiencing today, where many organization managers may perceive themselves wrestling with accelerated globalization, understanding the forces that are at work and the cross-cultural dynamics that are involved in their interactions is an essential prerequisite for maintaining healthy relationships with people whose performance we aspire to manage successfully, or who interact professionally with us in any shape or form. But understanding cultural factors that influence the behaviour of others is only one side of the equation. It is equally necessary to understand how those cultural factors impinge on each and every one of us as individuals (with our own cultural assumptions and values).

The welfare implications are often left unaddressed, yet the impact of stress, culture shock and returning to our own cultural norms raises significant issues for individuals, and as a consequence for their employing organizations. This chapter begins by examining national cultures, and continues by considering the impact of living and working abroad in terms of stress, culture shock and repatriation. The diversity of workforces today means that cultural considerations are particularly relevant to those remaining in their homelands but who work as part of multinational teams, as well as to those responsible for the remote management of foreign operations.

Indeed, even if we accept that issues of culture and welfare are implicit within the overall approach to managing expatriates and multinational teams in global organizations, we should also be cognisant of their significance to local people – those who act as the hosts to expatriates and foreign direct investment (FDI). Culture and welfare issues apply equally to those working at this local level, as parent firms and their subsidiaries experience the influx of potentially several alien cultures while simultaneously having to increase competitiveness in an increasingly globalized trading environment. Culture and welfare issues are therefore a 'networked problem' shared by all.

In addition, cultural and welfare issues go beyond the explicit employment contract, as they concern psychological matters which are 'unseen', usually unwritten, and frequently left undiscussed. We draw on the psychological literature to show the relevance of cultural misunderstanding and how welfare concerns affect the psychological contracts of both mobile employees and those whose working lives they affect. There are choices and consequences therefore in ignoring or paying lip service to culture and welfare issues, in terms of both individual satisfaction and overall organizational effectiveness.

THE INFLUENCE OF CULTURE

Global travel has become commonplace for the citizens of the industrialized world, and there are greater opportunities today to live and work abroad than ever before, and to be hosts to people from other countries who are there to work alongside or supervise us. As countries become multi-ethnic, so contact with people from other cultures also becomes a commonplace in the domestic environment, in both social and professional spheres. However, we often continue to assume that other people see things as we do, believing that everyone experiences the same physical, intellectual and emotional re-actions as ourselves. This is not, of course, the case.

So what do we mean when we refer to a national culture? We mean not only a country's music, painting or literature, but rather the whole manner and style in which the people of a country conduct their lives. A national culture involves a complete system of customs, habits, rules, values and be-liefs, shared by an overwhelming majority of the country's inhabitants. It gives them a particular outlook on life, a special mind-set; in short, it is their view of the universe.

Children learn their culture from their parents and members of the society with whom they have contact very early in life. The literature claims a range of ages, but it can be accepted that we have a firm moral code – a grounding of rights and wrongs – certainly by the age of 10 (and probably much earlier – some believe as young as age four). We learn how to behave and articulate the assumptions and values of our culture without even knowing specifically what they are. Besides telling us what is right and wrong, our moral code tells us what is good and bad, rational and irrational, normal and abnormal. These core values are rarely abandoned later in life.

Therefore at the centre of each person's being lies this nucleus of values; his or her core beliefs. When we meet someone from another culture, if we just look at them, we cannot see or be fully aware of these beliefs unless that person moves or communicates. There must be what we might call a cultural display before we get any information. For instance, if you walk along a street in a small European continental town, you can learn a lot about the national culture by two or three minutes of observation:

▌ Do people hurry towards their goals or are they relaxed?

▌ How important is time to them?

▌ Do they talk to each other much?

▌ Do they greet each other?

▮ Do they shake hands, bow or touch each other?

▮ How important is dress?

▮ Are they formal or informal?

▮ Do they show their feelings openly?

These cultural displays or events will have an effect on us. They might please us; we might find them strange; they might shock us. In our own culture people's actions meet with approval; we repeat them ourselves; the cultural trait develops; it becomes a national characteristic or tradition. In an alien culture our action meets with resistance; we might defend it; this leads to deadlock and eventual withdrawal. Similar cultures such as the Italian and Spanish might show semi-acceptance of each other's characteristics, and this would lead to friendly adaptation and essential cultural synergy: in this instance, close Latin understanding.

When international assignees and their families live and work in different countries, they take with them their own 'cultural baggage' – their preconceived ideas, attitudes and prejudices. Their view of the new host country and its people is coloured by a filter of their own norms and values, and often of stereotypes. And those with whom these people find themselves working carry the results of their own socialization, so that the newcomers' cultural baggage may inhibit their ability to embed themselves in ways conducive to organizational effectiveness. Their assumptions on strategic priorities and on the ways of conveying their intentions to colleagues and subordinates may be perceived as outwardly alien actions. Thus, dilemmas arise when people of different cultures form different views based on the same facts. It is important to remember that these views are different but not necessarily 'wrong'. For example, people from different cultures view aspects of life in contrasting ways. 'Man conquers Everest' is a Western viewpoint; 'Man in harmony with mountain' is an Eastern viewpoint. Cultures even view time differently: some emphasize punctuality while others reflect little sense of urgency.

There is considerable literature in the field of cross-cultural management, and our aim here is only to introduce some of the well-known theories and models in order to construct a framework to understand some of the issues that face assignees and others living, working or dealing with people in different cultural environments. This understanding can help in the preparation, management and repatriation of assignees, and in the everyday business dealings that assignees and others have with local nationals of various countries and regions of the world. It may also help those in host organizations to form a better appreciation of why incoming expatriate managers or colleagues appear to think and act as they do.

This will also provide a framework to understand the potential implications of choices made in business and personal life. To use the model introduced in the Introduction to the book, this commentary may be located among the 'business systems' and 'human capital' factors with which 'corporate strategy' aspects interact in pursuit of employee and organizational performance objectives. The notions of culture discussed below, generally emerging in the business psychology literature, may also be evaluated using the organizational strategy theories (transaction costs, agency, resource-based, and institutional) in order to triangulate the context in which multinational managerial choices are being exercised.

Definitions of culture abound in the literature. Hofstede is one of the most well-known theorists in this field, and his definition reflects his view that societal culture can be measured. He defines culture as 'the collective mental programming of the people in an environment' (1991). Trompenaars and Hampden-Turner (1997) define culture as 'the way in which a group of people solves problems and reconciles dilemmas'. Both definitions share the notion that culture refers to group behaviour in response to environmental issues. Culture effectively distinguishes the members of one group of people from another.

The concept of culture may be subdivided into:

▍ implicit culture: this relates to basic assumptions which produce

▍ values and norms: which reveal themselves as

▍ explicit culture: such as artefacts, behavioural models and rituals.

Explicit culture is usually 'broken down' into layers – with the visible symbols being the artefacts of culture. Language is an example of a symbol of culture, along with architecture, dress, food and so on. Cultures also have heroes or behavioural models that represent the culture of the group. Rituals or collective activities are other visible representations of culture. However, although these are all visible, the underlying values and basic assumptions that drive the visible practices are invisible and have to be inferred.

Hofstede's 1981 study, *Cultures Consequences*, of cultural dimensions in IBM attempts to analyse these values, as does the Trompenaars and Hampden-Turner (1997) research. Hofstede's research, carried out in IBM, made use of questionnaires to analyse culture in numerous countries. From the data, he constructed cultural dimensions so that culture could be 'measured' along four scales.

▌ **Power distance:** the extent to which a culture accepts inequalities in the distribution of power.

▌ **Uncertainty avoidance:** the extent to which a culture feels threatened by uncertain situations and so tries to establish rules.

▌ **Individualism/collectivism:** individualism refers to a loose social framework ('people look after themselves') while collectivism refers to a tight social framework ('people look after their group and show loyalty to it').

▌ **Masculinity/femininity:** masculinity refers to assertiveness and the value of money, while femininity refers to equality and the importance of quality of life.

Hofstede's later work (2001) includes a fifth dimension, **long-term/short-term orientation**, which refers to attitudes towards the past, present and future. For example, the United States ranks a little below average on power distance and well below average on uncertainty avoidance, but it is also the most individualistic culture and is well above average on masculinity. It is below average on long-term time orientation, reflecting its future-looking approach and the emphasis placed on schedules and punctuality.

Trompenaars and Hampden-Turner's (1997) model examines culture within three main domains: relationships and rules, attitudes to time, and attitudes to the environment. Within the attitudes to relationships and rules domain, the authors list five dimensions:

▌ **Universalism/particularism:** universalism refers to people's obligation to the law – the culture places greater emphasis on the law than on relationships. Particularism refers to people's obligation to friends and family ahead of legal obligation.

▌ **Individualism/communitarianism:** individualism refers to self-orientation and working for one's own self-interest whereas communitarianism refers to orientation to the goals of others and working for the benefit of the group.

▌ **Neutral/affective:** neutral refers to keeping feelings to oneself, whereas affective refers to the display of emotions openly to others.

▌ **Specific/diffuse:** specific-oriented cultures segregate the task from the person whereas in diffuse cultures the task and the person overlap.

▌ **Achievement/ascription:** achievement refers to status being accorded through doing, whereas ascription refers to status accorded through being (for example by age, gender, education, profession).

Within the attitudes to time domain, the authors list two dimensions:

▌ **Sequential/synchronic:** sequential cultures see time as a sequence of passing events – for these cultures time is more important than relationship building. For synchronic cultures, the past, present and future are interrelated, there is less insistence on punctuality, and relationships are considered more important than schedules.

▌ **Past and present/future:** cultures that focus on the past draw upon history and tradition in decision making and activities; those focusing on the present live for today; those focusing on the future plan ahead.

Within the attitudes to environment domain, the authors give one dimension:

▌ **Inner-directed/outer-directed:** inner-directed cultures focus on aggressiveness towards the environment and are uncomfortable when the environment is perceived to be out of control; outer-directed cultures are comfortable with the external environment and do not try to control it.

We have outlined two well-known societal cultural models. However, models to categorize and measure culture (such as Hofstede's work) have been subject to considerable criticism. This is possibly because 'culture' is both difficult to analyse and also complex to construct, as the assumptions that underlie it are invisible and for many of us virtually impossible to articulate. McSweeney (2002a, 2002b), for example, points out that Hofstede assumed that a questionnaire can accurately measure cultural dimensions, but it might be a flawed instrument – the people interviewed in each IBM subsidiary might come from different social backgrounds and thus the responses given in each country are not comparable. Hofstede also does not consider that three cultures interplay – namely societal, organizational and professional cultures. In essence, Hofstede's work does not take the complexity of culture into account. In addition, cultures are not bound by geopolitical lines drawn on a map – there are ethnic groups sharing a common culture extending beyond national boundaries. There are also distinct subcultures within regions of a country.

However, despite the many criticisms, Hofstede's work has 'become the standard against which new work on cultural differences is validated' (Triandis, 2004). It is therefore useful to use his model as a backdrop to give some examples of the issues that assignees might experience while working abroad, and hosts may experience on the receiving end of foreign people and practices accompanying incoming financial investment and business development. We can also recognize other, additional cultural implications. It is important to remember that cultures are not static, and change over time. As countries become more affluent, their populations become more individualistic, for example (Triandis, 2004). However, it is not known how long it might take for a culture to change significantly.

International assignees have to learn to work in three different cultures – national, organizational and professional – and these cultures shift in emphasis over time. In many respects the same applies to host employee groups: at work within a multinational they may in effect be entering a foreign cultural setting. An analogy is with embassies representing different nations in various host countries: inside the embassy building, visitors are deemed to be on a little segment of that country's turf. Organizational culture may reflect the local societal culture as well as the culture of the country where the organization is headquartered. Within it, professional groups have their own subcultures. Managerially, the challenge is to find ways in which diversity across these various cultural settings may be blended to secure overarching corporate aims, especially if the 'transnationally networked' model of organization is being pursued.

The assumptions underlying the corporate governing norms will also overtly, or more subtly, be interacting with the dynamics of the three cultural contexts described above. Are the host employees to be evaluated purely in transaction cost terms? Is there a mistrust regarding the likelihood that their agency will be directed in ways that complement or compete with corporate managerial priorities? On the other hand, is the managerial orientation one in which the very diversity of the employee resource is perceived to represent a source of value, inimitability and non-substitutability? And to what degree do the inward investors attribute responsibility to themselves and their managerial representatives to transplant a corporate, home-based institutional framework, or alternatively to choose to accommodate local cultural and institutional phenomena, or to negotiate a framework that blends sources of ideas and practice to deliver optimal organizational outcomes?

In short, different cultures hold different conceptions and assumptions about organizations and their management. Managers from different cultures may hold contrasting assumptions about the nature of management, authority, structure and organizational relationships. These assumptions shape their value systems and are translated into a range of different management practices. In turn these reinforce the original assumptions. These set the parameters within which progressive managerial reflection may take place, mindful of the hypothetical consequences that follow particular cultural and strategic choices, before multinational action plans are put in place.

In general, there is a continuum of practice in organizational behaviour from the instrumental view (found in the United States, the United Kingdom and Australia), placing transaction cost and agency considerations to the fore, to the social view (such as that found in Latin cultures), where people and longstanding institutional arrangements may be viewed as valuable as ends in themselves rather than means to others' ends. Within the instrumental view, the organization comprises a set of tasks that are achieved through a problem-solving hierarchy. Positions are defined in terms of tasks and functions, and authority is drawn from functions. By contrast, within the social view, the organization is seen as a collection of people managed through a formal hierarchy. Positions are defined in terms of levels of authority. Authority is exercised by individuals rather than through attachment to functions.

When entering into any project or working with nationals of other countries in order to deliver performance transnationally, it is helpful to analyze the economic and cultural profiles, and to explore the scope to empathize with them, by working through the following list of factors.

Economic background

❚ Area.

❚ Population.

❚ Population per sq km.

❚ Life expectancy.

❚ GDP.

❚ GDP per capita.

❚ Principal exports.

❚ Principal imports.

❚ Main trading partners.

Cultural characteristics

❚ Religion.

❚ Cultural classification.

❚ Values.

▌ Concepts including:
- leadership;
- status;
- space;
- time.

▌ Cultural factors in communication:
- communication patterns and use of language;
- listening habits;
- behaviour at meetings and negotiations;
- body language;
- other.

▌ Manners and taboos.

▌ How to empathize.

Hofstede's dimensions of culture can be applied to business practices in different countries to gain some understanding of how and why management is conducted in a particular fashion. For the internationalizing organization, paying attention to these culturally determined local practices, by displaying local responsiveness in management actions, can aid the introduction of headquarters policies and culturally different modes of operation. For example, France has a relatively high score for power distance in Hofstede's rankings. Structures are typically hierarchical, and communications flow downwards from the top of the organization via the hierarchy. An expatriate manager from a relatively low power distance country (such as Sweden), working in France, would need to understand that the authoritarian management style used there is likely to be more respected and effective than the Swedish consultative or participative approach. Hofstede's dimension of uncertainty avoidance records that Germans prefer to avoid uncertainty – they expect explicit rules to govern what they do. By contrast, the United Kingdom has a greater tolerance of ambiguity. A German assignee working in the United Kingdom will need to be aware that managers have greater autonomy in the United Kingdom than in Germany. For a British assignee working in Germany, a more prescriptive approach to management is necessary, as Germans prefer to follow rules more directly than in the United Kingdom. Equally colleagues and subordinates on the receiving end of interventions designed and supervised by enterprises and managers from countries beyond their own need to be aware of the socially informed sources, and be ready to interpret and act on these from a culturally attuned position.

The United States is the most individualist country in Hofstede's rankings. Employees in the United States prefer individual rewards and performance management based around the contribution of individuals. The United States is also future- and short-term oriented, and so performance rewards based on the organization's future performance would be accepted, with performance rewards being applied annually (recognizing short-term gains). In collectivist countries such as China, the preferred way of working is more group-oriented, and relationship building is more important than short-term individual gain. This clearly has an impact on the likely effectiveness of western-style individual performance-based rewards (although as research evidence presented in Chapter 5 illustrates, stereotypical responses do not automatically follow in the reward management domain). The masculinity and femininity dimension also has implications for the workplace: masculine nations value money and achievement (like the United States), whereas feminine countries (such as Sweden and France) value quality of life. In essence, masculine societies live to work whereas feminine societies work to live. An American manager working in Sweden may expect employees to work extra hours and forgo holiday to meet targets as would be the case in the United States. Swedes, however, are typically less motivated by the monetary rewards that this might deliver, preferring leisure time with their families.

Dealing with people in different cultures will entail communication – which could be face to face, indirect, oral or written, using body language, and using technology such as e-mail and videoconferencing. When we think of communication, we naturally try to convey our values to other people. We say or do something which impacts our listener or observer. A kind of cultural ripple is created, where our performance, rituals, admiration for certain heroes or national figures, our use of speech or body language, reveal our values. Hall and Hall (1990) consider communication in terms of low and high-context cultures. Americans, Australians and British are examples of low-context cultures – they communicate directly and to the point, with communication placing value on straight-line logic. Communication is explicit. At the other extreme are the Japanese and Chinese, who are high-context communicators – they value a more indirect approach to communication, with emphasis on saving face. Communication is more dependent on the person and the situation or context in which it is taking place. Ambiguity and subtlety are valued, and being able to read non-verbal cues is of critical importance. Each side considers its use of language to be normal. There is no mutually or universally accepted way of convincing someone that you are right, or even of showing them exactly what you mean. To manage communications effectively when organizing and working across different cultures it is necessary to try in the first instance to identify areas of shared practice where communication can be conducted more easily, but failing that to devise methods to reconcile differences (Trompenaars and Hampden-Turner, 2004) in order that communication can progress.

To operate successfully in different cultures and for the business overall to succeed, a cross-cultural approach needs to be taken to ensuring that performance is managed. Here we take a cross-cultural perspective on this issue and suggest that 10 prompts be considered in managing performance internationally in different cultural environments:

▌ **Focus on outcomes, rather than inputs and processes.** Process measures and compliance procedures are important indicators of performance achievement, but are a means to an end, not ends in themselves. Organizations report that they seem to make progress when they move away from the traditional (western) emphasis on inputs and efficiency, and focus instead on outputs, and even better outcomes, results and effectiveness.

▌ **Make sure that measures applied to individuals, teams and projects are linked to long-term corporate goals.** Processes should not encourage short-termism in behaviours for short-term gain if this may be detrimental to the business overall in the longer term. Remember that different nationalities have different attitudes to time, and motivation tools need to reflect these, with the long-term corporate objective at the heart.

▌ **Use quantitative and qualitative measures of performance in combination.** In cultural terms, not all employees may respond well to masculine values of achievement and targets. Qualitative evaluation through observation and review of project teams may produce complementary or alternative information.

▌ **Involve customers, suppliers and your own staff in developing appropriate measures and feedback.** Remember the cross-cultural challenge of high power distance societies where feedback mechanisms requiring upward and all-round 360-degree appraisal are likely to prove unworkable.

▌ **Carry out pilot introductions of performance measures.** It is always important to test any new initiative before introduction – remember that 'measurement' may be an alien concept and employees' trust needs to be built. Remember too that measurement does not guarantee accuracy – in terms of international assignees, their performance is subject to the newly encountered variables of societal, organizational and professional cultures – and family pressures during adaptation.

▌ **Be wary of perverse incentives which might encourage the opposite behaviour to that which is intended.** Affiliation may prove to be a stronger motivator than achievement in collective and particularist societies. Incentives aimed at the individual could 'break up harmonious relationships and damage the business longer-term.

▌ **Don't get so sophisticated that people cannot understand the measures.** Remember that the management of performance needs to be communicated across languages. In some languages there may not even be a direct translation of this concept.

▌ **Provide for auditing and checking.** A system is needed to ensure that the measures applied are achieving their objectives and that information and data remain 'honest'. The management of performance in high-context cultures can prove to be especially challenging, as face saving can override the performance process.

▌ **Get the supporting systems right.** The success of any performance measurement system in a cross-cultural context rests as much on the strength of the supporting systems as on the measures themselves. Systems are needed to gather a variety of information, both formally and informally, but any measurement against competencies can improve this process, as competencies reflect the application of skills and knowledge through the use of appropriate values.

▌ **Use measures in combination with close reporting relationships.** Complex measures cannot replace the need for appropriate management controls and monitoring. As one organization put it: 'If your day to day management control is poor, then no amount of measures will get it right.' This is particularly important in international projects where geography can reduce the formal and informal contact between the individual and supervisor, and also in international team working where the team leader may change depending on the nature of the project. For international assignees, the reporting manager may remain in the home country and contact is limited.

In summary, the inter-cultural dynamics must be appreciated, together with the diverse corporate and political influences, in managing individual and team performance in a multinational setting. The choices multinational managements face will be influenced by these complex phenomena, interacting with the assumptions conditioning how they evaluate them, and the actions likely to be preferred, derived from theoretical influences on management strategy. This strategy might take a transaction cost, agency, resource-based or institutionally oriented perspective (or some combination of these).

CULTURE SHOCK

The previous section has highlighted only a few of the cultural considerations that people experience when living and/or working together across different cultures. It is therefore expected that most people will experience cultural surprise when interacting with other cultures, and culture shock, to some degree, particularly when living and working in another country. Culture shock is a normal and predictable phenomenon, although those experiencing it may feel that they are inadequate or weak, even believing that they are suffering some form of mental illness. According to Oberg (1960), feelings of strain, rejection, confusion and incompetence are common. Individuals may also experience a sense of loss, feelings of deprivation, feelings of surprise, anxiety and even disgust. All these are normal, and hence it is crucial in preparation and training programmes, either for expatriation or to receive/partner with individuals and groups from another culture, that the effects of culture shock are known and explained (see Chapter 4).

One of the key issues involved in culture shock is the need to cope with ambiguity. Most research evidence comes from the expatriation literature, reflected in the illustration that follows, but similar considerations may apply to host country organization members too. Assignees and their families, for example, have to try to make sense of what is happening around them when actions and behaviours that would work at home fail to achieve the desired result in the foreign environment. Culture shock is stressful because it requires readjustment in coping with differences in assumptions and values, patterns of thinking, behaviours and styles of communication.

Competencies associated with success in the international environment (see Chapter 3) include cross-cultural communication skills and tolerance of ambiguity, but despite being able to listen actively, observe and avoid making quick decisions, it is a normal reaction in times of stress to become judgemental and to interpret behaviours from one's own assumptions and values. The application of one's own 'moral code' can lead to ethnocentrism – hence feelings of disgust and/or hostility towards local people and/or their environment (or towards the 'foreign invaders'). Likely expatriate stressors include security concerns; time management; ignorance of the local language; climate differences; health management/environment; attitudes to women; failures/unreliability of services such as transport, communications and utilities; non-availability of goods that were available at home; excessive bureaucracy; role changes for the individual and partner (who might be a non-working spouse, managing servants, or a spouse acting as company representative).

Readjustment to the new environment has been described in terms of a U-curve theory (Torbiörn, 1982). In this theory, expatriates arriving in a new country will experience a short *'honeymoon'* or tourist phase. During this stage the new environment is exciting and challenging – it is like being on holiday in a different country. This phase is critical, as unrealistic expectations may be created, leading to later feelings of being let down when they are not realized. After this, a longer period of *'culture shock'* or crisis follows, characterized by disillusion, disenchantment and lowered morale. At this stage, Oberg's descriptors are particularly apt. In terms of the individual's reaction to this stress, the so-called 'fight or flight reaction' is particularly prominent (see below). Typifying the fight reaction is hostility towards the local culture, taking a defensive attitude, complaining and even engaging in aggressive behaviour. The flight reaction may be characterized by withdrawal from interaction with natives, immersion in one's own cultural group (the expatriate ghetto), and alcohol/drug dependency as a result of using such substances initially as a coping mechanism. Another flight reaction is to 'go native' – engaging in superficial acculturation, although this is often merely escapist behaviour. In the third stage, the assignee experiences a period of recovery leading to *'adjustment'* (in Torbiörn's terms) and resolution. In this stage the assignee learns to operate appropriately in the new environment before reaching the stage of *'mastery'* or adaptation. At this final part of the U-curve, the assignee has adjusted to the new culture while affirming and retaining his or her own cultural identity.

As every person reacts to stressors differently, there can be no prescribed timetable for the culture shock cycle. However, it is generally thought that it takes around six to eight months to move through the various stages and reach adaptation. Those who make frequent international moves may go through the cycle quickly or barely experience it all. Alternatively, frequent moves may take their toll on psychological well-being. Organizations transferring people on short-term assignments or as part of a mobile cadre may wish to consider the likely effects on productivity of employees if they barely have time to adapt before returning home or moving on to another position. And productivity among host organization members may be equally disrupted as a result of frequent changes of home country overseers disrupting the equilibrium of locally institutionalized operating norms around work employment arrangements. It could be hypothesized that a transaction costs or agency-oriented managerial style by the expatriate manager may particularly amplify the consequences of frequent expatriate substitutions, but even a resource-valuing multinational people-management strategy may be undermined if relationships between expatriates and locals are destabilized too frequently.

MANAGING INTERNATIONAL ASSIGNMENT STRESS

The term 'stress' originates from the Latin *stringere*, meaning to draw tight. It is the result of outside forces or pressure placed upon us, and may be thought of as being people's response to a disturbance in their personal equilibrium. Many of the definitions of stress refer to external stressors as forces or strains placed upon an individual. Maund's (2001) definition, for example, is typical: 'Stress is any force that puts a psychological or physical factor beyond its range of stability, producing strain within the individual.' Stress may alternatively be defined as the state of affairs that exists when the way people attempt to manage problems taxes or exceeds their coping mechanisms (Stoll, 1991). This latter definition is helpful in that it shows that the experience of stress is an individual reaction. This means that what is perceived as stressful to one person may be viewed as excitement or a challenge to another (again with scope for cross-cultural differentiation between organizational members).

The impact of stress on health and welfare has been known for many years. Stress results from the over-application or misapplication of Seyle's general adaptation syndrome (Seyle, 1946 reported in UCL/CBI, 1991). Seyle considers this as a three-stage reaction that takes place within us as we prepare ourselves for potential threats. The first stage is *alarm*, when an individual's defence mechanisms become active. At this point the body's sympathetic nervous system is activated, and hormones (such as adrenalin) are released to trigger the 'fight or flight' reaction. The second stage of the stress process is *resistance*, considered to be the stage of maximum adaptation. If the coping mechanism employed is successful, then the body returns to equilibrium. However, if the stressor continues or the coping/defence mechanism does not work, the body enters the third stage, *exhaustion*. At this stage adaptive mechanisms collapse.

The natural reaction to stress is fight or flight. It is these reactions that result in the engagement of the parasympathetic nervous system which, in effect, winds the body down, naturally through exercise. Although the fight/flight reaction worked well for our ancestors and still protects us today, the main problems faced by people now are that there are increasing numbers of stressors and reduced opportunities to fight or flee in the modern world. Our bodies prepare themselves to undertake a physical reaction to potential threats and release hormones accordingly. When the source of threat does not require a physical response (or there is no natural outlet), the hormones still produce the stimulus for energy metabolites but these remain in excess in the body and can be responsible for later degenerative disease. Hormone imbalance can also trigger mental health problems (UCL/CBI, 1991).

Behavioural symptoms of stress include irritability, difficulty in making decisions, lack of humour, difficulty in concentrating, suppressed anger, feelings of being targeted or threatened, being unable to cope, and lack of interest in home life after work. Physical symptoms include lack of appetite or alternatively craving food under pressure, indigestion, insomnia, eczema, constipation/diarrhoea, impotency/frigidity and fainting. Serious illnesses are known to result from long-term exposure to stress, including heart problems, ulcers, colitis, hypertension, migraines, skin disorders and clinical depression.

The general adaptation syndrome is triggered by the need to adapt and adjust to changing circumstances. The reaction is not sensitive to the 'quality' of the event, although magnitude does affect it – both the strength and length of reaction. Everyone is subjected to stressful events in their everyday lives, at home and at work. Changing environments and situations require adaptation, with consequent readjustment by the individual concerned. The mental and physiological adaptation process is a prime cause of stress. This stress is, in turn, responsible for loss of performance in the short term and potentially degenerative mental or physical ill-health in the longer term (UCL/CBI, 1991).

Research in the United States (Holmes and Rahe, 1967) resulted in the development of a 'social readjustment rating scale', which identifies life events that require readjustment, and hence cause stress. Major events identified included death of a spouse, divorce, marital separation, detention in jail, death of a close family member, major personal injury or illness, and being fired from work. Interestingly, more positive events such as getting married or marital reconciliation also emerged from the study as being significant causes of stress. This indicates that stressful factors may be both negative and positive in their outcomes – stress is about readjusting to different circumstances, not just about dealing with negative events and situations. The desirability of the event is therefore not a factor; rather the greater the need to readjust, the greater the stress. If an event is encountered frequently and there is no requirement to change behaviour, the general adaptation syndrome does not apply and stress is not encountered. Where the individual desires the change of circumstances and prepares accordingly, the magnitude of the readjustment required is also likely to be less (UCL/CBI, 1991).

Holmes and Rahe (1967) suggested that scores be attached to each different stressful event, and that these be summed to give a total score, reflecting the number and intensity of stressful events encountered and thus degree of readjustment required. This score could then be used to predict the likelihood of stress-related ill-health occurring in the future. This research cannot be used to predict ill-health with any degree of accuracy: after all, as Stoll's definition indicates, we all experience and deal with stress differently. Nevertheless, individuals who experience a number of stressful situations simultaneously are more likely to suffer stress and potential ill-health as a result, than those people needing to make few readjustments. Research into personality also demonstrates links with stress-related ill-health. Those with so-called Type A personalities (who are highly competitive, tense, pressurized individuals) are more likely to suffer stress than Type B personalities (those who are more relaxed, in little need of displaying achievements and not easily frustrated or angered). Type A individuals are therefore more likely to suffer stress-related ill-health than Type Bs (Friedman and Rosebaum, 1974).

Besides issues in our personal lives, stress is also likely to be encountered in the working environment. Intrinsic factors such as physical surroundings, lighting, communications mechanisms and frequency, long hours of work, daily commuting and new technology are just some examples of stressors over which we may have little control. Role ambiguity, role conflict and responsibility without authority are other significant causes of stress. Added to these are relationships at work, career development (or lack of it) and work–life balance, which also impact on stress levels. The organizational structure and climate (whether individuals have a sense of participation, control and are involved in decision making) is a yet further example of stressors at work.

In the United Kingdom there have been a number of employment tribunal cases, taken by employees against their employers, claiming compensation for stress-related ill-health. There is statutory provision requiring employers to carry our risk assessments to protect employees from foreseeable risk, and a number of cases have been successful, in that the claimant successfully argued that foreseeable psychiatric harm had been caused from stressors such as long hours and workplace traumas (Cooper and Earnshaw, 1996).

Individuals involved in an international lifestyle involving travel and living and working abroad, and as the recipients of transplanted managerial ideas and supervisory agents from outside the host environment, are subject to yet further stressors, directly linked to their 'international' environment. The UCL/CBI (1991) research explored this in some depth via a survey of 206 international assignees and international business travellers. It found that the top 10 stressors were:

▌ living or working somewhere hostile or threatening;

▌ geographical separation from spouse, over one month;

▌ geographical separation from children, over one month;

▌ major change in responsibilities at work;

▌ spouse/partner unable to pursue career;

▌ change in residence – finding accommodation;

▌ working in a culture where language is unfamiliar;

▌ change in residence – moving self and belongings;

▌ identifying/arranging suitable education;

▌ return to home after stay abroad.

It is not surprising that the most stressful event identified is living in a hostile or threatening environment. Although companies aim to protect their employees from potential threats, even the tightest security measures can prove to be ineffective, particularly in today's climate of international terrorism. Having to live and work amidst security measures – such as in a secure compound or travelling under armed escort – requires significant readjustment. It is crucial to ensure that employees and their families are adequately prepared to live in areas of potential danger, and an understanding of the local language is important to be able to communicate effectively and know what is happening within the local environment. Known danger areas and situations can be identified and appropriate measures taken (emergency evacuation plans, rest and relaxation stress breaks, and so on). However, in some cases a perceived danger may prove as stressful as a real one to the individual and family. The fear of a potential threat may result in individuals being unable to prepare and initiate a coping response – the perceived threat, rather than an actual threat, can act as a stressor.

While actions to minimize exposure to stressful situations are important to safeguard the internationally mobilized, corporate managements may wish to reflect also on the likely consequences of such measures in further increasing the sense of segregation between expatriates and their hosts. They can act as a drag on organizational effectiveness, measured against the benchmark of the transnational model (Ghoshal and Bartlett, 1998).

Action may be taken by organizations to minimize the risks to assignees working in dangerous locations at both the corporate and individual level. At the corporate level, research should be carried out into the environments where operations are conducted and potential business partners researched.

Emergency planning for dealing with crises should be carried out, including the preparation and training of individuals in the headquarters to respond appropriately in an emergency. Security consultancies may be engaged to provide updated advice on local operations, and insurance policies put into effect. At the individual level, security measures should be put in place as necessary, briefing provided and stress breaks (such as rest and recreation leave) be included in policy.

Separation from family is the norm in most short-term assignments, commuter assignments and business trips. The duration of the separation is relevant as a stressor, with periods of separation of over a month being highlighted as particularly stressful. This is an important consideration for organizations when determining their mobility strategies. Couples may not want to relocate abroad as a family for dual career and educational reasons, but if an employee undertakes short-term or commuter assignments instead of traditional family mobility, a significant source of stress is introduced to the employee and family members. Measures may be needed within international assignment policies to provide for home leave, but even this may not be sufficient to reduce this source of stress.

In the case of expatriates, the change of job itself is a source of stress for the employee. There is the need not only to cope with aspects of mobility and cultural differences, but to perform well in a new job in a different environment. For locals, the stressor is the change in the expatriate presence, requiring coping strategies to overcome the uncertainty associated with a change in management practice, as to whether new relationships will have positive or negative outcomes. This source of stress should be taken into account within performance management processes.

The inability of a spouse/partner to pursue his or her career is also a significant source of expatriate stress. The UCL/CBI survey separated this from loss of income which, interestingly, was not ranked as stressful by the survey respondents. In order to maintain their careers, the couple may request an unaccompanied assignment – but as mentioned before, this solves one problem (the spouse continues in his or her career) but the separation results in another source of stress. If a spouse does accompany the assignee and is unable to pursue his or her career, this is likely to bring about a change in the dynamics of the family, with consequent needs for readjustment. If the spouse is unable to work at all but was used to following a demanding career, the situation is likely to be exacerbated. Assignment policies may contain provision to assist the spouse both practically and financially.

Change in residence is a further stressful event experienced by mobile personnel. This is an ongoing source of stress, with assignees continually adjusting to preparing to move, packing and storing items, moving belongings, settling in and moving on again, with the continual worry of housing at home and how it is being maintained. For those who are part of a mobile cadre, or who regularly expatriate, a sense of 'home' has to be constructed in each new location every few months or years, and familiar objects take on an even greater significance than they would in a stable home environment. Concern is therefore particularly high that household goods sent to the assignment location by air or sea freight will arrive safely. Relocation service providers offer practical assistance in terms of home search, home sale and lettings management. Specialist removals companies may be employed to handle international moves (Shortland, 2003).

Working across cultures presents considerable challenge and need for readjustment, and is therefore particularly stressful to mobile personnel and their hosts. Being able to communicate in the local language aids local understanding and acceptance, and is therefore a particularly useful coping mechanism. Language training can be deployed as a coping mechanism, in the sense of reducing the likelihood of stress from this particular factor. Language training is also crucial in terms of safety and security, as discussed above. Language training is frequently offered by organizations to the employee and spouse/partner (and sometimes to children). It tends to be a requirement for employment for locals to be able to communicate effectively in the language of the 'home' or inwardly investing organization. Two-way (or, where third-country nationals are involved, even multi-) cultural training is also crucial (see Chapter 4).

Children's education is also a significant cause for concern among internationally mobile personnel. As people are not prepared to sacrifice their children's future for their own job/career, this presents one of the major stumbling blocks to mobility. However, where suitable educational provision is available locally (or through boarding in the home country), decisions have to be made on finding and securing places for children. On the whole, the trend today is for children to accompany their parents rather than remain in the home country – separation from children has already been identified as a source of stress. Specialist consultancies may be employed to conduct school search and thus reduce the stress associated with this aspect of international living.

Returning home after the stay abroad is also identified as a major stressor. This aspect of the assignment process is often neglected, yet it requires a significant degree of readjustment. Frames of reference held by the individual and family are out of date on return home. Indeed if the assignee's frame of reference has shifted significantly towards that of the host country – or there has been a series of assignments in numerous countries – the sense of 'home' can be lost altogether. If the repatriation process is unsupported, the assignee and family can be demoralized, the employee's productivity will be reduced and turnover may result (see Chapter 3). Repatriation training and debriefing on return can help in this area.

REPATRIATION AND REVERSE CULTURE SHOCK

Although it may not be expected, returning assignees are likely to experience reverse culture shock – that is, they are affected by culture shock once back in their home country. This requires readjustment in much the same way as when they were assigned abroad. Initially, the returnee may be delighted to be back home, meeting up with family and friends and experiencing life in the 'home' environment. However, disenchantment usually follows when little interest is shown in stories and experiences abroad and 'home' is unfamiliar. Depending on where the assignment was, the returnee might see his or her home country as materialistic and wasteful, or the standard of living might not be as high as he or she had experienced as an assignee – particularly when assignment packages no longer apply. Loss of status is also an issue for many, as employees return to an environment where they are not 'expatriates'. These feelings of loss may be experienced by other family members too. Children, for instance, might leave international schools to return to local education provision. Common readjustment difficulties include sleeping difficulties, fatigue and tearfulness. These symptoms usually pass within a few weeks, although more serious illnesses such as clinical depression can result. The most common problem is the lack of acknowledgement that readjustment is required after repatriation, and that treatment may be needed.

Organizations may offer employee assistance programmes (EAPs) which provide confidential counselling. The use of such services is to be encouraged. However, if returnees do not recognize that they have readjustment issues, they are unlikely to seek help. Organizations should therefore provide an awareness of reverse culture shock within repatriation training, and offer confidential personal debriefing on return, as this can help returnees to acknowledge any difficulties and seek further counselling as necessary.

According to Lovell-Hawker (2004), debriefing can mean many things, and it is therefore helpful to consider the options available and their potential uses. She defines three forms of debriefing: operational, personal, and critical incident debriefing. Operational debriefing is defined as:

> asking for information about the work performed, and what was achieved. The aim is to learn what was done well, what could have been done better, and what changes should be made.

Lovell-Hawker defines personal debriefing as:

> asking how the experience was for the individual (what was best/worst? How is the readjustment process going?). Aims to help them integrate their experience into their life as a whole, perceive the experience more meaningfully, and bring a sense of closure.

Critical incident debriefing is:

> a highly structured form of personal debriefing, which can take place after a traumatic experience... Goals are to educate about normal stress reactions and ways to cope with them, to promote the expression of thoughts and feelings about the incident, to bring a sense of closure, and to provide information about how to access further support or help if required.

In terms of welfare of the returnee, operational debriefing indicates an interest in the work performed overseas, and shows that the contribution is valued. It should be carried out prior to any personal debriefing. Operational debriefing would usually be carried out by someone involved in managing the assignment objectives/project. On a practical note, returnees may be willing to share their experiences with others due to go on assignment and thus provide a 'real life element' to the preparation process. Personal debriefing should be offered, and if taken up, carried out confidentially (not by someone within the organization). It is generally appreciated by returnees as, again, it indicates that their efforts are valued and it can help to reduce feelings of loneliness and isolation which are common on return. Such debriefing can help to identify stress-related symptoms, provide reassurance that minor difficulties experienced are normal, and help to resolve issues and bring closure, helping returnees to move on with their life. In addition, such debriefing may help to prevent anxiety and depression from developing, or if severe symptoms are identified, encourage take-up of medical help. It is important to allow sufficient time for the debriefing to take place without the returnee feeling pressurized.

Critical incident debriefing is offered after traumatic events, and should be carried out confidentially. Lovell-Hawker recommends a seven-step process to allow for a 'gentle "step down" into discussion of the more emotional aspects, and then "climb back up" so that the session ends positively by thinking about support and the future'. She suggests:

> Step 1 – introductions; step 2 – the facts about the experience; step 3 – thoughts during and after the experience; step 4 – the sensory impressions and emotions; step 5: teaching about normal symptoms; step 6 – discussing coping strategies, and future planning; step 7 – ending the session.

INTERNATIONAL MOBILITY AND IMPLICATIONS FOR THE PSYCHOLOGICAL CONTRACT

The difficulties that may be encountered in working in different cultural environments – within international teams, as a manager responsible for performance in another country, or as an international assignee – are likely to have an impact on the individual's psychological contract. The imposition of culturally different policies and practices on local people by a foreign-based headquarters will also affect the psychological contract that locals have with their multinational employer. The psychological contract is important to working relationships, employee productivity and performance because it concerns how people perceive fairness and how they are treated by their organization. It is defined by Guest (2004) as 'the perceptions of both parties to the employment relationship, organization and individual, of the reciprocal promises and obligations implied in that relationship'. Effectively, the employment relationship is seen as an 'exchange' – 'a set of perceived reciprocal promises and obligations between the individual and the organization' (Makin, 1999).

The psychological contract comprises two parts: the economic contract or transactional deal, and the social contract or implicit deal. The transactional element is explicit, and is based on reward of contributions – an economic exchange. However, the social contract is not usually discussed openly, and is based on reciprocity – an interpersonal exchange. Together these produce the 'inferred deal' that comprises the psychological contract. Both the employer and the employee need to deliver on their promises to create a psychological contract of fairness, trust, commitment, well-being and performance. The state of the psychological contract between the individual and the organization concerns 'whether the promises and obligations have been met, whether they are fair and their implications for trust' (Guest, 2004). If one side does not fulfil its promises as perceived by the other side, trust is lost and performance and organizational commitment is damaged. This translates into lower job satisfaction and intention to quit on the part of the employee.

A greater part of the lives of internationally mobile personnel is dependent upon the organization than is the case for domestic, headquarters-based and local employees. Research by van Ruitenbeek (1999) indicated that the employer's side of the psychological contract regarding international assignees differed significantly from that of the assignees themselves. She noted that whereas the employers expected hard work, loyalty, commitment, the winning of new business, the management of local operations, skills transfer, cross-cultural effectiveness and for assignees to complete their assignment and not complain, the expatriate employees expected a whole range of different concerns to be addressed. These were listed as pay and benefits, career development/training, cultural orientation, housing, spouse employment, children's education, social life, personal security, elderly relatives and pets. When the psychological contract is broken, the individual tends to focus on the economic aspects of the contract. Although every attempt should be made to preserve the psychological contract, this reinforces the need for fair and equitable reward policies (see Chapter 5), training and development (Chapter 4) and good, transparent communications.

CONCLUDING REMARKS

The history of relations between nations is fraught with the consequences of false assumptions about motivations, intentions, thought patterns and feelings. To do business successfully in the international arena requires us to explore differences in perception, ways of thinking, styles of communication and customary behaviour. We need to be able to explain what happens when people who come from business systems in contrasting cultures meet, eat, joke, argue, negotiate and cooperate with each other. Awareness should be developed of the feelings people have about each other, their expectations, the effect their interactions have, and the manner in which one embarrasses, frustrates, angers or impresses the other. Such insights help to predict the outcome of encounters between cultures. This will help us to clarify what one must do to become a competent competitor, a trusted colleague or partner, and the human capital choices that flow from this. Indications are obtained as to what degree of adaptation may lead to producing the right impact on representatives of the other culture.

The author Robert Louis Stevenson once said that there are no foreign lands, it is the traveller who is foreign. This is a particularly apt statement when considering the influence of culture on those living and working in another country, and those who remain in their homelands but have dealings with people in other lands. One of the keys to success in a foreign environment in terms of a performance-focused relationship rests in consideration of employee welfare – the impact that the foreign organization will have on the working lives of local nationals, and the impact of international mobility on those employees who are asked to travel or relocate to serve the interests of the business. How multinational managements weigh these complex issues is likely to be significantly influenced by their strategic orientation towards the workforce: whether employees are viewed in transactional cost or agency terms, or whether a resource-based position is adopted, possibly cognisant of the implications of institutional practice. Organizations have legal and social responsibilities for employee welfare, but such responsibilities also make for sound business practice.

Productivity, performance and business success in a highly competitive environment depend on employees being physically able and mentally willing to perform their roles to the best of their ability, and in some instances to engage in extra-role behaviour. Stress causes ill-health affecting employees' physical and mental abilities, so steps taken to reduce stress levels must improve both employees' lives and their contribution to the working environment. A healthy psychological contract is also needed to increase motivation and organizational commitment. It follows that business strategy should not include these as an add-on when the going gets tough; rather it should incorporate them in the early stage of strategy formulation and strategic choice when considering operating in an international environment.

YOUR TURN

▌ What is culture and why does it matter within IHRM strategic choice?

▌ How can cultural differences be reconciled to mutual advantage by strategic business partners?

▌ Is employee welfare and well-being becoming of increasing significance in SIHRM? Why? Or why not?

▌ How might key organizational actors improve their psychological contract and that of others upon whom they – and their business dealings – depend?

▌ Examine some examples of SIHRM choices that have been made by your organization, or one known to you, in the light of cultural issues. How might these choices have been amended or changed to (potentially) result in more favourable consequences for the organization and its social actors?

REFERENCES

Cooper, C and Earnshaw, J (1996) *Stress and Employer Liability*, Institute of Personnel and Development (IPD), London

Friedman, M and Rosebaum, R (1974) *Type A Behaviour and Your Heart*, Knopf, New York

Ghoshal, S and Bartlett, CA (1998) Managing Across Borders: The transnational solution, Random House, London

Guest, D (2004) How people feel about work – the new psychological contract, annual conference proceedings, Chartered Institute for Personnel and Development (CIPD), London

Hall, E T and Hall, M R (1990) *Understanding Cultural Differences*, Intercultural Press, Yarmouth, ME

Hofstede, G (1981) *Cultures Consequences: International differences in work-related values*, Sage, Beverly Hills, CA

Hofstede, G (1991) *Cultures and Organisations: Software of the mind*, McGraw-Hill, Maidenhead

Hofstede, G (2001) *Cultures Consequences: Comparing values, behaviours, institutions and organizations across nations*, Sage, London

Holmes, T H and Rahe, E M (1967) The Social Readjustment Rating Scale, *Journal of Psychometric Research*, **2**, pp 213–18

Lovell-Hawker, D (2004) *Debriefing Aid Workers: A comprehensive manual*, People In Aid, Oxford

Makin, P (1999) The expatriate psychological contract, conference proceedings, Centre for International Briefing, Farnham

Maund, L (2001) *An Introduction to Human Resource Management*, Palgrave, Basingstoke

McSweeney, B (2002a) Hofstede's model of national cultural differences and their consequences: a triumph of faith – a failure of analysis, *Human Relations*, **55**, pp 89–118

McSweeney, B (2002b) Fundamental flaws in Hofstede's research, *EBF*, **9**, pp 39–43

Oberg, K (1960) Culture shock: adjustment to new cultural environments, *Practical Anthropologist*, **7**, pp 177–82

Shortland, S (2003) Managing international assignment stress, *Managing Internationally Mobile Employees Briefing*, **37**, pp 12–15

Stoll, K (1991) Stress and international mobility, unpublished conference proceedings, University College London and CBI Employee Relocation Council

Torbiörn, I (1982) *Living Abroad: Personal adjustment and personnel policy in the overseas setting*, Wiley, New York

Triandis, H C (2004) The many dimensions of culture, *Academy of Management Executive*, **18**(1), pp 88–93

Trompenaars, F and Hampden-Turner, C (1997) *Riding the Waves of Culture*, Nicholas Brearley, London

Trompenaars, F and Hampden-Turner, C (2004) *Managing People across Cultures*, Capstone, Chichester

UCL/CBI (1991) *Survey on Stress and International Mobility*, University College London and CBI Employee Relocation Council, London

Van Ruitenbeek, D (1999) The expatriate psychological contract, conference proceedings, Centre for International Briefing, Farnham

3

Choices and consequences in resourcing global business operations

---

CHAPTER AIMS

This chapter sets out to do the following:

- explore 'employee resourcing' issues associated with the increasing pace of internationalization and management of strategic international investments;

- provide practical considerations underpinned by theoretical frameworks informing international employee resourcing;

- examine international employee recruitment and selection policy and practice;

- highlight the role of 'diversity' within international employee resourcing;

- consider the whole cycle of resourcing including repatriation or localization of internationally mobile personnel.

INTRODUCTION

Not all internationalizing business development projects are of the same type. Some are purely acquisitions of existing enterprises ('brownfield'); others involve the development of the business – often including operational site construction – on a 'greenfield' basis. These represent opposite ends of a scale. Between the extremes of sole ownership acquisition and development from a start-up, mergers, partnerships and joint ventures play an increasingly significant role in international business development. In a number of cases, international ventures will be at some intermediate phase, for example, the acquisition of a part-completed manufacturing or process plant.

The second major source of variation lies in location. Business operations may be located in the developed world or the developing world. The developed world is defined as those countries of North America, Europe, Japan and Australasia where the capitalist system can be deemed to be mature. Developing countries lie in the emerging markets of the Far East, particularly the Chinese, south-east Asian and Indian subcontinent regions, the Middle East, and the previously communist Eastern bloc. Business opportunities are also being pursued with varying degrees of enthusiasm in Central and South America, and Africa, particularly the south, now it has emerged from isolation. Cultural, political and background economic factors in different parts of the world will significantly affect the approach taken to resourcing the business, which will in turn affect the achievement of strategic business goals.

The choices of business location, types of operation and resourcing strategy are almost endless. The consequences of getting them wrong can be the success or failure of the organization. This chapter considers resourcing choices within a theoretical framework, recognizing that growth in the global marketplace is by no means linear and that resourcing must be recognized as a complex and continuing process. The chapter continues by providing discussion on recruitment possibilities before considering the crucial issue of capabilities identification within the selection process. It also focuses on the cultural and psychological implications of resourcing business operations. Resourcing is seen as a cyclical process, and thus consideration is given to repatriation and localization of international assignees as part of a strategy of talent retention. Throughout the chapter, attention is drawn to diversity issues such as resourcing using local talent and the increasing participation of women in senior international roles.

THE INCREASING PACE OF ORGANIZATIONAL RESOURCE INTERNATIONALIZATION

There is plenty of evidence for the increasing pace of internationalization in the ways business operations are resourced, with direct consequences for the division of labour across the world's economies. Newspaper headlines reflect this, with stories of 'offshoring' in which thousands of jobs are exported to countries such as India, where highly skilled workers are available to take on communications and IT functions, more cost-effectively for businesses than can be achieved in western developed economies. This international 'export of jobs', as it is often emotively described in the western press, reflects tight labour markets in 'exporting' nations, the ability to service operations globally through advanced information technology, and the increasingly international nature of labour and people resourcing.

Commentators such as Wallerstein (1983) regard these developments as a product of the historical evolution of capitalist economic organization, as those engaged in the accumulation of profits from commercial enterprise struggle with competitors to maximize the benefits available to these interests – and with other interest groups, such as state agencies and working people in employment systems around the world. We reflect on some of these issues when discussing employment regulation in an international context, in Chapter 6. For now our focus is more functionally inclined: what issues might concern multinational managements when pursuing a strategy of transnational resourcing of the needs of the enterprise?

THE PROCESS OF ORGANIZATION AND EMPLOYEE RESOURCE INTERNATIONALIZATION

The process of internationalization may take many forms. The 'greenfield' start-up, for example, refers to the situation where a corporation sets up a foreign subsidiary from scratch. It is not unusual for this to be achieved through the use of expatriation – either an employee from the parent organization is sent to head up the operation, or a small team of key individuals is deployed. The 'greenfield' approach is a relatively slow approach to building an international business, and as such its cultural risk might be argued to be limited. The subsidiary will tend to select individuals who match the organizational culture, and these people will be socialized by the expatriate managers sent out from the host country.

At the other end of the spectrum lies the foreign takeover. Under this approach, a local company is purchased wholesale by a foreign buyer.

Clearly, this provides immediate entry into the local market and the possibility of fast expansion – but the cultural risk is extremely high. Integration of the two organizations is typically difficult. One solution might be an arms' length approach to managing the foreign operation, but this will preclude the integration of knowledge and the likelihood of capitalizing on this when further ventures are undertaken. To achieve integration, headquarters or other parent company staff might be drafted in, possibly replacing key local individuals, to instil the corporate culture within the new acquisition. This could be regarded as a destruction of human capital, as an ethnocentric resourcing approach might damage local responsiveness, but not necessarily create international vision.

International mergers are relatively common but, on the whole, tend to have a relatively low success rate. It might be debated whether the merger is a true merger of equals (by size, importance of operations and so on) or a disguised form of takeover. Cultural differences – in terms of societal, organizational and professional cultures – need to be addressed, but frequently are not given sufficient attention. Citing Child, Faulkner and Pitkethly (2001), Goodernham and Nordhaug (2003: 19) observe that 'as many as 50 per cent of M&As fail'.

Partnering with other organizations to collaborate on specific projects or to capture certain markets for mutual benefit may prove to be a prudent way to internationalize. Such partnering is less likely to be viewed as threatening or hostile, and could pave the way for a merger later, when the partners learn of each other's cultures and how to work effectively together.

Joint ventures also provide a mechanism for global expansion. A new business is created by pooling resources from two or more founding parties. Although culturally they should be lower risk than mergers or acquisitions, attention needs to be paid to which partner supplies particular resources. Lack of attention paid to cultural factors can often cause difficulties in joint venture operations. The common mistake is for emphasis to be placed on visible issues such as the legal framework, financial and market analyses. Cross-cultural differences must be given attention, including the relationship of the organization to the social and political frameworks operating locally. The structure of the joint venture company, as well as selection, development, performance management, reward, reporting and decision-making systems must all be given sufficient attention.

The role of our model is critical here. Although business system aspects such as financial and legal considerations must be explored fully, the human capital and social issues must also form part of the due diligence process, and these must work in tandem with business strategy to ensure that whatever the form of the new international venture, focus is placed on ensuring strong performance within the employment relationship. The assumptions underlying strategy formation, as this extends to decisions on employee re-sourcing, will have a material effect on organizational outcomes. Is the prevailing ideology based on transaction cost theory, or agency theory, where a wholly instrumental posture will locate employee resource planning as subsidiary to more financially and technically oriented considerations? Or will managerial choices privilege, or at least equalize, the people dimension and associated embedded systems and processes alongside inanimate factors of production (money, equipment and so on), reflecting adoption of a resource-based and/or institutionally informed theoretical stance? The latter may be judged to be instrumental in the final analysis – treating employees as a means to organizational ends – but the edges are tempered somewhat by consideration of a wider range of contextual factors.

Such assumptions and resultant choice making are likely to colour the ways in which multinational managements invest in positioning the organization in employment markets; how potential human capital is identified and attracted; and the care with which selection, socialization and 'corporate memory-building' is undertaken. The degree of direct involvement by senior line management in resourcing activities offers another tangible indicator of the perceived value of human capital management in the governance of the organization as a whole.

MANAGING STRATEGIC INTERNATIONAL INVESTMENTS

We now look specifically at some mechanics in relation to making acquisitions, mergers, joint ventures and greenfield developments work, in people management terms. So often, once the deal is done and the commercial people have flown home, existing management teams are left wondering how best to ensure the success of a new international venture. That venture will be successful through the combination of the efforts, commitment and talents of the people involved. Those people include both the successful investor and any local people whose services have been acquired as part of the venture.

It is of great benefit to internationalizing businesses to stop to think seriously and systematically about the way in which they will enable all those concerned with managing business unit investments to meet their strategic goals. In our experience, it is useful to undertake this series of steps:

▌ Establish guidelines on the company's strategic objectives in asset development and acquisition, which will assist at the time that targets are identified.

▌ Review core capabilities to ensure the organization is well organized to handle turnaround situations.

▌ Identify people across the parent organization best placed to provide support to the project, and team leaders in the valuations, development, due-diligence work, and implementation of their projects.

▌ Provide focused training and business awareness, to ensure financial and commercial success from implementation.

▌ Provide suitable capabilities development modules to add into corporate training programmes (see Chapter 4).

The matrix in Table 3.1 provides a useful guide to addressing some of the questions which will come to light in trying to align capabilities with business objectives.

Hofer and Schendel (1978) suggest several theoretical business strategies that business units can follow, ranging from aggressive market share growth through to consolidation, exit and liquidation. For the sake of simplicity in developing the matrix in Table 3.1, three generic stages are used: growth, sustain and harvest.

1   In the *growth phase*, internationalizing businesses are at the early stages of their life-cycle. They have products or services whose growth potential is significant. To realize this potential, considerable resources may have to be committed to develop and enhance the new products and services, and to create an operational and distribution infrastructure which will support local and global relationships with partners, suppliers and customers.

2   International businesses in the *sustain phase* will still require investment and reinvestment, but are expected to earn sustained high returns on the capital that investors have supplied. Management focus will be on enhancing continuous improvement in market share and operational efficiency, rather than the long-payback and growth-resourcing investments necessary during the first (growth) phase. This is where the majority of businesses will be in their domestic operations, and they will expect to move into this phase as soon as possible during their international expansion.

Table 3.1 Matching capabilities to strategic business requirements, retaining core capabilities which differentiate the business to win, and outsourcing non-core activities

	Strategic themes			
	Market development: building local network + equal opportunity identification	Deal making	Long-term market development	Business operations
Growth	Strategic alliance with local partners – hire local business development team	Acquire local company with in-house business deal-making talent	Short-term expertise import/ long-term capabilities development	Expatriate expertise for skills transfer
Sustain	Joint venture – marketing operation – local agency	Hire specialist 'internationalists' (expats) + key local expertise if available	Local team with corporate capability developed in-house with 'centre' coaching	Local team recruitment
Harvest	Mature joint venture – expansion opportunities – exit strategy/asset realization group from 'centre'	Core business team (in joint venture with local partners?) combining limited expatriate input with mainly locally developed key capability	Host team transferring know-how locally and as corporate memory to other projects in region and globally	O&M* distribution using own local team or agency: limit operations to residual capital investment repatriation

* O&M: operations and maintenance activities.

3 The *harvest phase* will apply to business units that have reached a mature phase of their life cycle. Investors will be seeking payback on capital investments made during the two earlier phases. Such 'profit centres' no longer warrant significant investment, simply enough to maintain equipment and capabilities rather than to create new ones. The main financial goal is to maximize cash flow back to the corporation.

Facing up to the reality of matching international business development aspirations with the current capability pool, organizations find benefit in defining employee resourcing programmes to cover distinct but interrelated phases.

Following business forecasting exercises, internationalizing businesses will identify a number of priorities. These will include the requirement to improve both the management process for business development and execution, and the capabilities deployed on international projects. As experience is gained, further issues will emerge of a behavioural and cultural kind. For instance, some organizations in benchmarking their capability with advisers, clients and customers have feedback that indicates that 'we talk down overseas'. Despite the best efforts of those involved, in developing from a long-standing domestic business, organizations often find there remains the feeling in some quarters that they retain a 'two-business' culture. Such businesses have much to learn about developing and managing overseas projects, and especially joint ventures, in a way which continues to give both the investment community and their boards the confidence that their long-term interests are secure.

In assessments that have been undertaken of organizations attempting to internationalize through the development of a portfolio of investments overseas, the need has been emphasized for clear lines of responsibility within the project management process. The roles of key individuals and functions need to be clearly defined and understood. Increasing importance is being placed on the part played by project managers during both development and operational phases, in leading and coaching multi-disciplinary teams. Cross-cultural sensitivities must be recognized and managed to ensure project objectives are met. Also, the project manager has a key 'corporate' function: namely, ensuring lessons learnt on a specific exercise are distilled and captured, so they may be transferred within the sponsoring organization, as a source of competitive advantage in approaching new or repeat business opportunities.

Reporting controls are also necessary so that executive and functional management have the information they need to be assured that the quality is right and projects are on track. Organizations also need to develop a 'corporate memory', setting down in a more structured and formal way best practices, so that these can become common practices. This will reduce the risks inherent in having valuable project knowledge and expertise residing solely with a small number of individuals.

INTERNATIONAL LEADERSHIP RESOURCING: THE INTERNATIONAL CADRE

The 21st century is the age of the multinational executive, accompanying attempts to construct the globally networked corporation. The world's major businesses now invest heavily in the development of a distinctive *international cadre* capable of transferring the enterprise's commercial and operational philosophies and systems into every location in which they wish to have a profitable presence. This group – capable of thinking global, acting local, and vice versa – will be among the premium capital to which any organization will wish to have access.

The shortage of talented executives with the abilities and background to run global businesses is one of the most significant challenges facing organizations everywhere. Most multinational employers are, at present, embarked on the process of finding a distinctive framework within which they can adequately describe their present or future internationally mobile executive grouping.

Empirical studies have brought to the surface tensions surrounding the categorization of corporate or 'headquarters' executives. In practice, there are clear indicators that assist in placing individuals. Those supporting international business activity as a fundamental part of their job definition (with the need for frequent travel, with its impact on lifestyle which differentiates such individuals from their domestically bound colleagues), and who accept they are obvious candidates for postings outside their 'home' country, can usually properly be placed in the international cadre category. For example, a few years ago, a US-based telecommunications company undertook an exercise to determine what steps were necessary to form a pan-European executive cadre. After much deliberation by a cross-functional management group, they resolved that their European workforce could best be categorized on the basis of 'career trajectories'. The trajectory might be wholly domestic; it might involve some 'international' working – even assignments lasting over a year. 'Transnationals' were categorized as those judged able and willing to accept a flexible career path where mobility was central to what people did – there was no 'home' base to which to 'return' in any conventional sense.

DEFINING MULTINATIONAL CAREER PATHS

∎ **Parent**   Parent company staff who may be deployed at some point in their career to an overseas location for 'skills transfer' reasons, but who are likely to return to the domestic operation subsequently (and certainly to 'retire' in their country of origin).

∎ **Transnational**   Staff who may begin a career with a multinational organization from anywhere in the world, and whose professional skills may be used in a variety of markets; who accept that their next posting location cannot be predicted, take this as a condition of employment; and have no preconceptions about where they might conclude their career.

∎ **Domestic**   Staff hired locally and whose career is unlikely to take them outside the domestic market other than in the most infrequent and unusual of circumstances: a one-off project, or for training, say, at parent company headquarters.

Building on this empirical example, the career trajectories model with its three distinctive multinational career paths, as summarized in the box, is not only useful in reflecting on employee resourcing choices and consequences. It also forms a context for reward strategy formation (discussed in Chapter 5). For the telecoms multinational, this was an important departure from previous practice, where international assignment duration tended to be the measure against which individuals were differentiated. The new approach created a simple model against which to identify people, and for those not in 'the cadre' something possibly to aspire to. It also served to legitimize inequity of treatment between different categories of staff, accepted throughout the organization. The model is not only simple to apply; it also makes sense in managing employee relations.

Frameworks that theorize international business development may be drawn on to assess the degree of fit of employee resourcing categories. Perlmutter's (1969) and Heenan and Perlmutter's (1979) classic models describing 'ethnocentric', 'polycentric', regiocentric' and 'geocentric' stages of internationalization are particularly helpful in guiding the evaluation of employee resourcing choices and consequences.

Organizations internationalizing their businesses through greenfield start-ups are likely to take an ethnocentric approach to employee resourcing. Adopting a centralized structure, they usually export policies and practices from the headquarters operation. The export of parent country nationals (expatriates from the headquarters) is common practice to transfer organizational culture, means and methods of operation and control, and to socialize newly recruited local staff. However, there are a number of disadvantages in using this approach to resourcing key positions. Parent county nationals (PCNs) may take a long time to adapt to the local environment and therefore are not locally responsive. Promotion opportunities for locals are restricted, potentially leading to the lowering of morale and the raising of turnover, and there are issues of inequity between PCNs and locals in terms of remuneration (see Chapter 5). Nevertheless, the use of PCNs is a common approach, frequently also adopted in takeovers and acquisitions.

As organizations' foreign operations begin to become more widespread, with the launch of subsidiaries in different countries, so the control exerted by the headquarters may become weakened and a greater degree of decentralization takes place. There is typically a rise in local autonomy and consequently local responsiveness. At this polycentric stage, in Perlmutter's terms, host-country nationals (locals) are increasingly selected to fill key positions, while PCNs remain at the corporate HQ. (It should be noted that PCNs may still be used at this stage to train locals as necessary, although the focus now is not to keep them in the foreign environment unnecessarily.)

There are clear advantages in using local nationals to resource international subsidiaries. They are culturally attuned and speak the local language, thereby providing local responsiveness. There is continuity of management locally, enabling career opportunities for local people. The cost of staffing locally is lower than if expatriates are used. In areas where security is a key issue, the deployment of local nationals lowers the firm's profile in the host country. That being said, there are some significant disadvantages in the polycentric resourcing approach, unless specific actions are taken. A gap might potentially develop in communications between the parent and the host countries, as local nationals' efforts at communicating with HQ become stymied by language barriers (for both national and corporate language). As a result, the internationalizing business can become a loose federation of independent units rather than an integrated network sharing knowledge. If senior management has limited international experience, this may become a liability in the highly competitive international environment.

In the regiocentric and geocentric resourcing strategies, people are deployed within business units on either a regional or a global basis. This means that employees are either recruited and deployed within a region, or drawn from anywhere in the world to service operations. Both approaches result in a pool of senior managers with international experience, and the tendency for national identification with particular units to be reduced. Regional approaches can work well where there is freedom of movement for nationals of that economic area (as in the European Union). A regional approach to resourcing may also be appropriate where true global mobility would prove unacceptable to employees. The true geocentric or transnational firm would, however, expect to draw and deploy its talent from anywhere, and to anywhere, in the world. There are a number of problems surrounding global mobility, however. These include the impact on the lives of the employees concerned and their families, the discouraging approach of many immigration regimes which require time (and therefore money) to be spent organizing visas, together with the increased costs of training and preparation, and compensation for relocation.

Now we have briefly located the internationalization of employee resourcing in the context of addressing needs for various types of organizational formation and the phases of development, and have touched on 'leadership cadre' implications and some of the alternative ways employee resourcing may be theorized, we turn to two practical questions. First, what considerations do multinational managements face in specifying roles and determining the capabilities they seek to acquire, which necessitate the recruitment of people to resource the operation? Second, how is employee selection to be handled given the transnational focus? Many of the issues raised and discussed in the following section apply to managerial employees working for multinational organizations in general. However, given the administrative, cultural and psychological complexities associated with internationally mobile working, we have chosen to devote much of the narrative to expatriate executive management considerations.

INTERNATIONAL EXECUTIVE RECRUITMENT

It is important to remember in international recruitment that there are very many role specifications that involve international activity. Sparrow (1999) gives examples of a wide range of international job roles, ranging from the home-based manager but with a central focus on international players and markets, through to transnational managers who move across borders and are detached from a single headquarters. Other examples include members of multicultural teams, internationally mobile managers who are loyal to the parent culture and make frequent or short visits abroad, skills and knowledge transfers, and expatriates on lengthy assignments who represent the parent company in a limited number of countries.

Besides the varying roles that might be undertaken in international working, the people undertaking them have different motivations. We have found that 'free agents', for example, may be regarded as being committed to the host location and willing to work for the highest bidder there – but they may not be committed to the parent company. Those devoted to their home countries may agree to work abroad but do not integrate well in the host location. Their dedication to home country practices may help them to transfer the parent country culture, and they may act as an agent of control from the HQ, however. And they are likely to repatriate willingly. By contrast, those committed to the host location may not want to return to their sending country – they 'go native'. These assignees are more suited to permanent transfers or to 'localization'. Employees who have reached a plateau in their careers at home may be willing to move abroad for a challenge – but this is likely to provide insufficient motivation to make their international career a success. Those being recruited to international cadres need to be 'dual citizens' in the sense that they have high allegiance to both the home and host countries' operations and the corporation itself.

Recruitment practices in the international arena require cross-cultural sensitivity. For example, cross-national advertising can be expensive and prove to be ineffective if the same approach is taken in each country. Knowledge of the best recruitment media in each country is needed, along with knowledge of how job advertisements are phrased locally. Executive search agents may also be used to identify talent. With the significant numbers of mergers, acquisitions and alliances taking place in the growth areas of China, India, South Korea and Malaysia, as well as Eastern Europe, these regions provide a good source of talent. Internet recruitment can also provide an avenue into new areas of the world in terms of attracting talent.

International graduate recruitment programmes are well-known sources for identifying potential international cadres. However, although new graduates may prove to be mobile and willing to work internationally in the short term, such development programmes require a long-term outlook in terms of talent development. The process of developing senior international management is slow, retention rates are typically low, and as the graduates' lifestyles change, so international mobility becomes less attractive to them. Compensation for such mobile groups is also complex (see Chapter 5).

Dual careers and family issues play a major role in international employee resourcing. Dual-career couples may be unwilling to take an assignment that would involve one partner in the relationship having to give up his or her job and/or career prospects. Practical approaches to dealing with this include the use of short-term or unaccompanied 'commuter' assignments in place of more traditional expatriate postings or international cadres requiring long-term mobility. The resourcing approach taken needs to be linked into alternative mobility strategies if the right person is to fulfil the role required.

IDENTIFYING INTERNATIONAL EXECUTIVE CAPABILITIES

Although the appropriate mix of capabilities can be secured in the short term through acquisition (by recruitment of individuals who already possess such skills, or through alliances and partnerships), a resource-based strategic orientation may be translated into the development of existing resources, over the medium to longer term, using structured training, and through career development (planned experience) initiatives managed corporately.

The situation may in time be addressed by virtue of the fact that executives with potential are being deployed on a multinational basis from the earliest stage of their careers. In this way, individuals will be acclimatized to the implications of international working throughout their employment, and will normally form relationships which reflect those circumstances. (This has long been the case, for example, in global oil businesses.)

However, developing new international business formations as a strategic priority means that experienced executives are needed to spearhead development and implementation, as a matter of urgency. 'Globalizing' organizations often find it essential to learn from early mistakes which result from acting in haste in deploying capabilities. In Stephen's experience, mistakes arose by virtue of the fact that the organization's corporate management had picked 'winners'! These were individuals who had had a track record of continued success in developing technical and/or commercial careers in the United Kingdom. Such winners in many cases quickly became dubbed 'losers' when deployed on new ventures around the world.

SPECIFYING INTERNATIONAL COMPETENCIES

Innumerable surveys have been conducted on the competencies considered to be essential (or certainly desirable, recognizing that no one will have all these attributes) in international managers. Competencies may be considered to comprise skills, knowledge and the application of these via values. The cross-cultural sensitivity of international competencies therefore cannot be stressed too highly. International competencies we have seen endorsed by multinational managements over the years include:

∎ strategic awareness (global view);

∎ adaptability to new situations: able to deal with ambiguity;

∎ sensitivity to different cultures;

- ability to work in international teams;

- ability to manage change and transition;

- ability to learn and to transfer knowledge;

- language skills;

- cross-cultural communication skills;

- international negotiating skills;

- open, non-judgemental personality;

- awareness of cultural background;

- intellectual ability;

- self-reliance/self-orientation;

- self-esteem: realistic and thorough degree of self-knowledge, self-confidence and self-acceptance;

- relationship-building skills;

- social orientation – people-orientated: respect for others, trust in people;

- managerial skills;

- high task orientation;

- result-oriented;

- understanding international marketing;

- understanding of international finance.

Furthermore, internationally capable executives are characterized by the following:

- subjective, flexible and relative in their perception and assessment; seeing themselves and their impressions as changing;

- use of cultural stereotypes in a self-conscious and tentative way;

- forward-thinking in trying to understand *what* is going on and not just *why* things occur as they do in different cultures;

- flexibility to reframe fields of reference (as opposed to looking for certainty, tidiness and rationality);

▌ action-oriented, willing to take risks, with multi-dimensional vision.

The following aspects may also be added:

▌ **An open approach to contrasting cultures:** proof of interest through travel, or study, in other business or geographic cultures; recognition of different, or conflicting, moral standards; an enquiring, yet objectively analytical, intellect.

▌ **Individual motivation level:** what are the individual's true aspirations; how can they be met? What is the benefit to the organization?

▌ **Balance between open/closed behaviour:** independent, good judgement; recognition of host business unit culture and expectations.

▌ **Ability to listen, analyse, persuade, motivate and direct:** total, persistent, communication; consensus normally the ideal (dependent on business unit culture) but confidence to provide direction.

▌ **Constant, yet responsive style:** even temperament; provides a recognizable, consistent role model in adverse, or favourable, circumstances; recognizes and responds to significant changes, yet rides out minor deviations.

▌ **Creating teams; being player and leader:** sensitive, balanced behaviour; confidence to allow experts to lead; ability to contribute factual as well as managerial skills, sustaining team aims above those of individual.

▌ **Self-confident and decisive:** able to operate when isolated, both by distance and host culture; independent intellect, confident of corporate core values.

▌ **Reliable:** resilient; able to retain a separate sense of perspective.

▌ **Being in control:** establishing credibility; providing an effective influence.

Clearly it is possible to construct long lists of desirable competencies, but it is important to remember that the requirements for these will vary with the nature of the international post. In joint ventures, for example, the role of the manager frequently involves working through partnerships and collaborations. This requires a different skills set from the more traditional hierarchical managerial role. The likelihood of being able to recruit all the competencies needed is slim, and thought must be given to competency development (Chapter 4), and recognition given to the time-consuming nature of this.

International competencies may therefore have immense rarity value, and careful thought also needs to be given to retention of talent – a point of particular significance in relation to internationally mobile executives, requiring managerial attention on repatriation from international assignments (discussed later in this chapter). In essence, recruitment and selection are only a part of the international assignment cycle. For organizations to retain competencies honed in international working, effort must also be put into preparing, supporting and repatriating (or localizing) the assignees and their families.

There are various philosophies concerning the resourcing of an assignment. These include predicting international assignment competencies via traditional psychometric approaches (for instance, using exercises conducted in an assessment centre), clinical risk assessments that investigate the transitions and adaptations that international assignees will have to manage, and designing assignments around the individual (in career developmental approaches). Let us briefly sketch some of the theoretical considerations.

PSYCHOLOGICAL RESEARCH ON INTERNATIONAL ADAPTATION

Theoretical models of psychological research on cultural adaptation focus on life events, change and potential stress. The basic assumption is that working in a different country and/or culture puts high demands on the individual, and depending on personality and external factors, could result in maladaptation and psychological disturbance. Psychologically, international assignments fall into the category of 'life events', defined as major life changes requiring modification of one's behaviour (that is, adaptation skills). Life events, especially negative events, can put the individual at risk of psychological difficulties, such as depression, anxiety disorders or alcoholism. Research in this area has shown that there is a definite link between the number and severity of life events (such as moving house, loss of a loved one or unemployment) and psychological disorders (see Chapter 2).

Individuals deployed as expatriates are exposed to several such life events: changing country, changing job and changing house; consequently, there is a high risk to their psychological well-being, and hence a risk of deteriorating job performance and company profitability. Moreover, these changes are not restricted to the individual, but usually concern the entire family.

The following factors influence the extent of stress an individual experiences, and these factors ought to be considered alongside competencies and capabilities when identifying individuals to work outside their country of origin:

▌ **Personality factors:** general personality profile; stress vulnerability (pre-disposition to react strongly to difficult situations in an emotional sense); internal versus external locus of control (whether a person believes that events are influenced by his/her own behaviour or by powerful others or fate); self-efficacy and mastery; motivation for expatriation.

▌ **Predominant coping styles.**

▌ **Social support system** (with the assumption that strong social support – of an affective, instrumental and informative nature – can buffer potential stressors and thereby facilitate emotional well-being and adaptation).

THE SELECTION PROCESS FOR INTERNATIONALLY MOBILE EMPLOYMENT

Research by UMIST/CBI/CIB (1995) highlights the necessity of having a thorough and formal approach to international employee selection. The research recommends:

▌ A detailed job analysis is conducted for all international assignments. The strategic purpose of the assignment must be identified and the global assignment context assessed. From this a job description can be formulated.

▌ If assignments are used for career development, the specific set of international competencies to be developed, both corporately and individually, should be identified.

▌ Selection criteria must be established. A detailed person specification can be drawn up. The organization must ensure that the competencies required to operate effectively in the foreign environment are considered, and not just the technical skills required.

▌ Consideration should be given to advertising the post internally and/or externally, in order to draw on a wider pool of candidates. Indeed, organizations should develop strategies to develop employees' skills systematically so as to build a candidate pool for the future.

▌ Consideration is needed to the use of selection methods that have reasonably high validity (such as structured interviews, psychometric tests and assessment centre exercises) for both internal and external recruitment. Ideally, several selection methods should be applied and the selection decision made by a cross-culturally aware selection team.

▌ Consideration to be given to involving the spouse/partner in the selection process.

The selection process should not simply conclude with the issue of the assignment letter; the preparatory training programmes should begin sooner, rather than later. Although training and development is dealt with in more depth in Chapter 4, it is important to highlight here, as part of selection, the role of preparation. Indeed, as part of the selection process, it is important to clarify that the assignee has:

▌ a clear understanding of the purpose of the assignment, his or her role within it and the objectives;

▌ the opportunity to identify any training requirements (both pre-departure and on arrival in the host location) so as to meet the requirements of the post;

▌ a clear understanding of the terms and conditions of the assignment, and realistic expectations about the impact of the assignment on his/her career prospects;

▌ an understanding of the methods that will be used to prepare the assignee and his/her family for the assignment, and the impact of these on their expectations;

▌ an understanding of how any previous international experience might be utilized in this new role.

Selection tools

Most usually an interview is used as the basis of the selection process, backed up by references. However, as many writers have noted, the interview is probably the least reliable selection tool. Interviews can have increased validity if they are structured and conducted by a panel, preferably representing the countries involved in the international assignment process. Tests may be used to provide certification of knowledge and skills, and psychometric testing conducted to identify various characteristics such as personality and resilience. Work samples may be given to see how candidates might respond to work situations or exercises. Another option is the use of biographical data to correlate personal characteristics with work success. Graphology is popular as a selection tool in some countries.

Many of these selection methods are combined in assessment centres where candidates from several countries may be brought together for a period to undergo team and individual exercises. All of these selection methodologies have drawbacks. It is important to consider the candidates' familiarity with various tools and their likely responses to them. For example, in some countries such as the United States and the United Kingdom, senior personnel are used to undertaking psychometric tests and participating in assessment centre exercises. Nationals from other countries may never have experienced these, and their lack of familiarity with the process and potential outcomes may put them at a disadvantage. The tests themselves may be culturally biased and/or the testers' ability to interpret the test results may be coloured by their own cultural assumptions. The candidates may believe that the whole process is 'insulting' if they come from cultures where status is ascribed (Trompenaars and Hampden-Turner, 1997), while those emanating from achievement-oriented cultures relish the challenge. The simulation of new work duties provides a reasonably realistic measure of the candidates' potential ability and approaches to deal with duties in the new environment. However, simulation in an assessment centre can never provide a substitute for the 'real thing'.

The cultural differences that can emerge in the international selection process need to be considered carefully, and anyone participating in a transnational selection team needs to be fully trained for the role. Sue learnt from a senior Korean assignee that when asked a detailed (and potentially difficult) question in an interview, the assignee chose to wait a while before answering. In the Korean's view, this was to show 'respect' for the question and to preserve the 'face' of the questioner. The American interviewer expected a speedy response as it was thought that this indicated 'knowledge' and 'keenness'. It is no surprise that cross-cultural misunderstandings were affecting the interviewee's chances of success.

In collectivist nations (Hofstede, 1994), the selection process may favour the appointment of family members over strangers. In universalist nations (Trompenaars and Hampden-Turner, 1997), the pursuit of equal opportunities in accordance with legislative requirements would render the selection of family or friends potentially illegal. Sue spoke to one British assignee who had spent his life in the United Kingdom but whose family roots were in India. On returning to India to seek work there, he failed to be selected for jobs that he was well qualified to do. In the interviews that he attended, he was always asked about his family connections within the organizations where he was seeking employment. Having none, he found himself deselected from the process. (He has since returned to the UK to work.)

Consideration of diversity can help to widen the potential pool of applicants, in both local and international recruitment and selection. For example, the role of women in the international assignment arena provides an interesting issue – with increasing talent shortages, employers cannot afford to disregard them in their international selection process. Yet, historically, this does appear to have very much been the case.

WOMEN AND INTERNATIONAL ASSIGNMENTS

Women have made considerable career progress in the international environment over the past two decades. In the early 1980s only around 3 per cent of international assignments were carried out by women (Adler, 1984a). Sex stereotyping faced women trying to enter management, and presented a barrier to their advancement in an international environment (Altman and Shortland, 2000). Research indicated that women did want to pursue international careers but that employers appeared reluctant to send them, assuming that foreign operations would not be willing to accept them (Adler, 1984b). Yet further research indicated that women were accepted and did well on assignment, even in particularly masculine societies (Adler, 1987), but still they were not selected in significant numbers to fulfil these international roles.

By the early 1990s women had still made little progress into the masculine world of expatriation. A UK-based study put women's participation in expatriation at only 5 per cent (ORC/CBI, 1992). Later in the decade the percentage increased, reaching just under 9 per cent by 1995 (UMIST/CBI/CIB, 1995) and 14 per cent by 1996 (Windham/NFTC, 1997). However, as Altman and Shortland (2000) argue, expatriation lost some of its glamour in the 1990s as reward packages were trimmed back, career progression became uncertain and concerns over job security on repatriation came to the fore. The authors note that it is perhaps cynical to believe that women's increasing participation in international assignments has resulted simply from the fact that men were not so keen to accept them. More likely the increase in the percentage of women expatriates in the late 1990s can be explained by the larger participation of women in management in general. If expatriates are typically selected from a managerial pool and there are more women in that pool, then their chances of selection should be higher. Nevertheless the percentage of women expatriates rested at around 13 per cent in 2002 (Moore, 2002).

The nature of expatriation has changed over the past decade, with more developmental assignments, mobile cadre movement and skills/knowledge transfer assignments, and with fewer long-term managerial postings, such as 'country manager'-style expatriations. This shift in emphasis is likely to favour women's appointment in international roles, as employers become more willing to select junior or specialist staff (that is, from the ranks where women are more strongly represented). However, as Altman and Shortland (2000) argue, where posts require senior managers, there are still relatively few women in the senior managerial hierarchy to choose from. It is likely, they argue, that although the percentage – and numbers – of female international assignees is rising, their participation at the more senior level remains disproportionately low.

Research has shown that employers are more willing to select less senior men for top international jobs than women – in other words, women have to do more to prove themselves capable in senior roles at home before they are selected for senior jobs abroad (Linehan and Walsh, 1999, 2000). Further research has indicated that where an effort is made to select against specific job criteria, in a formal and transparent manner, there is an increase in women's representation in the international assignee workforce (Harris, 1999).

Although women are increasingly being represented in the internationally mobile workforce, it is questionable whether their participation will ever equal that of men. The paucity of women mentors and role models and organizational networking opportunities for women, together with women's work–life duties, have in the past served to reduce women's likelihood of promotion. Dual career relationships are also thought to have disproportionately affected women's participation in expatriation in comparison with men (Altman and Shortland, 2004). But the authors argue that women are more career active now, are capitalizing on their own networks and are equipping themselves with the necessary competencies for future international careers. Furthermore, Altman and Shortland (2001) argue that women are used to being visible, being seen as different, having to try harder and coping with dual roles. These abilities place them in a good position for international roles in the future. Indeed, data in 2005 (ORC, 2005) indicates a rising trend in women's participation – they now represent 16.5 per cent of the international assignee workforce.

REPATRIATION OF INTERNATIONALLY ASSIGNED EMPLOYEES

When the assignment ends, international assignees might remain in the host location (and be subject to localization – see below), move to a new international location (as part of a mobile cadre – and if so they should be subject to the selection process again), or repatriate to their home country. Repatriation causes both emotional and financial upheaval, as families have to learn to live in their home country once again, pursue career paths and return children to local schooling. Reverse culture shock is not typically expected on return home, yet it frequently results in the returnees having low morale and a lack of understanding about why they feel deflated. The welfare issues related to repatriation are covered more fully in Chapter 2. However, the stress associated with culture shock and the lack of interest others pay to their experiences abroad can result in poor performance and the returned assignee acting as a negative role model to potential future assignees. This is a critical issue for internationalizing companies – the pool of talent for selection will diminish if returned assignees spread the word that an assignment only serves to reduce career prospects for themselves and their family members.

Career counselling is increasingly made available to spouses as part of the dual career package of benefits (ORC/CBI, 1996). The assignee should not be ignored or 'warehoused', but in terms of the resourcing process, the skills and competencies developed by assignees abroad should be utilized as fully as possible on return. If this is not done, high turnover of repatriates may result. As assignees typically cost some three times as much as locals to send and maintain in post, clearly the financial investment made in these people is being jeopardized. But in addition, the rare competencies and experience gained while abroad are ripe for the taking by competitors – a very expensive loss to the organization indeed.

Returned assignees frequently speak of feeling like a 'small fish in a big sea', reflecting their loss of autonomy on return (Coyle, 1998). Many then wish to regain their autonomy and look for further assignments or experience in other organizations that will provide them with the 'big fish in a small sea' experience once again.

Repatriation actions are necessary throughout the assignment cycle, beginning with selection. The selection process should be mindful of the types of assignee and those who are likely to repatriate effectively. Free agents and those with a 'gone native' mentality are unlikely to want to return to their home country – indeed, they may not even see it as home. Preparation (such as briefing) and cultural training are necessary for repatriation, so that assignees are aware of the changes they can expect and prepared to deal with them.

Support while on assignment includes communication channels and media to keep in touch with events and developments at home. Maintaining such links acts as preparation and provides continuity with the home country. Mentors and sponsors can work with assignees and help them by advising on opportunities within the home-based operation. The critical issue, though, is for assignees to return to suitable job/career paths that use their international skills. Returnees can be used to brief those going out on assignment – this ensures that briefing is up to date for the newly transferring assignees, and shows that the returning international assignees' experiences are valued. The importance of international assignments and the return of the assignee can be stressed within career planning, and the value of international experience recognized in the performance management process. Nevertheless, all of this may not stop employees leaving – they have changed as people while away, their horizons have widened and their future career development may not fit within a company with rigid frameworks of operation.

Cultural factors can play a major part in decision making on repatriation. While they work in a different cultural environment, people may internalize elements of the local culture, and they may not recognize why they are unable to adopt a preferred working style on return. Sue worked with one German manufacturing company that transferred a number of senior German managers from the headquarters in Germany to the United Kingdom. These assignees found it difficult to work in the United Kingdom to start with. Many commented that their British colleagues did not seem to follow prescribed rules. 'It was as if the rules were made to be broken', said one German expatriate. The German managers found themselves having to make decisions without referring to policies and procedures in the way they had done at home. To begin with this was alien to them, but as they settled into their assignments, they came to like the degree of autonomy that the British way of working provided. The problem for their employer came on repatriation – having gained the cultural value of coping with ambiguity (in Hofstede's 1994 terms) and thus having enjoyed greater autonomy in the United Kingdom, they were less willing to be bound by the rules on returning home. The company found that its repatriates were leaving to work for competitors. This organization did much in terms of communications, mentoring and support for its expatriates during their assignment – but cultural training might have opened their eyes and those of the assignees to the process that was taking place in their expatriate population prior to repatriation (Shortland, 2002).

EXPATRIATE EMPLOYEE LOCALIZATION

Localization may be defined as the phasing out or removing of expatriate employment terms in the assignment location for any reason: for example, it might occur when it has become clear that the assignee chooses to be no longer mobile, or the company does not perceive the need for the assignee to move again in the foreseeable future (Ernst and Young/CBI, 1996). However, localization may also be viewed as the use of local nationals (in other words, a polycentric approach to employee resourcing).

Localization of assignees involves the removal or phasing out of expatriate allowances and benefits so that assignees are treated as locals. This emphasizes and formalizes their loss of mobility. It is usual for allowances such as housing and education to be phased out over a period of two or three years, whereas other elements of the package may be curtailed immediately the 'expatriate contract' comes to an end. Communication of the terms of localization should be made at the selection stage of the assignment cycle, so that assignees are aware of what will happen when the international assignment contract ends, and realistic expectations are set. If terms and conditions are reduced without careful communication, assignees may feel poorly treated, and the investment in them will be lost if they seek alternative employment.

CONCLUDING REMARKS

International capability can be created drawing on a variety of sources, including:

▌ organizational partnering;

▌ acquisition of relevant business units which possess the talent to make up capability shortfalls;

▌ talent spotting and attraction of leadership and know-how capabilities;

▌ potential identification and holistic capabilities development from within.

Organizations need to develop models that will help them in assessing the capabilities they will require, by acquisition, alliances or development, as an intrinsic part of actualizing international business strategy. This process will not only require clarity in forecasting the activity areas and markets into which organizations wish to grow their interests and the capacity to exploit opportunities. It will also be necessary to gauge the comparative capability advantages being developed by competitors. Moreover, aspirant international businesses will need to identify where, over the short, medium and long term, they can leverage the capability of talented individuals and work groups to win an advantage in their target markets and sectors.

In order to attract and retain the right people, cross-cultural sensitivity is required in the recruitment and selection processes used. In addition, alternative strategic approaches to the deployment of personnel may be required. Traditional forms of resourcing at senior management levels – such as ethnocentric approaches to expatriation – may no longer be appropriate in today's cost-competitive environment. But it is not just the organizational issues that have to be given consideration in resourcing terms. Work–life balance concerns such as family issues and dual careers are key determinants in employees' decision making. Flexibility is required within multinational resourcing strategy and policy to accommodate these factors.

Our experience of working with organizations attempting to internationalize their businesses has led us to a simple conclusion. Very few of us really know our executives well. It may be acceptable for domestic recruitment, selection and career development purposes to have only a two-dimensional, exclusively career-oriented view of our executive population. The challenges that individuals face when deployed on international assignments mean that a more rounded or '3D' perspective is required.

We need to know whether the executives can cope with the very different working environment from the one for which their training and past experience equipped them. Moreover, when deploying the mature executive overseas, the job does not stop at the office or factory door. It is part and parcel of the domestic environment. When put to the test, there are few companies who would claim to know intimately the full domestic circumstances of an individual employee; indeed efforts to do so might be deemed to be intrusive under normal circumstances. However, before inviting individuals to step on a plane to develop careers outside their domestic environment, companies are learning to have a more comprehensive understanding of their key executive group and their families.

YOUR TURN

▌ There are innumerable choices open to multinational managements in determining strategy to internationalize employee resourcing. What factors should be taken into account and why?

▌ What are the choices and consequences involved in 'growing your own talent' versus buying in from outside?

▌ Why is diversity an important issue in international employee resourcing? What difference could it potentially make to organizations known to you?

> What is the likely impact of new technology on strategic considerations for management of employee mobility and international assignments?
>
> What are the consequences of strategic interventions to reduce barriers to international mobility?

REFERENCES

Adler, N (1984a) Women do not want international careers: and other myths about international management, *Organizational Dynamics*, **13**, pp 66–79

Adler, N (1984b) Expecting international success: female managers overseas, *Columbia Journal of World Business*, **19**(3), pp 79–85

Adler, N J (1987) Pacific basin managers: a *gaijin*, not a woman, *Human Resource Management*, **26**(2), pp 169–91

Altman, Y and Shortland, S (2000) Women managers abroad: a bright future from the ashes of the past? *Managing Internationally Mobile Employees Briefing*, **10**, pp 8–10

Altman, Y and Shortland, S (2001) Women, aliens and international assignments, *Women in Management Review*, **16**(3), pp 141–45

Altman, Y and Shortland, S (2004) *Women and International Assignments: From the 1980s to the 21st century*, Academy of Management 2004 Meeting, New Orleans

Coyle, W (1998) *On The Move: The expatriate experience* (training video), Wendy Coyle and Associates, Sydney

Ernst and Young/CBI (1996) *Localisation*, Ernst and Young/CBI Employee Relocation Council, London

Goodernham, P N and Nordhaug, O (2003) *International Management: Cross-boundary challenges*, Blackwell, Oxford

Harris, H (1999) Women in international management – why are they not selected?, in *International HRM: Contemporary issues in Europe*, ed C Brewster and H Harris, pp 258–76, Routledge, London

Heenan, D A and Perlmutter, H V (1979) *Multinational Organization Development*, Addison-Wesley, Reading, Mass

Hofer, C W and Schendel, D E (1978) *Strategy Formulation: Analytical concepts*, West Publishing, St Paul

Hofstede, G (1994) *Cultures and Organisations*, HarperCollins Business, London

Linehan, M and Walsh, J S (1999) Senior female international managers: breaking the glass border, *Women in Management Review*, **14**(7), pp 264–72

Linehan, M and Walsh, J S (2000) Beyond the traditional linear view of international managerial careers: a new model of the senior female career in an international context, *Journal of European Industrial Training*, **24**(2/3/4), pp 178–89

Moore, M J (2002) Same ticket, different trip: supporting dual-career couples on global assignments, *Women in Management Review*, **17**(2), pp 61–67

ORC (2005) *Dual Careers and International Assignments*, Organization Resources Counselors, London

ORC/CBI (1992) *Update on Survey on Spouses/Partners and International Assignments*, ORC Europe and Confederation of British Industry (CBI) Employee Relocation Council, London

ORC/CBI (1996) *Dual Careers and International Assignments*, ORC and CBI Employee Relocation Council, London

Perlmutter, H V (1969) The tortuous evolution of the multinational corporation, *Columbia Journal of World Business*, **4**(1), pp 9–18

Shortland, S (2002) The impact of culture on international assignments, *Managing Internationally Mobile Employees Briefing*, **30**, pp 2–4

Sparrow, P (1999) International recruitment, selection and assessment, in *The Global HR Manager*, ed P Joynt and B Morton, Institute of Personnel Development (IPD), London

Trompenaars, F and Hampden-Turner, C (1997) *Riding the Waves of Culture*, Nicholas Brearley, London

UMIST/CBI/CIB (1995) *Assessment, Selection and Preparation for Expatriate Assignments*, University of Manchester Institute of Science and Technology, CBI Employee Relocation Council and Centre for International Briefing, London

Wallerstein, I (1983) *Historical Capitalism with Capitalist Civilization*, Verso, London

Windham/NFTC (1997) *Global Relocation Trends 1996 Survey Report*, Windham International and the National Foreign Trade Council, New York

4

Training and development in the global environment: choices and consequences

---

CHAPTER AIMS

This chapter sets out to do the following:

- examine training interventions typically used in the preparation and deployment of international assignees;

- explore the importance of employee development and the form of typical development initiatives for mobile personnel in international organizations;

- explain the role of learning theory in both training and development initiatives;

- explain the role of theoretical perspectives in strategic training and development interventions to support international organization effectiveness;

- examine training and development interventions at local level in international organizations.

INTRODUCTION

Multinational managements all want to win in the global market. But only those who understand and can commercialize their core competences (defined as 'the bundle of skills and technologies' (Hamel and Prahalad, 1994: 199) to attain organizational distinctiveness will break out from the pack. Uncovering gaps in the skills and capabilities embedded in core competencies, and finding ways to plug them, complements managerial actions associated with resourcing the organization to help achieve planned corporate objectives. Those who espouse the resource-based theory of the firm (rebranded by Hamel and Prahalad (1994) as a 'core competence' approach to competitive strategy), encouraged international employee capabilities identification (discussed in Chapter 3), and the use of skills training and capability development initiatives aligned with other organizational initiatives, to create competitive advantage through human capital.

This chapter examines the role of international training interventions and international development approaches, set within a theoretical framework which draws on both learning theory and theoretical frameworks within ISHRM. It is frequently said that international assignees represent around 10 per cent of the population but create 90 per cent of the problems within international human resource management. Reflecting this, the chapter focuses primarily on the internationally mobile employee. However, the requirement to gain competitive advantage through the use of local nationals is a significant issue, and so training and development at the local level are also addressed.

INTERNATIONAL TRAINING

To use Boydell *et al*'s 1991 definition, training comprises a relatively systematic attempt to transfer knowledge or skills from one who knows or can do to one who does not know or cannot do. In the international arena, training interventions aimed at people who will be living and working abroad may be categorized into five main groups:

▌ briefing;

▌ pre-assignment visits;

▌ language training;

▌ cross-cultural awareness training;

▌ 'culture shock' awareness training.

In this section, we outline the purposes, advantages and disadvantages of these training interventions from an international perspective, and set them within a theoretical SIHRM and learning context. The aim is to explore the degree to which such interventions may result in increased international assignee effectiveness.

Briefing

Briefings are the most commonly provided form of pre-departure training, and tend to comprise factual presentations on the country or region where the person is to be assigned. Country or regional briefings generally comprise background information to enable the assignee and family members to gain an understanding of the context in which they will experience life and work events. Briefings usually include information on the geography, transport and communications infrastructure, history, political and economic environment, the government, and general living and working conditions. Briefings are often highly practical in nature, going beyond what could be gleaned from a tourist guide and providing detail on the expatriate community and housing options as well as schooling opportunities for children (in developed areas), and housing and schooling alternatives if the destination location is problematic in this regard. Information on work opportunities for accompanying spouses and partners (and any visa or work permit implications of spouse/partner employment) is also usually included.

One of the key elements that should be included in country or regional briefings today is security. Awareness of potential security issues is crucial for assignees and families both in terms of their safety once in the destination location, and also as part of their process of deciding whether to accept the assignment as a family group or to undertake an alternative assignment pattern. An important part of the briefing process is the timeliness of the data presented. We are all aware that political instability can emerge overnight, and that security advice needs to be up to date. Data on housing costs and schooling options also must be current if assignees and their families are to plan accordingly, especially as organizations are tightening up on costs and limiting expenditure on items such as these within the assignment package.

Besides information available publicly, briefing courses may also provide access to data and tips provided by existing or previous assignees to that location. Such 'on the ground' information can prove particularly helpful to assignees when making decisions such as which personal items they should pack and which they can obtain locally. Such information can make a big difference in terms of the time it takes to settle in. Briefing programmes tend to be delivered fairly quickly, with courses running from one to three days in length. These are supplemented with books, videos, computer programs and so on. When employees and their family members are unable to attend formal courses, self-help training is available via these kinds of media. Briefing can therefore prove to be a relatively inexpensive form of training.

In terms of learning, the aim of briefing is to increase the participants' knowledge. It therefore has a strong quantitative flavour to it – the acquisition of facts and figures. There is a sense of the participants 'gaining more' with the intention to memorize and reproduce known issues (Marton *et al*, 1993). It is possible to view learning gained through briefing in the light of the behavioural group of learning theories, in which learning is defined in terms of outcomes – a stimulus presented generates a learned response. For example, an assignee preparing to go to Japan should be aware that when presented with a business card by the Japanese (the stimulus), the correct response is to study it carefully. This is crucial if offence is to be avoided. However, despite its many advantages, briefing does not usually provide an opportunity to change behaviour beyond that gained through surface-level learning. The training is 'passive' in nature, and this results in participants focusing on 'meaning' aspects, such as the significance of the tasks ahead of them through an attempt to gain an understanding of the signs and artefacts (Ramsden, 1992), as with the business card example given above. In terms of cross-cultural theory, only the visible surface level of culture is explored (Hofstede, 1994). As such, briefing might be considered a platform from which further training might be provided. Regrettably, however, it is often the only training provided.

Often ignored is the need to provide briefing prior to repatriation, particularly when assignees and their families have been away from their home country for several years. The requirement becomes paramount if the family have not used home leave or other opportunities to return home during their assignment. There is a danger that they will lose contact with changes at home, and that on repatriation, home will seem foreign and settling back in will prove problematic. This will impact on the employee's attitude to work, and as a role model for potential future assignees. Pre-repatriation briefing can be used to bring families up to date, although such passive learning will not engage them with any psychological or cultural changes they themselves have undergone while away.

Pre-assignment visits

Pre-assignment visits are sometimes known as 'look-see' trips, and their purpose may be twofold. Although here we are considering their role within training, such pre-assignment visits may alternatively (or additionally) be used as a selection tool. As part of the selection process, the assignee and, typically, the spouse or accompanying partner are offered the opportunity to visit the destination location to experience it first-hand and use this experience to decide whether or not they wish to accept the assignment. Pre-assignment visits are usually around one week's duration, during which travel, accommodation and subsistence costs are met. In terms of the overall cost of an assignment (should the couple accept the posting), this cost is only a small part, but as a selection tool by itself, the look-see visit is considered expensive – especially if the potential assignee and partner reject the transfer.

Not surprisingly, therefore, the use of pre-assignment visits is more usually part of the preparation process, and as such may be viewed as a training intervention. If a pre-assignment visit is offered to a married or partnered employee, then it is normal practice for both partners to undertake the trip. Some organizations will meet the costs of accompanying children as well. The aim of the visit is for the employee, couple or family to gain a deeper understanding of the environment where they will be based via first-hand exposure to the local culture. For the employee, the trip may be combined with business meetings to gain experience of the organizational culture as well. The use of a pre-assignment visit can generate a positive attitude towards the assignment – although it has to be accepted that this is not a certain outcome.

During the visit, it is usual for organizations to engage local consultants to assist with the identification of suitable housing and schooling. This has the added advantage for the employer that employee productivity may be improved once the assignment begins, as time that otherwise might have been spent on home search and school search is not wasted. The provision of a pre-assignment visit may also help to reduce temporary living costs once the assignment begins, as leases on rental property may be organized during this period. This period in the assignment location might also be used by spouses and partners to research local employment opportunities – again consultants may be engaged to assist in this process. If these factors are set against the cost of the pre-assignment visit, the cost–benefit analysis looks positive.

One of the major problems with organizations' approaches to the use of a pre-assignment visit lies in an unclear definition of its purpose. It is not uncommon for organizations to send employees and family members on such expenses-paid trips with the dual purpose of both selection and training. This sends a mixed message to the assignee, who may find it difficult to say no to an assignment while being expected to find accommodation and gain some cultural understanding in preparation for taking up a position in the location (Dowling, Welch and Schuler, 1999).

In terms of learning, the pre-assignment visit provides a brief opportunity for the potential assignee and family to begin to engage with the culture of the new location. They can begin to apply their learning from preliminary briefings to the real world. Learning in this situation might thus be considered as how we come to perceive and understand the world in certain ways and how we behave within it. This leads into the cyclical process of turning learning into knowledge, the latter comprising the organizing principles of these perceptions and behaviours in the mind (Richardson, 1985). Potentially, learning takes place at a deeper level as the assignee now has the opportunity to focus to a greater extent as to what the task is about, while operating within the local societal and organizational cultures.

Turning to repatriation, the offer of pre-repatriation visits to arrange housing/schooling issues and to re-familiarize with the home environment is rare. Organizations typically expect assignees to use home leave for such purposes. In practice, the repatriation can be a stressful, emotional and frantically busy period, as the returnees carry out all the various arrangements needed to return to life back home. Organizations may grant paid leave on return for this purpose.

Language training

When assignees and their families are to be living and working in a country with a different native language, organizations normally offer to meet the costs of language training for the employee. Such training is frequently offered to accompanying spouses and partners, and occasionally to children. It is considered that the ability to converse in the local language aids adjustment through the opportunity to develop social links. Learning the language also indicates willingness to integrate into the community. However, language training is sometimes considered to be unimportant, particularly if the business language spoken is the assignee's native language. Such an ethnocentric perspective (with the strategic emphasis on transactional costs rather than building on human resource potential) may have strategic and operational implications, as language – as an artefact of culture – plays a crucial role in cultural understanding at the local level.

Today, the majority of assignment policies contain clauses detailing assistance given to dual-career couples (ORC, 2005). Emphasis is increasingly being placed on assistance in job search, work permit/visa provision and career counselling/management. Organizations that regularly send assignees abroad have built databases of contacts and opportunities for spouses/partners in an attempt to prevent the partner from being the stumbling block to the assignee accepting the post abroad. Pressure is also being placed upon governments by multinational managements to operate more progressive working visa policies for accompanying spouses, so that immigration law can help to promote international mobility rather than restrict labour opportunities for such individuals. However, even where freedom to live and work in the foreign location is available, spouses and partners may be precluded from entering the labour market simply because they do not speak the language well enough to compete with local people.

Language training cannot necessarily turn someone into a proficient speaker overnight, but for those spouses or partners with some language knowledge/ability already, training might improve their skill and/or help them reach proficiency in business speech and thus aid them in the recruitment process. For those unwilling or unable to work while abroad, learning the language will help prevent them feeling isolated in their new environment. Thought needs to be given to the rationale behind the provision of language training to other family members within the context of assignee benefits packages. For example, because cost-cutting has affected the earlier tendency to send assignees' children to international or home-country schools, there is increasing emphasis in assignment policies on the use of local schools. Leaving aside the major issue of curricula, children might be able to adapt and settle into local educational provision but require preparatory language training if delivery is in the local language. Young children learn languages quickly (in comparison to adults) but may feel alienated and isolated in the first days at school without some rudimentary language capability. If local schools are to be used for young children, thought might be given to the provision of some language teaching in advance of the assignment.

It may take a considerable length of time to learn a language. Consideration therefore needs to be given to the timescale involved. Language training might begin in preparation for the assignment, but consideration should be given to continuing the training in the assignment location. This is likely to result in more effective learning, as the language can be practised regularly rather than being learnt in the artificial environment of the home country. Stephen witnessed a situation a few years ago where a small number of expatriate assignees, leading a business unit in a southern European location, continued their language training in the host location, building this around day-to-day work routines. This added to team bonding and the sense of co-operation around the project. It also added light relief, as the executives drew on the practical experience of struggling with a new language to show host country business unit members a lighter side of their engagement, shared jokes about their hesitantly accented speech, and showed a sincere effort to meet local colleagues halfway in more nuanced communication, even though business was generally conducted in English.

It is also worth giving consideration to training in the use of the organizational or corporate language. Although the business language used may well be English or the headquarters company's native language, the assignees' familiarity and use of this language will reflect the part of the organization where they have experience. Training may be required in local terminology and in the use of corporate communications channels in the local subsidiary. Attention to this aspect of language training can help to improve employee effectiveness and productivity (as exemplified above). Although extending beyond the use of corporate language, socialization within the foreign organization is crucial if individuals are to learn how an organization functions and their role within it.

There are cultural differences in the use of English and indeed other languages, where different countries share a common language but give different meanings to identical words or phrases. Such issues are not normally addressed as part of a formal language training programme, but should be addressed, perhaps, through being incorporated within cultural awareness training, discussed next.

Cross-cultural awareness training

The ability to function effectively in the home location is no predictor of success in the foreign location, and hence an understanding of how things are done locally (in other words, cultural awareness) is needed. Trompenaars and Hampden-Turner (1997) consider culture as reflecting how a group of people solves its problems and reconciles its dilemmas (see Chapter 2 for a fuller discussion of definitions and their implications). Culture is manifested in practices, although why people take different approaches is usually not obvious. Unseen values, beliefs and assumptions held by the particular cultural group drive the operation of practice, and it is these invisible drivers of culture that have to be interpreted by outsiders. Typically we are unaware of our own cultural values and assumptions, and hence it is particularly difficult to transfer knowledge and skills related to cultural assumptions to others.

One of the main objectives of cultural awareness training is to help assignees cope with unexpected events in the new country, and thus aid the improvement of productivity. It also aims to foster appreciation of the societal culture, so that assignees can act appropriately. According to Dowling et al (1999), although the benefits of such training are known, take-up has been slow and such training, where offered, is frequently voluntary. Employee resistance to taking part in cultural awareness training can result from a lack of understanding of its benefits as well as lack of time prior to departure.

Cultural awareness training may take one (or both) of two main approaches. The training given may aim to identify cultural differences in a general sense, for example by providing an explanation of theoretical models and their applicability in terms of understanding behaviours and relating them to the trainee's own cultural standpoint. Training may also be more country-specific by comparing and contrasting the differences between the home and the host countries, through an examination of the assignee's own cultural background. Such cultural awareness training is particularly useful to underpin specific practices such as managing local staff, building teams and negotiating, as well as in understanding culture shock (Shortland, 2004).

The delivery of cultural awareness training ideally uses approaches that go beyond surface learning, providing a deeper and more lasting effect (Marton *et al*, 1993). Delivery may include classroom-type activities but it is more usual for the training to include role plays and simulations of events, often with facilitators from the host country's culture. The aim is for trainees to be able to practise such skills as negotiating and running team meetings within an environment as culturally close to the real thing as possible.

Various models have been proposed concerning the factors that might influence the components and delivery of cultural awareness training programmes. Early work by Tung (1981) suggests that the degree of interaction that is likely to be required between the assignee and the host culture, together with the degree of dissimilarity in the cultures of the home and host countries, should determine training content and rigour. She suggests that if the level of interaction between the assignee and the host culture is likely to be small and the two cultures are similar, training content should focus to a greater extent on task issues than on cultural issues. Training rigour would be expected to be low. By contrast, if the assignee is likely to have considerable interaction with the host culture and the dissimilarity between the two cultures is great, then training content should focus to a large extent on cultural issues (as well as task issues) and training rigour should be high.

Mendenhall and Oddou (1985) propose three dimensions of cultural awareness training (subsequently revised by Mendenhall, Dunbar and Oddou (1987)), building on Tung's model. They consider the impact of cultural differences and assignment lengths on methods, rigour and duration of training programmes. For example, if the assignment abroad is to be relatively short, there is little expected interaction with the host culture and cultural similarity is high, information-giving approaches to training (such as country briefings via books and videos) may suffice. Training rigour is low and the duration of the training is short (say, up to a week). If the assignment is expected to be of longer duration (up to one year is suggested), cultural dissimilarity is greater and interaction with locals is expected to be greater, additional training approaches are required. The authors suggest affective approaches, such as role plays and cultural assimilation exercises. Training rigour is medium to high and the duration of any programme extends to around one month. Finally, the authors suggest that where the cultural dissimilarity is high and expected interaction is great, additional training rigour, methods and duration are required. Training should reflect an immersion approach and ideally include field experience together with sensitivity and experiential training, and be cross-culturally rigorous. The duration should be around two months.

The pressure on organizations to conduct global business speedily immediately adds a realism that only serves to undermine the theoretical models. It is unlikely that businesses can afford the time to enable employees to take part in such lengthy pre-departure training. Decisions to resource operations are made quickly and the selected candidate is required to be in place often within a matter of days. However, the models are valuable in drawing attention to the complexity and time-consuming process of gaining cross-cultural understanding. Organizations have to make the trade-off between expediency and cultural effectiveness. As ever, choices have consequences.

The cross-cultural training models are prescriptive in terms of how much training is needed and what type it should be. They make rather questionable judgements about whether cultural training is necessary, depending on the degree of cultural dissimilarity, length of assignment and expected degree of interaction. An assignee might enter a foreign business environment on a short-term assignment and not be expected to have any large degree of interaction with the local culture. However, one cultural misunderstanding in a meeting with a senior local customer could do significant and lasting damage to the business. The cultural similarity between the countries involved might be thought insignificant, but the subtle cultural differences might prove more difficult for the assignee to adjust to than more obvious differences.

It could be argued that it is easier to plan and prepare coping strategies in the face of major cultural shifts than it is to identify and engage responses to more subtle ones. We have heard from assignees who found moving between similar cultures to be far more traumatic than they had expected. Examples included assignees moving between the United States and Canada, and between Australia and New Zealand. Certainly there are numerous examples of Americans moving to the United Kingdom who have found the cultural differences, even use of language, bewildering – something totally unexpected and for which they had received no training. Such experiences are not the preserve of Western cultures. Research by Yu

(2003), reported in Shortland (2004), found that the subtle cultural differences between Taiwan and China proved problematic for the assignees involved.

TRAINING FOR TRANSFERS BETWEEN COUNTRIES WITH SUBTLE CULTURAL DIFFERENCES

The cultural differences between Taiwan and China are subtle (both cultures being based upon a similar root), and these differences raise issues regarding Taiwanese companies' requirements for particular competencies in their international assignees. Whether China is regarded as culturally similar or tough by Taiwanese organizations and potential assignees will impact on the content and rigour of training considered appropriate and delivered. According to Yu (2003), Taiwanese literature suggests that assignees leaving Taiwan to work abroad should receive preparatory training including language, law and culture in the host country, customs and habits, professional and technical knowledge, management and leadership skills, international manners, political sensitivity, managing pressure and lectures for family dependants. In terms of additional training content specifically for expatriates transferring to China, political perception, safety, understanding of the different cultures, leadership skills, making, implementing and following rules, relationship management, parent company communication, skills for collecting information and training skills are also mentioned.

Yu points out that language training is commonly neglected, as there is some common language between China and Taiwan. However, she argues that language training should not be ignored completely, particularly where partnerships are involved between Taiwanese enterprises and other countries with direct investments in China. She highlights the security and safety issues affecting Taiwanese expatriates in China and the importance of risk management training. She also draws attention to stress management training and the need for training in relationship management. Different approaches to communicating with customers and suppliers are required. Chinese businesses prefer to maintain a 'lukewarm' relationship with Taiwanese businesses. She notes that training should therefore include emphasis on attitudes towards association with those from China.

Drawing upon the relevant Taiwanese literature, Yu recommends that cross-cultural training for Taiwanese working in China should therefore comprise seven main elements:

▌ language training (including text book training and oral training);
▌ local legal regulations and cultural training (including cultures and habits in China, current economic and political situations, and living conditions);
▌ pressure (stress) management training;
▌ risk management and security, and hygiene management training (including training for political vigilance, precaution against natural calamities, and common sense regarding self-defence and personal safety);
▌ relationship management training (including human relationships, attitudes relating to associations with other people, training for maintaining good communication with the parent company, and cross-cultural communication training);
▌ training for international manners;
▌ relevant professional knowledge and skills training.

Yu's case study research set out to test these suggestions by examining training practices in a typical medium-sized Taiwanese company that had already opened an office in Shanghai, and had plans to establish subsidiaries in China and staff these with parent country national employees. She found that the expatriate selection was carried out directly by line managers, who stressed that professional knowledge determined the ability to take on the responsibility associated with the international assignment. The HR department surveyed the potential expatriates regarding their willingness to work abroad. Yu found that considerable emphasis was placed on this latter factor, although once employees' interest in undertaking assignments had been established, they were 'expected to be able to overcome the impact and challenge of the foreign environment with its different cultural background'.

The training programmes given to assignees prior to expatriation varied according to their roles, and reflected requirements from a management viewpoint. All received training on the local environment, and the majority on the local culture, adjustment and professional skills. Additional training for some included leadership, organizational culture (parent company), communication, social and working relationships, short-term practical training, and family adjustment training. Her research indicated that potential expatriates were 'therefore most likely to know something about the local environment and culture prior to their assignments'. However, although the interviewees believed in understanding local affairs in advance, they felt that adjusting to customs and living locally would require future attention. Furthermore, most interviewees considered that learning the local language or dialect would provide a valuable tool to extend social interactions, and would also make their international assignments more successful. The importance of training for family members was also acknowledged.

The competencies to be developed through training suggested by expatriates and their managers reflected the cultural difficulties experienced on assignment. They included language and communication skills, stress management, social skills, open-mindedness, cultural understanding, self-control and independence. Interviewees who had experience of assignments to China identified competencies more directly related to cultural differences than job skills requirements. In terms of training content, the research revealed unexpected issues and difficulties that expatriates experienced when transferring between culturally 'similar' countries, including language, stress, risk management and dealing with social relationships. In order to prepare assignees to cope with language and cultural differences, the rigour, depth and timing of training need to be considered. To provide such training effectively, it is unlikely that information approaches will suffice – affective and immersion approaches may be required, with their inherent timing implications.

Yu's research concluded that 'expatriates require competencies in terms of knowledge, ability and attitude that are applicable within the domains of work experience, living adjustment and cultural interaction'. Although the knowledge content may be addressed by briefings, the training rigour required (particularly for the ability and attitude components), implies the use of affective or immersion approaches. Work-related training such as business trips, international conferences and short-term assignments could be used. The timing of training delivery also required consideration, with the need for language training, for example, extending beyond the pre-departure period and continuing throughout the assignment.

Subtle cultural differences between the home and host countries are generally assumed to present little or no challenge to assignment effectiveness and ultimate success. Assignments from Taiwan to China may be used as an example of assumed culturally similar environments. However, as Yu's research study has revealed, transfers to culturally 'similar' countries may require significant attention to selection criteria, competencies and training content, of the level normally associated with international assignments regarded as culturally tough.

(This case study is drawn from Shortland, 2004.)

In terms of learning theory, cross-cultural awareness training attempts to move trainees from surface learning (such as via the passive delivery of information) into deep learning via action and involvement. In Ramsden's (1992) terms, the approach to learning moves on from the 'what aspects' into the 'how aspects' – from that which is experienced to the act of experiencing. Training in cultural awareness may be both holistic (focusing on the whole in relation to the parts) and atomistic (focusing on parts or segments of the whole). Relating this to Tung's and Mendenhall *et al*'s models of cultural awareness training, a more holistic approach to learning takes place where the training uses field experiences and simulations to gain cross-cultural effectiveness. An atomistic approach takes place where the training relies on isolated examples, perhaps via role plays that are set within a specific context. In Marton *et al*'s (1993) conceptions of learning, the trainees reach a watershed point in gaining understanding through meaning. Depending on the rigour and duration of the training, this may be limited to a 'study' situation or go beyond this to enable the trainees to 'see in a different way'. Through field and other real experiences, emphasis is placed on changing conceptions, learning is located in the real-world context and the trainee may be enabled to 'change as a person' through new ways of seeing him or herself in the light of his/her own cultural background. To provide this holistic perspective – so that the assignees can relate their conceptions of others' cultures within the framework of their own cultural 'baggage' – is the goal of cross-cultural awareness programmes.

Culture shock training

Assignees who live and work abroad are likely to undergo a period of culture shock. On arrival they may well experience a range of positive and negative emotions ranging from excitement to dread, although often there is an upswing in mood on arrival, as the new environment presents a challenge and an opportunity to those with a sense of adventure. However, this 'honeymoon' phase, as it is often known, wears off as the everyday reality of life in the new environment sets in. At this point, assignees typically experience disenchantment – a downswing in mood – and as Dowling *et al* (1999) note, this period is critical. How the individual copes at this point may determine the success or failure of the assignment. Coping mechanisms need to be brought into play to regain competence in the environment and to view the future in a more positive light, to enter a period of resolution. At this point, the assignee and family members come to terms with their new environment and reach a level of adjustment/acceptance that enables them to function effectively and productively in the new environment without losing their own cultural identity (Shortland, 2003a).

Each person is different, and this culture shock cycle may not be experienced by everyone. Different family members may have different reactions at different times. For some the cycle may take six months or more to complete, for others adjustment may be achieved in a few weeks. Experienced and frequent assignees may go through little if any culture shock – or may find that their experience of it diminishes with each assignment.

To set culture shock in a positive light in terms of learning, incidental learning theory might be applied in this context (Shortland, 2003b). Argyris and Schön (1974, 1978) contend that in conditions that require heightened attention, learning takes place through the element of surprise. Incidental learning theory therefore suggests that learning can result as a by-product of other activities, and can occur without intention – although the learner has to give meaning to the situation. Working in a different cultural environment continually results in the unexpected, and assignees and their families need to give increased attention to what is happening around them so as to cope with and understand events in their new environment. This aids their learning and thus their ability to deal with culture shock.

It is often totally unexpected for returnees to suffer culture shock on repatriation (reverse culture shock), yet perhaps this is why so many returnees find coming home stressful. They expect everything to be as they left it, although of course, previously familiar aspects of their home country will have changed and their own mindset will have altered too, especially if different cultural values have been internalized. In terms of learning theory, constructionist approaches to learning can be related to this problem. The constructionist view, as exemplified by Schein (1988), is that we change our behaviour by unfreezing ways of doing, cognitively redefine how to behave, and then refreeze these learning points to be used as future action. Using this model, the culture shock that can result on repatriation may be explained through assignees changing their ways of behaviour while abroad by unfreezing ways of seeing and doing, by taking in new ideas and locking them in to be used while on assignment. They thus construct their learning so as to operate effectively in a different cultural environment where ways of seeing and doing differ from those at home (Shortland, 2003b). On repatriation, or on moving to a different cultural environment, learning has to be carried out all over again to unfreeze accepted ways and to return to the original (or another) means of behaviour.

Culture shock training aims to prepare assignees and families for the various stages of the cycle. Understanding that experiencing culture shock is normal can be a great comfort when the problems and emotions being experienced cannot be simply explained by cultural differences alone. The training aims to aid assignees and family members to develop coping strategies, particularly at the point of disenchantment so that this does not lead to crisis, health failure and retreat (by returning home early, becoming part of the expatriate ghetto or becoming dependent on alcohol or drugs). As culture shock may be experienced on both expatriation and repatriation, and between similar and dissimilar cultures, it should form part of pre-departure training programmes for both outgoing and returning assignees and their accompanying family members.

Culture shock training may be incorporated within pre-departure cultural awareness training programmes, but in practice it is far less likely to be included when assignees are moving to culturally similar locations. Pre-departure repatriation training is relatively uncommon, and reverse culture shock is therefore rarely addressed prior to departure. When repatriates experience negative emotions on return, and so may act as negative role models to potential assignees, organizations are known to provide counselling services or various involvement initiatives to demonstrate awareness of the returnees' needs to share and use their assignment experiences. Formal reverse culture shock awareness training is, however, relatively rare.

INTERNATIONAL DEVELOPMENT

Whereas training may be viewed as a relatively short-term intervention concerned with skills transfer, development implies a longer-term initiative. In Boydell *et al*'s (1991) definition, development may be viewed as working with individuals or organizations so as to enable them to cross a threshold of qualitative significance to them and their life. Development in the international context typically involves spells of working abroad to experience different cultural contexts and how these impact on, and help to promote achievement of, organizational strategy. In terms of learning, developmental initiatives frequently rely on experiential learning, whereby in Kolb's (1984: 38) terms, 'learning is the process whereby knowledge is created through the transformation of experience'.

It is frequently reported that to reach senior management positions in multinational organizations, potential candidates are expected to have international experience. This is usually thought to refer to an assignment in a foreign location, although in today's networked world, virtual international experience and multinational team working might be deemed suitable. Learning from experience sounds straightforward – we experience events in various contexts every day. However, if experience is so valuable, surely we would be significantly more knowledgeable than we are!

Experiential learning theory contends that learning is a continuous process grounded in experience, but to understand learning, we have to understand knowledge creation. Knowledge results from a transaction between objective, social knowledge drawn from human cultural experience, and personal, subjective knowledge drawn from our own subjective life experiences. It is the transaction between these that underpins learning (Kolb, 1984). There is a difference, therefore, between learning from experience and experiential learning – we have to transform the experience into new knowledge. It can be a messy approach to learning, as we return over again to experiences and build them into knowledge to be applied in the future. The concept of experiential learning implies significant change within ourselves, and this has personal ramifications. Experiential learning should result not just in new understandings and the development of capabilities, but in changes in behaviour. As such, the learning and consequent development achieved can be initially unsettling, possibly threatening, but ultimately empowering. Experiential learning provides an appropriate theoretical framework within which to place development initiatives, as assignees observe, reflect, theorize and test out these findings in the foreign location.

In terms of models of global business growth, development initiatives may be categorized within frameworks such as those posited by Perlmutter (1969) and Bartlett and Ghoshal (1989). For instance, Perlmutter proposes four stages of global growth: ethnocentric, polycentric, regiocentric and geocentric. Although organizations do not usually follow a logical progression through these theoretical stages as they evolve into multinational corporations, rather growing via external activity such as joint ventures, mergers, and acquisitions, the stages can provide a framework for analysis of typical international development practices.

For example, at the ethnocentric stage of global development, there is concentrated use of parent-country nationals to resource key positions in the foreign subsidiary. Transfers are typically from the headquarters out to the subsidiary operations, and development initiatives tend to take the form of relatively lengthy expatriate assignments. At the polycentric stage, there is increased focus on the deployment of local nationals in key positions. To avoid subsidiaries losing sight of headquarters policy and practice, development initiatives for locals may include transfers to the headquarters for key, senior local personnel to gain HQ experience and to transfer values, policies and practices back to the subsidiary. At the regiocentric level, where organizations make use of regional groupings of operations linked by a regional hub, typically development initiatives involve a mix of parent-country nationals experiencing assignments to foreign operations, locals undertaking transfers to the HQ, and third-country nationals, parent-country and local nationals undertaking assignments between and among the various subsidiaries within the regional grouping. There might also be use of regionally mobile cadres, at both senior and junior levels. Examples might include senior managers undertaking development in a number of different country operations and newly recruited graduate trainees on graduate development programmes that involve multi-location experience and training. At the global level, human resource development initiatives expand beyond the regional level and thus involve development programmes extending throughout the global scale of operations.

In a similar vein, Walton (1999) sets international human resource development (HRD) within the framework of Bartlett and Ghoshal's (1989) model. Again as a four-stage approach, model A (multi-domestic) acts as the first stage. The organization is configured locally, and international strategy refers to a nuclear aggregation of domestic strategies. With each national operation relatively independent of elsewhere, expatriates are used to exert headquarters control. Model B (international) refers to the coordinated federation of subsidiaries. A certain measure of local autonomy is evidenced, particularly in developed countries. Walton contends that the key HRD task is knowledge and expertise transfer to countries less advanced in technology or market development. Specialists are sent to develop local talent. In this case the development initiatives rest more firmly in the arena of the local people, than in the specialists sent out from HQ to undertake the knowledge transfer. In model C (global), the organization comprises a centralized hub with cross-national operations. Assets, resources and responsibilities are centralized, with decision making and control from the centre. However, centralization and integration are applied together, and according to Walton, the structure of the business (as typically applied by Japanese companies) takes the form of cross-linked national operations engaging in worldwide competition. HRD rests in intensive communication and retaining complex management systems via centralized development procedures. In model D (transnational), the organization aims to be both locally responsive and globally efficient, via knowledge transfer across boundaries. The aim is to disseminate information, share common goals, and view local interests in the context of the global organization.

The Jones Corporation case vignette in Chapter 1 exemplifies how initiatives to expand and develop talent pools to support international business expansion may be taken by multinational managements as they attempt to steer the organization through the various stages outlined following either of the frameworks mentioned above.

Developing international executives

International talent may be developed via a number of initiatives. These include:

▌ international careers (including one-off assignments and mobile cadres);

▌ capabilities development via development centres;

▌ development of project team capabilities;

▌ networks of opportunity, action learning and virtual HRD.

International careers

Hall (1986, cited in Selmer, 2000) defines a career as a sequence of related work experiences and activities, directed at personal and organizational goals, through which a person passes during his/her lifetime, and which are partly under the individual's control and partly under that of others. Foreign assignments have long been recognized as an important mechanism for developing international expertise, yet Tung (1988, cited in Riusala and Suutari, 2000) finds that the relationship between international assignments and careers is unclear. Indeed, careers are increasingly characterized by discontinuity, interruptions and reformulation, particularly as a result of organizational changes in response to the fast pace of change in the external environment. Corporate restructuring, demographic and technological change, to name but a few issues, all impact on careers and career development.

Altman (1999) proposes a model of international careers that considers intensity of experience (frequent, infrequent and occasional) within an organizational framework. Frequent use of international assignments is made by three types of organizations, categorized as empire, colonial and professional.

Empire organizations are world-leading multinational enterprises (such as Shell) where careers comprise numerous assignments via international cadres or several out-and-back assignments. Developmental objectives are integral to such assignments.

Colonial organizations (now typical of Japanese and Korean companies, according to Altman) 'require' assignments to be undertaken in a home from home (expatriate) environment, and careers are seen as a 'mission'. Such assignments may have development of the transferee at heart, but the transfer of control and knowledge from the HQ to the subsidiary may be a more expected objective.

In the professional organizational framework, external hires are used for assignments abroad. They are free agents, and turnover is often high in this approach.

In the infrequent intensity category, the organizational frame comprises two types, peripheral and expedient. The peripheral organizational frame includes minor multinational enterprises and organizations in niche markets. Foreign assignments are considered desirable, and such postings are necessary for development of individuals if they are to be successful within their organizations. However, the organizations categorized by Altman as expedient have little experience of international careers, as suggested by the name, and the HRD strategy is ad hoc. Any development initiatives are therefore somewhat risky.

The final category – the occasional intensity – represents organizations undertaking their first attempts at internationalizing. Their managements experience international assignments as fringe activities. Those in this organizational frame have only occasional exposure to international activity, for example through business trips, visits and conference attendance.

Altman's model raises issues concerning how careers are viewed and categorized. The 'boundaried' career is perhaps typical of the empire organizations. It represents a traditional linear career, being specialized and continuous, often within one organization and providing a key to upward mobility. Today, however, careers are often viewed as 'boundaryless' – assignees use experiences and development for their own ends (Rousseau, 1996, cited in Eby, 2001). The boundaryless career transcends organizations and refers to sequences of experiences across organizations and jobs. Assignees develop new skills, increase their marketability and are sustained by external networks and contacts. Individuals 'own' their own career. The downside, however, is the loss of organizational identity, and organization managements may provide fewer developmental opportunities for the recognized free agent.

The boundaried and boundaryless career models can be related to the psychological contract (discussed in Chapter 2). The boundaried career represents the 'old' deal in terms of the psychological contract – where loyalty was given in return for jobs for life and the expectation of organizational development and support. The boundaryless career represents the 'new' deal where there are no job guarantees and self-development, using organizational opportunities as presented, becomes critical to maintenance of the perceived reciprocal promises and obligations between the individual and those leading the organization.

International cadres as mentioned in the first category of Altman's model are not as widely used as multinational managements might like in terms of employee development. This is primarily because of practical difficulties and cost constraints. Visa and work permit issues can present barriers to mobility, the requirements for cross-cultural adaptability and sensitivity are paramount to success, and perhaps even more important, employees need to be receptive to the idea of a mobile life. Dual-career and family issues pose a major hurdle in this respect.

The costs involved of using out-and-back assignments for development purposes are likely to be high (even though policy design may reflect the difference between developmental and essential skills in the transfer assignment rationale). The costs of mobile cadres in terms of support packages are likely to be even higher as employees transfer around several locations. The turnover rate among mobile cadres is often high, as valuable competencies are developed at one employer's expense, to be poached by another unwilling to make such an investment in the development of talent.

In order to maintain links with the home country and to support career management systems, assignees may be offered the support of a sponsor or mentor. Sponsors have responsibility for the assignee in terms of career re-entry to a greater degree than mentors, who theoretically at least act as counsellors and guides. In practice, however, the sponsor and mentor may be the same individual. For sponsor/mentor systems to be effective, the person appointed must be willing to serve in this capacity, be at a senior level, follow communication guidelines, be involved in career management and be appraised on the role. Their function is not only to 'look out' for the assignee but also to identify opportunities, communicate regularly and have a 'stake' in the assignee's career. Management needs to ensure that, should the mentor/sponsor leave the organization or no longer be able to carry out this role, arrangements are in place to ensure that the assignee is not left disconnected or isolated from career developments and other changes taking place in the sending organization. It is important to note that although the role of the mentor/sponsor is an important one in career management, assignees must also be willing to manage their own career – they cannot totally rely on others, or expect others to manage their careers for them.

While considering the rationale for using international assignments as part of employee development and the need for support systems during the posting, it is also important to factor repatriation into the development programme. Repatriation should be managed strategically via a formal policy supported by top management commitment. The benefits of development via assignments need to be demonstrated to those in the home organization, as this will influence the willingness of potential future assignees to accept such transfers. The returning employee should be encouraged to share knowledge gained abroad. This is critical regardless of the stage of globalization of the organization, although it is a particular requirement of transnational organizations. Local knowledge shapes global perspectives, and knowledge transfer is highly valued in international HRD. This leads to the efficient and effective use of international competencies, a requirement for both individual and organizational development.

Capabilities development via development centres

International assignments should be regarded as a cycle beginning with selection, going through the stages of preparation, support, and re-entry or transfer to another location, or localization in the host country. As part of this cycle, development centres may be used to develop the capabilities of assignees at any of the various stages – although most frequently they form part of the selection and/or early preparation stages. They may be used during the assignment, however, as part of the support given in-post or prior to return or reassignment. Capabilities development via development centres may also be aimed at local nationals and third-country nationals moving between several international locations.

Development centres may be run by a cross-section of senior line managers with specialist HR support and the input of psychologists. Individual development potential is assessed via a variety of group, team and individual exercises, and work simulations as well as interviews and psychological tests in some instances. The outcome of each development centre should be the preparation of a personalized, international development plan for each individual who wishes to proceed. The plan needs to be supported by the individual, his or her line management, and those responsible for international business development and operations. It means that, well before any decisions are taken regarding any particular international assignment, individuals are honing their strengths, and addressing development needs which have been identified in this systematic way. It also provides an excellent opportunity for the organization better to get to know the executive concerned, both through information gathering and by opening a dialogue with the family. In this way, recommendations for particular postings can be avoided which, based on the evidence, would clearly not produce the kind of results any of the parties to this 'new contract' would be satisfied with. In essence, development centres aim to develop human capital for business success.

This process works best when it is part of a wider capabilities development programme for international business. From our experience, this is a process whereby 'corporate memory' can be built and transferred across the executive population via a variety of formal and informal means, including both internal and external inputs. In order to maintain ownership of the programme right across the internationalizing business, it is helpful to identify a series of 'champions', experts or functional leaders in their field, each of whom takes responsibility for a particular element of the programme. Its application can range between informal exchanges to pass on experience and learning points – such as working lunches with individuals who have just completed successful international ventures – to more formal sessions. In the latter case, individuals can gain both know-how critical to the advancement of capabilities, giving the organization a competitive edge in the global marketplace (such as industry-specific contractual and commercial factors), and specific skill sets, deployed as modules relevant to the overall business development process (such as negotiating skills or communications skills). These are all set within the context of intercultural understanding.

The identification of a group of champions gives momentum to such a programme. It also provides a network within which feedback can be shared, in order to strengthen and improve the ongoing conduct of the programme, in all its constituent parts, over time. The champions, properly coordinated, become a capabilities development fraternity, collectively transferring know-how and experience, honing their own expertise in the process, and providing the life-blood of a continuously 'learning organization'.

A development centre programme should consider person- and situation-oriented assessments at different stages of the international assignment process, set and evaluated within the strategic business development framework, so as to pinpoint business 'technical' and business 'behavioural' capabilities. In the process, individuals may be matched and developed to organizational needs. Once gathered, sifted, identified and tested, these new capabilities become the basis for an ongoing programme of development centres, in which executives who have been nominated or have volunteered for international assignments can test their potential in a non-threatening and systematic way as part of a continuing process.

The results achieved through development centres may boost confidence among corporate management that it is possible to find 'round pegs' to fit into 'round holes' in international operations. The centres also provide individuals with an opportunity to deselect themselves from direct involvement within the international assignment programme, without loss of face, if they recognize, when faced with simulated reality, that they would simply be uncomfortable in such an environment. It is important that individuals have such opportunities, as achieving success on one assignment does not necessarily predict similar success on another.

Development of project team capabilities

A successful project is crucially dependent on the calibre and experience of the project manager and his or her team. Key personnel must be appointed and developed on the basis of need rather than expediency. From benchmarking a number of aspirant internationalizing businesses, we have identified the following key features for winning:

▎ Deploying well a number of significant company strengths, such as technical skills, operational capability, reputation, commercial understanding, the commitment of people, and ability in the management of critical raw materials procurement.

▎ Technical people who 'ask the best questions'. The strength of technical due diligence can be definitive in winning 'bankable' projects. Better definition of risk means a more informed basis for bidding on price.

▎ Handling aspects of the local element on some projects, such as setting up a local company and the deployment of local nationals in the project, which can contribute strongly to success.

▎ Efficient, cost-effective use of external advisers.

A set of competencies required of key project management team members needs to be established and developed. Company HR systems need to be utilized to identify potential project team leaders and in team formation.

The objectives of a successful programme of capabilities development are the creation of well-balanced international teams, operating to maximum effectiveness, sharing common goals (linked to strategic business plans). There will be recognition of cross-cultural sensitivities, an evolution of demonstrable international business skills, including interpersonal and negotiating skills, deal structuring and financial engineering, communication and project management skills. In addition, the process will be carried out with the involvement of key individuals within the parent corporation, affording the opportunity of a wide pool of talent and experience, while enhancing communication links and understanding between domestic and other parts of the internationalizing business entity.

To be successful, a programme of capabilities development must target the right population. It is critical, therefore, not only to define this population correctly, but to have a good understanding of their strengths, weaknesses, aspirations and development needs so that fit-for-purpose training and development interventions can be targeted at the right person at the right time. Furthermore, the programme should contain some distinct but interrelated components: assimilation of knowledge/information, and acquisition of business (technical) skills and business (behavioural) skills, giving a mix of 'hard' topics and 'softer' skills.

Networks of opportunity, action learning and virtual HRD

Alternative and less well-known approaches to HRD include the use of networks of opportunity, action learning and virtual development. An example is the use of a management course that is integrated into career development plans. Management course modules may be held in different countries, and participants have the opportunity to gain short periods of international experience while building networks with others from different locations. Action learning may be used for projects run internationally, where project teams join together through either visits or virtual technology to pursue a shared objective.

STRATEGIC HRD: LOCAL TRAINING AND DEVELOPMENT INTERVENTIONS

The majority of this chapter has focused on training and development of international assignees. Assumptions are frequently made that such interventions are aimed only at parent-country nationals. This may be the case in early stages of internationalization, but if a business is to expand and be successful in the global marketplace, training and development cannot simply be lavished on the home-country employees and those in the expatriate population. A strategic approach is needed if international HRD initiatives are to be carried out successfully. The aim should not be simply to train and develop the internationally mobile, but also to develop local staff and to establish a learning culture throughout the organization. Across the organization's sphere of operations, employees from all backgrounds need to be oriented towards the corporate culture, and a geocentric approach should be taken to knowledge sharing. Walton (1999) advocates respect of local cultures, minimization of expatriate numbers and the grooming of local talent, with local operations being able to fine-tune to match local skills.

Drawing upon Ferdows (1997), Walton suggests that HRD initiatives should address the contribution that the local operation can make to the whole organization. Beach-heads are used to gain access to markets in the early stages of globalization, and provide outposts to gain knowledge or skills needed by the company. Off-shoring is established to gain access to lower wage costs while 'server' operations supply specific local or regional markets. Source operations are established to develop, produce and distribute products for global markets. However, the big HRD challenge, he argues, is to provide the development opportunities that transform the server operations into contributor operations, and the source operations into lead operations. Contributors both serve local markets and assume responsibility for product operation, customization, improvements, modifications and development. The lead operations have ability to innovate and create new processes, products and technologies for the whole organization.

This philosophy concerning the use of training and development initiatives in the local context, therefore, becomes the final focus of this chapter. Organizations wishing to reduce their dependence on parent-country expatriates and to develop into a transnational organization are likely to make considerable efforts to train and develop local personnel and/or to extend their resourcing from beyond the parent country and local markets to make use of other nationalities (third-country nationals).

Let us turn first to the training and development of local nationals. In general, organizations' approaches to training and development are based on home-country practices. This is particularly true if parent-country nationals are sent abroad to train local staff. Training interventions that work well at home may not prove to be so effective abroad. It is important to consider the cultural environment in which the training will be delivered, the style of the trainer, and the capabilities and preferred learning styles of the trainees. For example, hands-on style training in which the trainee is free to ask questions of the trainer is common in the west. Cultures where trainees are used to more formal classroom-style training, and the culture precludes them from directly questioning the trainer, may render the western approach inappropriate, even counter-productive.

It is often assumed that the training required for local nationals should comprise technical and skills-based elements. This is not disputed, but cultural factors, even language, may need to be incorporated. In a global environment, local nationals working for a multinational enterprise need to understand and be able to function effectively within a different organizational culture and corporate language. The practices used in management represent different societal values and norms. The effectiveness of HRM practices may be undermined if locals are unaware of these. Training cannot necessarily provide a panacea, and it is likely that HRM practices may have to be adapted to suit local needs – but training can and should help to provide a basic understanding of why the organization is operating certain policies and procedures. Employee communication is considered crucial to organizational effectiveness. Language training in the parent country/corporate language for certain groups/levels of local employees may be necessary. Training interventions need to be language-sensitive at all levels, with training delivered in the local language where appropriate.

Development initiatives for local nationals have been mentioned already in this chapter, but to summarize, in a global organization, local nationals will need to be developed across country boundaries if they are to apply global understanding and vision to complement their local responsiveness. If organizations are to secure management (at all levels) with local/global competencies, development initiatives must widen the perspectives of local nationals beyond their own country's horizon. Development programmes may involve senior local nationals working for periods in the parent country's headquarters or in other destinations to learn corporate and societal practices. These may be regionally based initiatives or involve wider global mobility.

This raises the issue of the training and development of third-country nationals – where interventions are aimed at employees who are neither parent-country nor local nationals. Once again, cultural sensitivity is required if the format and delivery of the training is to be effective. International development programmes are particularly challenging to such personnel, as both the culture of the organization (which may reflect, in part, the HQ's country culture) and the country where they are working are foreign to them.

The use of training and development initiatives for local and third-country nationals via virtual means might be considered as an alternative to mobility. Again, the delivery of such interventions needs to be thought through carefully. International capability might also be considered via the development of international teams – although these require training and support. Mentoring and coaching might also be considered as ways of providing development initiatives across an organization operating internationally.

CONCLUDING REMARKS

A successful skills training and capabilities development programme is designed to meet the strategic needs of the internationalizing corporation and to reflect the framework and process for business development and operational management. It forms part of a holistic HRM framework incorporating establishment of an internal talent pool for international business development; the recruitment and selection process for key team members; and team-building techniques and processes to facilitate information flow and understanding within project teams and corporate management.

The development of skills and capabilities from within – built from turning learning into knowledge – must be integrated with those designed to augment capability by other means, including targeted recruitment, alliances and joint ventures, and strategic business unit acquisitions. These efforts together will generally assist in providing internationalizing businesses with a 'kick-start', providing an injection of targeted capability to complement existing core organizational competence, along with medium- and longer-term capability.

The evaluation of international training and development choices and consequences is aided by locating practically focused considerations within the context of a range of learning theory, as we have attempted to sketch in this chapter. Such theory needs to be tempered by considerations of varying cultural interpretation of specific initiatives. Equally, clarity is required regarding the strategic model adopted by multinational managements, which gives rise to their orientation to human capital building, expatriate and/or local national. The organization might perceive its employees as either costs to be minimized and troublesome agents to control, or scarce, valuable, inimitable and non-substitutable resources, gaining whose potential cooperation will necessitate navigating diverse institutional contexts.

YOUR TURN

▌ To what extent do you believe that training and development are considered as an input to business strategy in internationalizing businesses?

▌ How can organizations tailor training and development interventions taking into account cultural differences across their international workforces?

▌ To what extent should organizations continue to invest in training and development of employees whose tenure with them might be no more than transitory?

▌ How can local training and development interventions encompass global awareness?

▌ How can knowledge gained through training and development interventions for some be shared and utilized by others within an international organization?

REFERENCES

Altman, Y (1999) International HR: career management, in *The Global HR Manager*, ed P Joynt and B Morton, Institute of Personnel Development (IPD), London

Argyris, C and Schön, D A (1974) *Theory in Practice: Increasing professional effectiveness*, Jossey-Bass, San Francisco

Argyris, C and Schön, D A (1978) *Organizational Learning: A theory of action perspective*, Jossey-Bass, San Francisco

Bartlett, C A and Ghoshal, S (1989) *Managing Across Borders: The transnational solution*, Harvard Business School Press, Cambridge, Mass

Bloom, M and Milkovich, G T (1999) A SHRM perspective on international compensation and reward systems, in *Research in Personnel and Human Resource Management*, ed P M Wright, L D Dyer, J W Boudreau and G T Milkovich, pp 238–304, JAI Press, Greenwich, Conn

Boydell, T, Leary, M, Megginson, J and Pedlar, M (1991) *Developing the Developers: Improving the quality of professionals who develop people and organisations*, AMED Report, pp 14–28

Dowling, P J, Welch, D E and Schuler, R S (1999) *International Human Resource Management: Managing people in a multinational context*, South-Western College Publishing, Cincinnati, Ohio

Eby, L (2001) The boundaryless career experience of mobile spouses in dual-career marriages, *Group and Organization Management*, **26**(3), pp 343–68

Hamel, G and Prahalad, C K (1994) *Competing for the Future*, Harvard Business School Press, Boston, Mass

Hofstede, G (1994) *Cultures and Organisations*, HarperCollins Business, London

Kolb, D (1984) *Experiential Learning: Experience as the source of learning and development*, Prentice Hall, Englewood Cliffs, NJ

Marton, F, Dall'Alba, G and Beaty, E (1993) Conceptions of learning, *International Journal of Educational Research*, **19**(3)

Mendenhall, M and Oddou, G (1985) The dimensions of expatriate acculturation: a review, *Academy of Management Review*, **10**, pp 39–47

Mendenhall, M, Dunbar, E and Oddou, G (1987) Expatriate selection, training and career-pathing: a review and critique, *Human Resource Management*, **26**, pp 331–45

ORC (2005) *Dual Careers and International Assignments Survey*, Organization Resources Counselors, London

Perlmutter, H V (1969) The tortuous evolution of the multinational corporation, *Columbia Journal of World Business*, **4**(1), pp 9–18

Ramsden, P (1992) *Learning to Teach in Higher Education*, Routledge, London

Richardson, K (1985) *Personality, Development and Learning*, Unit 8/9 Learning Theories, Open University Press, Milton Keynes

Riusala, K and Suutari, V (2000) Expatriation and careers: perspectives of expatriates and spouses, *Career Development International*, **5**(2), pp 81–90

Schein, E H (1988) *Organizational Culture and Leadership*, Jossey-Bass, San Francisco

Selmer, J (2000) Usage of corporate career development activities by expatriate managers and the extent of their international adjustment, *International Journal of Commerce and Management*, **10**(1), pp 1–23

Shortland, S (2003a) Managing international assignment stress, *Managing Internationally Mobile Employees Briefing*, **37**, pp 12–15

Shortland, S (2003b) Learning through international experience, *Managing Internationally Mobile Employees Briefing*, **36**, pp 4–7

Shortland, S (2004) Selection and training requirements for transfers to countries with subtle cultural differences, *Human Resources and Employment Review*, **2**(1), pp 36–46

Trompenaars, F and Hampden-Turner, C (1997) *Riding the Waves of Culture*, Nicholas Brearley, London

Tung, R L (1981) Selecting and training of personnel for overseas assignments, *Columbia Journal of World Business*, **16**, pp 68–78

Walton, J (1999) *Strategic HRD*, Prentice Hall, London

Yu, P W (2003) *The Cross-Cultural Competence for Taiwanese Expatriates in China: A case study*, unpublished dissertation, London Metropolitan University

5

Choices and consequences in international employee compensation

CHAPTER AIMS

This chapter sets out to do the following:

▌ introduce you to the choices and consequences open to the management of multinational organizations in 'effort–reward' bargaining in respect of various 'international' workforce segments;

▌ consider 'strategic' issues around managing employee performance and compensation systems arising from pursuit of alternative modes of organization for international expansion and delegated leadership orientations;

▌ examine 'reward management' techniques for multinational application, and the underlying assumptions, derived from social and management science commentary, based on which they are designed.

INTRODUCTION

A recent survey of 90 multinational organizations (based primarily in Europe and the United States, but operating in up to 100 countries), reported that 85 per cent claimed to have 'a global pay *strategy*' (Edelsten, 2005, emphasis added), half of which had been adopted in the past five years. The remaining 15 per cent all said they intended to implement a global pay strategy over the next three years. The conclusion expressed on behalf of Mercer HR Consulting, the firm that had undertaken the survey, was that 'pay strategies play an important role in the success of multinational organizations... increasingly, pay is being managed from a global perspective' (Edelsten, 2005: 1). The survey found that ' typically these strategies apply to all employees, not just a select group, such as executives' (Edelsten, 2005: 1). The rationale for this choice to manage 'extrinsic' reward (see below for a definition) globally was described as multifaceted: 'to facilitate global expansion efforts, better manage labour costs, create internal equity, or ensure effective governance'. Of course, it may be unwise to accept uncritically the implied proposition that such an array of possible corporate aims will sit together harmoniously. As Bloom and Milkovich observe (citing Mahony, 1979), 'compensation systems cannot be understood abstracted away from the context in which they occur' (1999: 240).

A former Motorola director of compensation for Europe, the Middle East and Africa commented to one of us, 'You can do a lot more harm than good to employment relations with how you manage pay. My job will be done when it becomes a non-topic of conversation across the business.' What does this remark imply for managerial approaches to international effort–reward bargaining? First, for many years leading western multinationals relied on transporting management agents from 'home' country operations or 'corporate headquarters' to oversee internationally dispersed operations. The practice has come under severe scrutiny over the past decade, as greater competition has placed downward pressures on corporate costs. Second, as reported above, managing 'compensation' or 'reward' systems (that is, systematically combining management of pay and benefits structures and processes) from a global perspective may be translated into attempts by corporate management to standardize practice internationally. The following two anecdotes in a 'picture postcard' from a management consultant with long-time exposure to practices in central and south American countries hint at the need for caution before choosing reward system 'solutions' that rely too heavily on home-country expatriate assignments to overseas operations, or naïve adoption of common techniques.

Lorraine Zuleta identifies a problem where western companies send expatriate staff to Central and South America to work alongside key employees recruited locally. This is particularly pronounced at the middle-managerial level. She says major issues can arise in relation to brand or product line managers, for example. A few years ago Kraft assigned a project manager from the United States to Venezuela for 'career development' purposes. Enjoying a traditional US 'expatriation package', the 'trainee' was in fact paid more than the local general manager. Such practices severely distort pay comparability levels, and may lead to distrust of corporate management intentions while demotivating those on whose cooperation successful country market development depends.

Toh and DeNisi argue that discontent and resentment may be created among executives located in host countries for foreign direct investment (the commentators cite the case of China), on which the organization relies to secure 'embeddedness' in the target business market. Such key employees may perceive themselves being treated as second-class citizens relative to expatriates, who are locally perceived to be less qualified than the host country nationals in terms of work qualifications, expertise and experience (Toh and DeNisi, 2005: 133).

On the question of standardized reward system techniques, Lorraine Zuleta says:

> One of the biggest follies has been to try rolling out job evaluation systems worldwide (which is why some proprietary systems have become so discredited). When head office is intent on imposing standardization, everyone locally simply works on how they can beat the system. One used to overhear conversations between managers in the oil industry in Venezuela along the lines of: 'What do we want to pay, how many points do we require, and how do we write the job description to ensure this delivers the desired evaluation outcome?'

Such cameos are not intended to imply that corporate objectives are unattainable; simply that those choices, and the underlying assumptions, need to be weighed carefully, being mindful of the likely consequences – which may be unintended or downright undesirable.

In this chapter, we reflect on some of the issues surrounding the determination of rewards in the multinational organization, segmenting the 'global workforce' into two primary categories – internationally mobile or 'expatriate' employees, on the one hand, and employees sourced in the host country for international operations, on the other hand. We also take into account two additional subcategories: third-country nationals (individuals working outside their country of origin, but not from the 'home' employment system), and ex-host-country nationals (individuals who have left their home country to study or work abroad before returning to rejoin the local labour market). Trends in expatriate pay and benefits packages are reviewed against the backdrop of growing international competitiveness and cost pressures. Issues surrounding effort–reward systems of management applicable to 'local national' and other groups of employees are explored in relation to debates around the extent to which people management approaches may be said to be converging on a single model worldwide.

DEFINITIONS: SUBSTANCE AND PROCESS IN REWARD MANAGEMENT

Before moving on to the detail, let us first clarify what we mean when discussing, first, the notion of 'employee reward' (or 'compensation') as it finds expression in the literature, and second, how rewards can be 'delivered'. We follow Kessler (2000) in distinguishing between *extrinsic* reward within the 'effort–reward' bargain underlying employment relations between individuals and organizations, and *intrinsic* reward. Our focus here is on extrinsic rewards: material factors such as pay, perks, share-based reward and other long-term benefits (such as pensions). Intrinsic rewards may include aspects such as environmental factors and development opportunities. In some commentary, the term 'total reward' has become popular, combining both extrinsic and intrinsic aspects. This is valuable in the sense of drawing attention to the need for a more holistic approach to the effort–reward bargain. However, there is a danger that discussion may become vague and over-generalized. For the purposes of focusing our discussion below, the emphasis remains on extrinsic reward phenomena. (A clear introduction to the notion of total reward may be found at www.cipd.co.uk/subjects/pay/general/totrewdqf.htm.)

To situate the discussion of choices and consequences surrounding reward systems designed and administered across multinational operations, there is value in reflecting on what managements actually expect from the structures and processes they put in place to that end. In other words, what are the consequences managers anticipate contingent on their 'strategic' decision taking? Kessler (2000) is critical of commentary based on imposed assumptions about the goals underlying managerial practice: they might fail to account for the actual range of goals managers are pursuing, explicitly or implicitly. In terms of evaluating 'how to motivate and compensate the foreign employees' multinational organizations recruit, Rehu, Lusk and Wolff (2005: 82) attempt to state simply the 'real' managerial problem to be addressed: 'employers want to motivate their employees to work towards the organization's goals'.

A significant issue for reward management theory is what motivates workers to do what without stimulus they otherwise might not do. Reward structures and the dispersion of rewards reflect fundamental social values (Drucker and White, 2000) which may interact with a variety of ways in which multinational managements choose to organize the delivery of extrinsic reward, in pursuit of the aim summarized above. The focus may be on rewarding the *results* of employee effort: Kessler (2000) uses the term 'output' to summarize this reward management orientation. He contrasts it with managerial decisions to focus on '*input*' – that is, the enabling factors workforce members contribute to efforts to secure organizational (output) goals.

Kessler (2000) reminds us that managers may choose to focus reward delivery on *individual* employee performance. However, given a requirement for collective effort to achieve organizational goals, and a corporate governance orientation towards *corporate* performance, managers may decide to focus to some extent at least on collective units of performance.

The types of reward delivery format may be perceived as following from the relative emphasis on input/output and individual/collective contributions to organizational goal attainment. Individually oriented reward delivery in recognition for input may result in managerial decisions to pay for employee competence and/or skills (the specific capabilities and/or behavioural factors employees bring to the organization). This can be organized in a structured fashion, such as 'skills-based pay' programmes, or based on more subjective managerial judgement of individual employee merit. Output-related reward focused on the individual may include schemes such as paying commissions on sales, or for piecework production. It may be delivered in the form of individual bonuses or salary-related individual pay for performance (sometimes labelled individual performance-related pay, or iPRP).

By contrast, more collectively oriented output-related reward delivery schemes include team pay, 'gainsharing' and profit sharing. The first two are focused at the level of work teams, possibly across operational sites; the second is pitched more at the company, or at least divisional, level, where 'profit' is accounted for. Gainsharing has had a long history since its emergence in the United States, and is generally linked with managerial efforts to enlist employee effort in pursuit of cost reduction/saving, where a proportion of the 'gains' achieved is made available for distribution among the workforce segment(s) involved.

In the case of input-related collective reward delivery mechanisms, the focus tends to be longer-term, such as through the use of employee share ownership plans. Here there are potential problems for multinational managements, because there are differences across jurisdictions in the regulation and fiscal treatment of share-ownership arrangements.

A further point of clarification is necessary. Once we have attempted to specify the conceptual basis for discussing multinational compensation system choices and consequences – in terms of a focus on extrinsic reward, the underlying intentions that may be attributed to managements, and the variety of reward delivery channels – we need to position the alternative systems in the wider social context of 'employment relations'. It is necessary to keep in mind that the core of the employment relationship is the exchange contracted for, in terms of effort from the worker and payment by the employer. Marsden (1999) explains that as the basis of this 'bargain' is not unambiguously delineated (and is indeterminate), there is scope for each of the parties continuously to manoeuvre – workers for more pay than effort, employers for more performance than they pay for. Managerially this has given rise to attempts to limit the employer's risk and/or transfer the risk to the employee, through 'contingent' or 'at risk' reward. (Examples have already been provided in the overview of reward delivery vehicles.) On the part of employees there is the scope to attempt to secure greater capacity to influence pay – either through limiting entry to an occupational group, or through state regulation, or through collective mobilization to force employers to agree a bargain that offers a premium over the deal that might have been offered to non-organized workers.

Normative HRM commentary encourages managers to create structures and processes that offer employers a greater capacity to align the value created through labour employed, and the share allocated to the workforce. This is determined under managerial rather than collective discretion. In parallel, ideological devices ('employee communications' initiatives) have been used to underscore the warrant held by management for this. Employers are also encouraged to be seen to share the wealth created through profit share schemes, gainshare plans and the like, as referred to above. For this purpose they should arguably hold back some material rewards that might have accrued directly to labour through collective organization. Rather than using principles of equity to organize the occupationally informed distribution of wealth created, these changes have sought to increase the capacity of management to discriminate between individual workers, based on managerial judgements of performance achievement. Such developments go to the heart of debates surrounding the fundamental values underlying reward systems (Drucker and White, 2000), which we mentioned above, as these may be identified across organizations and employment systems internationally.

Hence, a variety of complex phenomena may be perceived to be in play when considering the choices and consequences surrounding reward management. The framework outlined in the introductory chapter, which drew attention to the interactions around work-related performance aspirations from the three perspectives of organizational strategy, business systems and human capital, can be applied to help evaluate theoretically informed pre-scription and empirically observed practice.

CULTURE AND BEYOND: NATIONAL, INDUSTRY AND CORPORATE CONTEXTS

We now move from definitional context setting to more practically focused concerns. How may effort–reward management practice be situated con-textually, recalling Mahoney's (1979) exhortation (cited in Bloom and Milkovich, 1999)? Under the HRM paradigm, reward strategy has as its very essence the requirement to align organization and workforce to achieve su-perior levels of corporate performance, sustained over time. From the point of view of simplified administration, global policies on reward might be ideal. But multinational managements face the broad question of how the interface between reward strategies and 'multi-domestic' contexts (Bradley, Hendry and Perkins, 1999) impact on corporate performance delivery.

As a starting point, the strategic challenge of managing pay and benefits systems transnationally may be perceived as involving a 'cultural' dimen-sion (Hofstede, 1981, 1991). Unravelling 'the complex set of influences' that national culture can have on the efficiency of 'various pay formulae and tech-niques' has become a focus for researchers' attention (Sparrow, 2000: 203). Corporate HR specialists in internationalizing organizations face the prob-lem of designing policies and practices that management will be able to apply across various geographies in ways that avoid conflict with the local national culture ('how we do things around here'). However, that is not the only requirement. If strategic alignment is the goal, multinational compen-sation systems also need to be fitted to the governance system and manage-rial style chosen for the organization overall (Milkovich and Bloom, 1998). And culture – including the value systems that inform the ways in which people can be expected to respond to economic and social phenomena – is not the only factor to be weighed in choosing how to structure and admin-ister reward systems internationally. 'Institutional factors' operating with-in different business systems may make some approaches easier or more difficult to adopt than others. Here we are referring to laws, economic conditions and political trends in the country concerned (Schuler and Jackson, 2005, citing von Glinow, Drost and Teagardem, 2002).

Because of the inherent limitations in any attempt to define and measure culture with any degree of accuracy, and the risk of 'blatant stereotyping' (Milkovich and Bloom, 1998: 18), we believe it is not enough to look solely to 'cultural difference' studies to guide the design and management of reward systems. Cultural sensitivity in multinational compensation management needs to be combined with attention to national, corporate and industry effects, not forgetting the aim of encouraging a corporate or 'global' mindset (Milkovich and Bloom, 1998) across the entire workforce. All this needs to be done in accordance with the empirical aspirations that Edelsten (2005) reports. Managerial choices in a multinational enterprise (MNE) might therefore be seen as involving resolution of the conflict between two pressures: one for internal consistency, and one for 'isomorphism' with the local institutional environment (Rosenzweig and Nohria, 1994).

On the one hand, seeking internal consistency by developing common compensation and benefits policies would facilitate employee reward management across borders, including cross-border mobilizations, while preserving internal equity. On the other hand, pressures to conform to local practices may be too great to ignore. National, industry, and organizationally specific factors may impact on the extent to which different practices can be designed to be global or 'multi-local' (Bradley *et al*, 1999). For example, pay determination of manual operatives is likely to be highly regulated, and the scope for subsidiary policy coherence may be limited. In contrast, 'performance management' is relatively free of host country regulation: management concern may be focused more readily on striving for cross-national consistency.

These are the key elements of national business systems infrastructure as summarized by Bradley *et al* (1999):

∎ the extent to which factors of production (location, physical, human and financial resources) differ from country to country;

∎ the extent to which economies differ in terms of their sector contributions (manufacturing, service and agriculture);

∎ the human/machine balance, productivity and competitiveness levels;

∎ the country's welfare state.

The relative effect of national values on reward systems will be influenced also by organization-specific factors such as:

∎ the degree of centralization or decentralization;

∎ the role of 'line' management;

∎ the composition of the line (expatriates or nationals);

∎ growth patterns;

▮ degree of technological sophistication;

▮ strength of 'corporate branding' (for example, the strength of corporate image may make it easier for firms like Coca-Cola or McDonald's successfully to adopt global reward strategies, regardless of national culture).

THINKING THROUGH CHOICES AND CONSEQUENCES IN INTERNATIONAL REWARD SYSTEMS

It has been estimated that all but 10 per cent of the total payroll for multinational enterprises comprises compensation for local nationals. It is not entirely appropriate, then, that most of the writing on international reward focuses on expatriate staff – and by implication ethnocentric (Perlmutter, 1969) employment policies, although it may be understandable, because of the disproportionately high cost of such individuals to multinational corporations. This focus on a small percentage of the global workforce, in the academic literature as well as in corporate practice, has become a matter for concern among some commentators, given the increasing need for multinational organizations to attract, motivate and retain an effective workforce in a variety of foreign locations (Lowe *et al*, 2002). Indeed, Milkovich and Bloom claim to perceive 'a worldwide restructuring of compensation and reward systems' (1998: 15). The analysts' rationale is 'globalization pressures' and 'market-based economies', which they argue create unprecedented opportunities for multinational employers, who recognize that 'global mind-sets are required to meet these challenges' (1998: 16):

> A global mind-set means adopting values or attitudes to create a common mental programming for balancing corporate, business unit and functional priorities on a worldwide scale [carrying with it] enormous intellectual and thus competitive advantages.
>
> (Milkovich and Bloom, 1998: 16)

In short, this involves emphasizing so-called 'networked knowledge management' (Scarborough, Swan and Preston, 1999) and getting 'the best ideas from everyone everywhere' (Milkovich and Bloom, 1998: 16). As will be discussed below, adopting a 'transnational' organizational form (Ghoshal and Bartlett, 1998) implies a range of choices for reward systems, compared with those that might apply where multinationals are structured along alternative lines.

Research reported by Roth and O'Donnell (1996) suggests that it is particularly important to look beyond expatriates when examining the area of reward systems management by multinational organizations. In a study of foreign subsidiary managers, the researchers found that variance in compensation practices increased with 'distance' from headquarters. Another way of expressing this is that reward arrangements designed for more senior managers (typically expatriates) tend to be closer to pay and benefits designed for home-country operations (Lowe *et al*, 2002). Further, Roth and O'Donnell (1996) found that nationality was the strongest predictor of reward system design. It may be short-sighted to focus on expatriate compensation over arrangements applied to the variety of 'local-national' workforces, whose constituents may supply multinationals with language, culture and skills that make them more valuable to the organization in the long term than headquarters-country nationals (Tilghman and Knight, 1998, cited by Lowe *et al*, 2002).

As a direct consequence, it may become increasingly important for multinational managements to make efforts to understand the needs and preferences of these locals (locating them within the attendant range of cultural and institutional variables), as high costs encourage organizations to reconsider the blanket use of expatriates for the oversight of globally dispersed operations. Milkovich and Bloom (1998) argue that it is in multinational managers' competitive interests to develop new reward models, with the flexibility to tailor the overall compensation system to fit the context in which they compete, within a framework of corporate principles. That is to say, the objective becomes 'to structure the total value of employment so that employee contributions support organizational goals' (Milkovich and Bloom, 1998: 22), while offering some opportunity for employees to select forms of returns from their employment that meet their individual needs as well.

While we support the view that 'expatriate myopia' (Lowe *et al*, 2002) needs to give way to more comparative research into reward system management internationally, we feel it would be inappropriate to fail to review the vast literature devoted to expatriation-linked reward, however. And indeed there is innovation in managing compensation for international mobility, especially where greater mutual flexibility between the individual and the organization and greater attention to performance alignment are introduced. Therefore, we first focus below on compensation management approaches associated with international (managerial) employee mobility. We then look at the emerging field of analysis of how multinationals are making choices related to their 'multi-domestic' workforces (Bradley *et al*, 1999), whether or not these choices involve the explicit adoption of 'global' reward strategies. Before turning to this detailed material, we briefly consider three interrelated phenomena to situate the subsequent discussion.

These are definitions of the various categories that distinguish the multinational workforce; 'best practice' organizational formations that prescribe movement towards a specifically 'transnational' structure; and orientations towards those to whom corporate managements delegate international leadership functions.

DEFINING 'MULTINATIONAL' EMPLOYEES FOR REWARD MANAGEMENT PURPOSES

In international companies there are two major categories of employee: 'expatriates' and 'local nationals'. Expatriates are employees sent from their 'home' countries by their employer to another country – the 'host' country – on a temporary assignment (generally one to five years). 'Headquarters expatriates' – those sent overseas from the headquarters country of the organization – are often called simply 'expatriates' or 'parent-country nationals' or 'home-country nationals'. Additional 'internationally mobile' employee categories may be identified: 'in-patriates' – those sent to the headquarters country from another country, possibly for corporate socialization and/or skills training purposes – and 'third-country nationals (TCNs)': those working temporarily in a second country for an employer headquartered in a third country. 'Local nationals' are people recruited and employed to work in the country in which they are resident. Generally, they are citizens of that country. They may also be known as 'host-country nationals'. This group may also include ex-host-country nationals – those who have left their home country to study or work abroad before returning to rejoin the local labour market. As noted in Chapter 3, some organizations have identified distinctive 'career trajectories' applicable to employees located throughout their various international operations, which may help multinationals to address choices about which approaches to reward and recognition to adopt in particular cases.

STRATEGIC CHOICES: ORGANIZATIONAL FORMATIONS AND LEADERSHIP PROFILES – IMPERIAL GOVERNORS, EXPATRIATE GHETTO RESIDENTS, GLOBAL CHAMPIONS?

Now we have defined categories of multinational workforce members, a second major consideration to help locate multinational reward management approaches is the choice of organizational form to structure international operations. Perkins and Hendry (2001) developed the model in Table 5.1, building on the work of Ghoshal and Bartlett (1998), to assist in systematically considering the interface between organizational and reward system design factors. It should be emphasized that the model represents a series of organizational 'ideal types'. These are abstractions against which empirical aspirations and practice may be evaluated. They are unlikely to be replicated exactly in practice.

The reference to empirical research by Perkins and Hendry brings a third significant factor to the surface. The researchers found that corporate management orientation towards those deployed to lead international business development may be a critical factor, and that this also demands attention in attempting to make sense of multinational managerial practice. A tendency was identified whereby corporate managements had moved:

> beyond straightforward acceptance of organizational design identified as 'leading edge' in the literature. Scaling back the stress on aspects of formal structure, emphasis was being placed more on the formation and development of a *cadre* of individuals occupying leadership positions within firms' global operations.
>
> (Perkins and Hendry 2001: 54)

The response to the question how multinational managements perceive leaders deployed beyond the 'home' country sets the context for choices about the detailed architecture, which conditions the bargain between multinational effort (performance) and reward, and the interface between members of the internationally mobile and local-national workforces.

Perkins and Hendry (1999a) review commentary on ideal-type multinational organizational formations in order to contextualize managerial choices and the consequences for international reward and recognition. They emphasize that prescribed 'best practice' needs to be situated within an understanding of the way employees and reward have traditionally been managed:

> vested interest, conditioned expectations and managerial traditions in structuring and practising performance and reward management will be embedded in the organization's culture. Such culture, research suggests, is likely to reflect a unidirectional organizational form, rather than the integrated settings configured in the transnational.
>
> (Perkins and Hendry, 1999a: 118)

Table 5.1 Multinational structures and international employee reward principles

	Decentralized federation	Coordinated federation	Centralized hub	Synthesized (transnational)
Operational focus	Local identification/ exploitation of discrete opportunities	Adaptation and deployment of parent organization core competencies	Implementation of corporate strategies	Diverse but interdependent perspectives and capability exploitation
Resourcing	Local self-sufficiency	Core capability sourced centrally/application dispersed	Centralized and globally scaled	Multiple and flexible coordination
Knowledge management	Locally emergent/ retained learning	Centralized innovation and core learning transferred to 'overseas' units	Centrally developed/ retained learning	Shared corporate vision and individual commitment
Reward architecture	Minimal consistency of approach: benchmarking to local labour markets; performance rewards based on value created in discrete markets, share of which is returned to core investor at discretion of local 'imperial governors'	Blueprint reward system transfused by roving parent organization agents at top levels. Disconnect between parent and local reward practice and performance goals and recognition other than for piecemeal 'initiatives'	Discrepancies of treatment between expatriate 'headquarters' employees and 'locals', both in levels and delivery of reward. Emphasis on maximizing return to centre from operational 'franchises'	Respect for diverse traditional and local market regulation, but common performance/ reward infrastructure, emphasizing shared value creation and integrative dispersion among stakeholders

Source: based on Perkins and Hendry (2001), following Ghoshal and Bartlett (1998).

Ghoshal and Bartlett (1998) describe four ideal forms of international organization, which are used in Table 5.1. The first two summarized here are federated structures, the second of which is a structure that emphasizes centralized control over corporate direction. The third recognizes the interdependency of resources used in the pursuit of sustainable multinational business development.

The 'classic multinational', which falls in the category of 'decentralized federation', reflects the traditions of family-centred ownership among European businesses. Offshoots of such businesses, developed beyond the country of origin, have tended to be run by trusted appointees, sent to govern overseas corporate 'empires' which are recognized as fundamentally different from the parent organization. Business units are located across the various territories to which finance capital investment is targeted, with investment capital outflows and returns the only common denominator.

Accordingly, each 'offshoot' from the parent was managed as a separate entity, to optimize trading in the local environment, and the corporate governance of these organizational arrangements appears to have reflected simple accounting consolidation. The tendency among governors has been to 'go native', integrating themselves into the local environment, and adopting local commercial and cultural norms over the term of a typically long assignment. The consequence was a fragmentation in employee reward management. Except perhaps for the 'country manager', the structure of compensation and its relationship to performance were linked to the outcomes achieved by the quasi-independent business units. The overall principle was one of 'subsidiarity' – the presumption that it is in the best interests of the constituent parts to address issues independently, with central initiatives only where local entities believe it will be to their advantage to permit them, or basic managerial capability is absent.

In strategic terms, we can think of this as a transactional cost economics model: continued support for specific business units and their imperial governors will be a function of the perceived immediate cost–return equation. Implicitly at least, assumptions derived from institutional theory may also be in play: the attitude of corporate management might be that the embedded material and ideological phenomena found in each country are not susceptible to significant adaptation and transnational coordination, and that to try to do so would carry overly burdensome transaction costs.

An alternative version of the 'classic' model may be described as the 'coordinated federation'. This places a greater degree of influence at the centre of the multinational, reversing the unidirectionality of operational management influence associated with the decentralized federation, while still maintaining the effective separation between the variety of local operations to which investment may be directed worldwide. The model came into widespread operation in the years following the Second World War, with the spread of US influence around the globe. Unlike the European tradition of family owner-managers, businesses in the United States enjoyed a predominantly 'professionalized' managerial population, and their governance arrangements favoured sophisticated financial management systems to enable delegation while maintaining overall corporate control within the 'home' institution. This form of internationalization was driven by the search for growth potential during the Cold War era in 'third-world developing' nations, where technical and managerial know-how was less advanced than in the 'developed' Western nations. The primary objective was therefore efficient transfer of capability in return for income generation. Again we can see this as having a transaction cost orientation, which pursues institutional dominance by the 'foreign direct investor' in ignorance or disregard of local institutional factors. The assumption appears to be that detailed corporate practice can be transplanted as the 'scientific' one best way.

In terms of reward and recognition, one consequence of the organizational culture of dependency under the coordinated federation model was the overriding value placed on parent company managers and other employees who were deployed on short- to medium-term expatriate assignments to transfer 'corporate know-how'. Localization of management was deemed rarely appropriate. In terms of strategic managerial ideology, we can see an agency orientation conditioning SIHRM decision taking. The role of corporate overseers was not only to ensure that there were predetermined returns on investment, interpreted and mediated through a series of multi-local lenses operated by the expatriate 'governor'; it could also be seen as ensuring compliance with parent company norms. This lessened the room for manoeuvre on the part of local management, who were placed under more sophisticated corporate scrutiny, in both product and financial terms.

In this model there is limited encouragement for capability development and reciprocal alignment of interests between the various constituencies that comprise the multinational across its various theatres of operation, underpinned by reinforcement-encouraging reward systems. Both expectation and general practice tended to emphasize the notion of preserving expatriates' 'at home' lifestyles, and this was done through a series of 'build-ups' of guaranteed, rather than performance-contingent, financial allowances on top of existing remuneration. Continuing the theme of expatriation 'compensation' (for a sense of loss of 'normal' lifestyle), among other things additional provision was made for company-provided, or company-funded, residential and related domestic facilities, security and 'clubs' to enable the expatriate community to maintain the sense of being 'at home abroad'.

At least to an extent, this logically reflects the circumstances faced by western company executives who had been deployed in remote locations away from an urban environment, associated for example with mineral extraction operations. But this model was adopted widely, and such 'packages' came to be expected even when the relocation was between cities. The consequence of the 'build-up' approach (commonly referred to as the expatriate 'balance sheet' of pay, allowances and other expatriation provisions) was to encourage the formation of expatriate ghettos. This in turn had the effect of amplifying the divisions between expatriate and local staff, particularly where the expatriates enjoyed a lifestyle far superior to that available to individuals on local incomes.

The idea of 'hardship premia' to induce expatriates to temporarily interrupt their career and personal lifestyles reinforced the sense of difference between the material and psychological contract available to employees associated with different corporate and federated organizational units. This was also an expensive model. The revenues to fund such generous provision were often available at a time when competition internationally and financial strictures were less pronounced, but the majority of multinationals subsequently came to experience economic 'globalization' pressures which caused them to rethink this type of package.

The scope of multinational business now extends well beyond the mineral extracting enterprises for which the balance sheet expatriate 'deal' was initially formulated. Even in those organizations, business streamlining has become a priority: gone are the days when to quote Jonathan Fry, former chief executive of lubricants business Burmah Castrol, 'you simply scooped up the product that was lying on the ground', enjoying a virtual monopoly on distribution so that costs were little more than a pass-through to the end-customer (Perkins and Hendry, 1999b). The increasing challenges in commercial environments during the 1980s and 1990s forced many coordinated federations to rethink this model, and with it their international reward management framework.

While the overriding corporate focus had come to be on cost control, more 'resource-oriented' theories of the firm may have exerted some influence on corporate thinking. We can draw on a 'core competence' strand in the literature reaching managerial audiences, to conclude that 'competing for the future' (Hamel and Prahalad, 1994) in international markets requires executives and professionals in organizational networks to be willing to align their talents, and knowledge of local business systems, with corporate goals. Divisive reward and recognition symbols could be perceived as a hurdle in the path of achievement of sustainable success in competitive markets, and of satisfying shareholder demands.

All the same, there is evidence to suggest that the most common expatriate terms and conditions continued to reflect 'balance sheet' principles (albeit in a variety of derivative forms, discussed below), in spite of their apparent organizational deficiencies. Management consultants ORC Worldwide surveyed international assignment compensation practices at almost 800 multinational companies from over 20 industries in 2002. They reported:

> Despite the use of alternative pay systems for expatriates, most participants still follow the ORC-pioneered balance sheet methodology. The majority of worldwide respondents (80%) apply this approach to cost-of-living, housing, and tax components of the expatriate pay package. Japanese firms top the list of users at 93%, followed by the Americas (84%), Europe/Middle East (70%), and Asia-Pacific (60%).
>
> (www.orcworldwide.com/surveys/wws2002.html)

Ghoshal and Bartlett (1998) describe a third organization and management model for international business development, referred to as 'centralized hubs' (again, see Table 5.1). They argue that this configuration particularly suited the managerial norms and practices of Japanese companies. In this model, multinational managements place greater emphasis on 'world' markets than appears to be the motivation for adopting either of the 'federated' variants. However, the centralized hub model depends on centralized decision making, suiting top managers and owners from cultures where group-oriented behaviour provides the cornerstone of management systems (Perkins and Hendry, 1999a). These institutional values reflect a complex system of personalized commitments and interdependencies, which it is notoriously difficult to transfer abroad. With managers based in headquarters and a tight control on subsidiary operations, the flow of materials, knowledge and support was even more one-way than under the coordinated federation. The result was that overseas-based international managers formed only a limited appreciation of the unique features of the local environment, against which commercial opportunities could be evaluated and exploited.

In this model, careers and associated reward structures remain firmly embedded within the parent company. In some cases there is an almost clinical distinction between 'corporate' and other staff. Access to career development and recognition at the highest levels tends to be effectively closed off to non-parent-country nationals, and as a result building a sense of reciprocal commitment and cohesion throughout the global firm is problematic, to say the least. Institutionally based strategy ideas appear to be firmly in evidence here, and the view that tends to underpin the coordinated federation is shared: that the norms and practices of the parent organization should not be subject to variation. Here the idea is to roll out the blueprint to achieve standardized assembly of patented products, and idiosyncratic managerial styles. This emphasis is particularly relevant to the efforts of manufacturing sector organizations to expand across world markets.

It may be perceived that the centralized hub multinational reflects a resource-based view of the core (that is, parent company) managerial talent: it is valuable, scarce, inimitable and non-substitutable (Barney, 1991), combined with an agency and transaction-cost orientation towards non-core employees on the periphery of the organization. Indeed, empirical work demonstrates that Japanese management running large companies in Japan have applied the same model: 'The primary core of regular employees [in Japan] constitutes only about one third of all employees' (Kuwahara, 2004: 283). However, it could be argued that resource-based thinking is in even greater evidence when Ghoshal and Bartlett (1998) prescribe a 'transnational solution' to facilitate effective international coordination of management systems across geographic borders, to match contemporary strategic conditions. Under this construction the 'transnational' corporation develops multi-dimensional strategic capabilities aligned to the pursuit of sustained competitive advantage in global markets.

The transnational model relates efficiency to global competitiveness, with the consequences for reward management that it is necessary to recognize appropriate behavioural inputs and performance outcomes that are supportive of this aim. Simultaneously, the transnational approach demands local responsiveness to diverse market conditions and continuous innovation, where knowledge transfer is realized through the medium of a multi-dimensional organizational network. Possible vested interest and conditioned expectations among expatriate staff are issues that multinational managers need to weigh carefully in considering moving towards such an organizational ideal type. And as many devolved organizational units comprise international joint ventures and strategic alliances, a plurality of governance agendas among investors and their managerial agents may also need to be factored in.

Reward management choices will need to reinforce, not undermine, corporate efforts to resolve the continuing conflicting pressure to balance centralization and decentralization. Milkovich and Bloom turn the 'think globally, act locally' aphorism on its head; organizations that wish to encourage their managers to develop 'global mindsets' to compete on a worldwide basis should 'think globally but act locally' in reward management practices, they say (1998: 16). If networked executive capability is to be applied in pursuit of sustainable networked competitive advantage, multinational reward and recognition systems may need to be audited to weed out practices likely to inhibit such voluntary interdependency between internationally mobile and other organization members. In Stephen's discussions with pay specialists in multinational companies such as BOC and BP, they emphasized corporate efforts to refocus the reward system with the intention of encouraging what they labelled 'federal behaviours' on the part of managers everywhere, reflecting this, for example, in performance appraisal objective-setting, appraisal and reward administration.

Against the backcloth of the four-part model of multinational organization and associated reward management philosophies we have outlined (and summarized in Table 5.1), we now turn to the mechanics of reward systems management, beginning with the extensive literature on expatriation. In the following section we draw on our experience to describe ways in which reward has been applied to facilitate international mobility, highlighting perceived positive and negative aspects. This will set the context for subsequent discussion of the choices and consequences that corporate management face in managing the interface between expatriates and non-parent-country employees.

REWARD STRATEGIES FOR INTERNATIONALLY MOBILE EXECUTIVES

We explained in the previous chapter that our experience of working with organizations attempting to internationalize their businesses has led us to the conclusion that very few of us really know our executives well. Not only do we, as HR people, need to understand our international employees better, it is fundamental that we engage the attention of our senior line management in this process too. In the past, managing an expatriate group has often been something that line managers have sought to shuffle off to the HR professional, as too complex or too emotive an issue for them to become embroiled in. The result has been that HR professionals have found themselves with the worst of all worlds. On the one hand, they have frequently had employees – possibly those who have not been identified with the degree of clarity required to fully appreciate the demands and the benefits implicit in an international assignment – angling for the best possible 'deal' they can strike. And on the other, they have line management impatient to 'get the individual [frequently trailing family members] on the plane as quickly as possible'. In our experience, it is only when senior line management responsible for deploying individuals on international assignments accept their true role as the pilot of the exercise, with the expatriate the co-pilot and with a new value-added role for HR as the navigator, that the process can be managed effectively, with all parties signing on to the strategy.

Principles for developing international assignment policies

From our experience in supporting organizations pursuing the strategic objective of internationalizing, the merits have been recognized of choosing to employ local national staff wherever possible. But, in virtually all cases, organizations conclude there are circumstances where using internationally mobile expatriate staff is the preferred option. This experience has revealed four key messages:

❚ No two assignments and no two assignees are alike.

❚ It is in the interests of the corporate HR specialists involved in supporting the mobilizations that line managers are fully involved at the outset in weighing and formally accepting responsibility for managing the excess cost and value equations associated with expatriate postings.

❚ Attention is required to ensuring that there are both incentives and rewards for the successful completion of overseas assignments and their associated performance objectives.

❚ Pragmatism may be called for if organizations are to remain competitive with their international employment offering, to attract and retain high-quality staff with global mindsets, while continuously striving for overall cost containment.

Competitiveness might be defined in terms of the organization's own industry group, regional comparators, or more generally. Pay posture choices are needed: for example, the organization might wish to position total reward opportunities within the top quartile of comparators. But is this for all categories of international employee? To what extent are elements of the pay and benefits package to be guaranteed irrespective of organization or individual performance?

The choices also include whether assignees' packages should aim to be equitable with home-based peers, host-based peers or other mobile assignees. An international assignment policy that provides equity with home-based peers is typically used for short-term assignments, for longer-term assignments where repatriation is expected, and for moves from countries with high pay and living standards to those with low pay and living standards. An international assignment policy that provides equity with host-based peers is typically used for longer-term assignments to countries with similar pay levels and living standards, where repatriation is not expected, and for permanent transfers. An international assignment policy that provides equity with mobile peers is typically used for globally mobile cadres.

Whichever strategic position is chosen, consequences will follow in terms of:

▌ the level of assignment acceptance among those nominated for mobilization;

▌ ease of understanding of principles and their detailed application among international assignees and assignment administrators alike;

▌ cost-effectiveness of administration;

▌ career and performance management over the medium/long-term;

▌ integration with employee attraction, retention and development policies;

▌ degree of commitment to the system among home and host management.

In the technical appendix at the end of this chapter, we outline a statement of principles that may be followed in the design and evaluation of an international assignment policy.

Assignment policies: documentation and detail

A well-designed and internally publicized international assignment policy should not only enable organizations to achieve strategic goals and operational objectives. In addition, it can help to control costs and manage assignee expectations, thus helping to support the psychological contract.

Assignments typically fall within three separate and distinct categories:

▌ Business trip (less than 31 days duration per single trip). Established company policies governing business travel and expenses generally cover this scenario. Some organizations define a business trip as a period extending as long as three months.

▌ Short-term assignment (over 31 days but less than 12 months, ranging to over three months and up to 12 months – again company definitions vary). Short-term expatriation may be prompted by situations such as the need for training, an assessment of the local or regional market before launching a new product/service, opening a new facility, or a quick troubleshooting effort. During this period, the assignee moves on to the headcount/budget of the project, with selected assignment terms applied, matched to individual circumstances. Career management remains the responsibility of the employee's home department, while performance management may be a shared responsibility.

▌ Full assignment (over 12 months – usually to a maximum of five years, after which localization or repatriation applies).

Additionally, so-called 'commuter' arrangements may be used as substitutes for either short-term or full international assignments, generally where individuals preserve their domestic arrangements intact in the country of origin. Representative consultant survey data indicates that, worldwide, a large proportion of participants are using shorter assignments, on an increasing trend over recent years. ORC Worldwide (2004) reported that three-quarters of those surveyed were using short-term assignments (under 12 months): 72 per cent in Asia-Pacific-headquartered organizations, 74 per cent in the Americas, and 78 per cent in Europe/Middle East. Japan is the exception, where 66 per cent of respondents report a tendency to prefer longer-term assignments (ORC Worldwide, 2004).

A documented assignment policy may be used to ensure consistency of treatment of assignees. The use of the same documentation can ensure that both the sending and receiving locations work to the same guidelines and principles, so that the elements that comprise the relocation package promised at home are delivered, as agreed, in the host location. Any policy should provide remuneration, benefits and allowances specific to the type of assignment. For example, all assignees on short-term assignments would be covered by a policy specific to their needs. Those on longer-term, full international assignments would have their own policy. Similarly assignees involved in 'commuter assignments' might be subject to a specific set of terms and conditions.

Assignees who are part of a mobile cadre might also be subject to an international assignment policy that more fully reflects the type of commitment the individual contracts, and the organization recognizes. Again, international cadre mobility may apply on a short-term or long-term basis. The aim of the policy, despite all these permutations, is to preserve equity among groups of assignees aligned with the types of assignment. However, there are also different types of international transfers to take into account, and once again preserving equity is an important issue. For example, transfer types might include skills transfers, developmental transfers, regional/country managers, volunteers, permanent transfers, localized assignees and/or repatriated assignees.

The intention of the international assignment policy is to provide equitable treatment for all assignees *within* each of these transfer types. However, it may not be necessary to provide equity *between* the different types of transfer. As a result, the international assignment policy should be sufficiently sophisticated to provide terms and conditions that distinguish between, and yet cover, all of the above.

The socio-political context of expatriate effort–reward bargaining

Although much discussion in the literature on expatriation concentrates on technical factors, we believe that to make sense of the choices and consequences involved, attention is needed simultaneously to socio-political considerations. Shortland (2002: 2) comments that a key issue is the 'balance of power' in the relationship between the assignee and the employer – not at the individual level (this would simply lead to individual negotiations) but at the level of the rationale for the assignment within corporate strategy. She states:

> Employees asked to work abroad because they are required to fill a skills gap may be in a stronger position to negotiate a higher level of relocation allowances and benefits than, say, an employee being offered an international assignment for developmental reasons. In the case of the skills gap, the employer needs the employee to take that assignment. The 'balance of power' lies with the employee. However in the case of the developmental assignment, there is 'something in it' for the employee – namely the opportunity to gain experience and career development. The international assignment package for the developmental assignee may not need to be as rich as that for the skills gap transfer.
>
> (Shortland, 2002: 3)

Drawing an example from volunteer assignees, she continues, 'If employees put themselves forward for assignments for personal reasons, the "balance of power" lies more with the employer. Generous relocation packages are unlikely to be necessary for volunteers' (Shortland, 2002: 3).

Distinctions may also be drawn between permanent transfers and localized assignees. Permanent transfers are likely to be sent abroad on packages that closely reflect local terms (assuming that there is not a huge disparity between the receiving location and the sending location in terms of living standards and remuneration levels). Their relocation packages are likely to be fairly limited (Shortland, 2002). Assignees who are sent abroad on expatriate contracts but who are 'localized' at the end of their term are likely to have more complex packages. Localization may be defined as the phasing out or removing of expatriate employment terms in the assignment location for any reason. At the end of their term, if assignees are asked to remain abroad, they are unlikely to be switched immediately on to local terms. Instead, some of their relocation allowances and benefits are likely to be phased out (for instance, housing and schooling allowances) rather than being taken away immediately, recognizing their need to deal with housing affairs at home and to not disrupt children's education (Shortland, 2002).

The underpinning principles of policy design – consistency and equity – lead neatly into the third rationale for developing an international assignment policy, namely cost control. If the sending and receiving locations implement consistency of treatment, this will ensure that assignees do not negotiate upwards. Equity within groups likewise helps to keep costs under control. If it is possible to apply different packages to different assignee types, employers can benefit from not paying more than is needed. A well thought-out policy can also be tax-efficient, and this can save considerable sums of money.

However, difficulties may arise if assignees with different motivations for the assignment (for instance, skills transfers, volunteers and developmental assignees from the same sending location) end up side by side doing the same job but on different packages. The reward policy must be linked in to the resourcing strategy, not operated in isolation. Clear communication is needed to ensure that the rationale for any differing treatment can be explained and justified.

Communication between management and assignees is improved through the provision of a documented policy. This is of particular importance when assignees are to be localized. If assignees find out only at the end of their assignment that localization means that their expatriate benefits are to be taken away, they are likely to suffer damage to their psychological contract, resulting in resentment and loss of organizational commitment. If the employee realizes this in advance, via clear communication, there is less likely to be potential hostility with its consequent effect on motivation and productivity. Provision of policy statements at the beginning of the assignment, detailing the transition that will take place on localization, can aid a smooth transfer from one set of terms and conditions to another (Ernst &Young/CBI, 1996).

Further benefits of a written policy and clear communication are transparency and the management of expectations. Assignees are aware of the benefits available to themselves and to others in similar situations. They cannot claim unfair treatment, and they are able to make more informed decisions concerning their futures. Does the package make international mobility worthwhile?

The objectives of having an international policy may be summarized, therefore, as:

▮ covering all transfers and types of assignment;

▮ comprehensibility among employees (assignees cannot be motivated by the policy if it is too complex for them to understand how it applies to them personally);

▌ administrative ease and efficiency (thus saving time and money);

▌ cost effectiveness;

▌ tax efficiency.

Effective international assignment policies constitute an umbrella covering the whole expatriate cycle – from selection through to repatriation, localization or the next assignment. Some sections of the policy (for instance, training) might be core to all transfers and assignment types, with the policy containing subsections for the different assignee types/groups as described above. The assignment policy should not be a straitjacket, however, as if it is, it will be unlikely to meet organizational objectives. A degree of flexibility within the sub-policies can be applied to meet individual needs. But multinational managements are likely to want any flexibility within the policy to be designed to fall within an overall budgetary constraint: the design should ensure that flexibility is permissible without 'cherry picking'. This is discussed further below; some examples are given on implementing efficient and effective expatriation policies.

Designing/redesigning policy

One of the most important issues to consider in the design (or redesign) of an international assignment policy is the need to gain the buy-in of all stakeholders. Without this, individuals in either or both of the home or host countries may bypass the policy by offering terms and conditions outside it. In this way the policy is undermined, and ultimately so is organizational strategy. It is advisable for the policy design process to involve consultation with home and host-country managers at all levels affected, to include both line and HR functions, the budget holders and those responsible for communication and implementation. Benefit is to be derived from consulting the assignees themselves as well – those on assignment, those who have returned and those who are in the pool of talent for the future. Sue found in her work in designing policies for international organizations, that assignees were surprisingly realistic – although they would have liked generous packages, they did understand organizational constraints. In her experience, employees were usually keen to point out areas where extra assistance was required, but also were prepared to indicate areas where benefits were not serving a useful purpose. Hence, involving them in policy design helped Sue to identify how organizations' limited resources could be targeted to best effect.

Gathering information about employees' expectations and needs, set very firmly in the domestic circumstances as well as the business case circumstances that will apply, is a fundamental part of developing reward management arrangements for individuals operating internationally (Dowling and Welch, 2004). In recent years, securing the full involvement of line managers in the process has been facilitated, as they have come under pressure corporately to keep costs carefully under control. In the days before intensive international business competition, when expatriates were sometimes identified and deployed in a rather careless way, money often appeared to be no object (as with the Burmah Castrol example cited earlier, reported by Perkins and Hendry, 1999b).

The approach to expatriation management discussed above – where international assignments are resourced not only for reasons of efficiency, but also to provide genuine personal and career development opportunities – reflects a combined resource-centred and institutional conceptualization of expatriation principles, rejecting both agency and transaction cost theory in this regard as incompatible with a sustainability perspective. Of course, such an orientation carries with it 'sunk investment' risks which are likely to be criticized by those persuaded by the alternative theoretical positions.

In summary, multinational organization managements will wish to be confident that, in deploying expatriate personnel, they will bring value to the assignment greater than the cost of their employment and support outside their country of origin, compared with the alternative of engaging local talent. The expense of expatriates is acceptable in the short term since, for a while, they can create greater value than a local. This issue is illustrated in Figure 5.1.

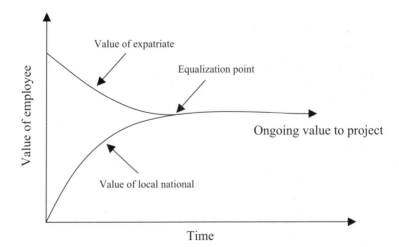

Figure 5.1 Excess cost versus excess value of using expatriates

Expatriate remuneration systems in practice

In the technical appendix at the end of this chapter, we discuss in detail the alternative ways in which the terms and conditions of international mobility may be structured. Whichever approach to assignee remuneration is selected, once explicit and implicit expatriation terms have been determined, individuals will still wish to be given greater flexibility to customize the organization's investment in them, tailored to their own diverse needs and expectations. Care needs to be taken here so that individuals' needs are addressed but within the framework of the policy, to ensure that equity and transparency remain.

To give an example of how this might work, Stephen worked on the development of an approach starting with the rate for the job and then delivering additional components flexibly and cost-effectively, as illustrated in Table 5.2. This represents a flexible 'pot' available to an expatriate, capturing the overall investment available for financing his or her deployment, signed on to by the relevant line manager, with particular reference to the comparisons between what an expatriate would cost and a similar local employee (assuming one was available). The line formally accepts accountability for delivering the excess value from the assignment in return for the excess cost to the company involved.

When this 'expat-flexible-pot' framework was adopted, the development of expatriate terms was better informed, it was owned by line management as well as the individual being deployed, and was more of a partnership arrangement, rather than one party seeking exclusively to negotiate with HR, to get a better deal over the other. As far as possible, accountability for determining the value and make-up of international assignment terms and conditions rested with the line manager on whose budget any costs would fall.

Table 5.2 The 'expat-flexible-pot' approach

	Designated currency values
Salary	
Variable bonus payment(s) (if applicable)	
Hypothetical 'home' income tax and social insurance deduction (1)	
Net base and incentive pay	
Location 'mark up' incentive payment for assignment to… (2)	
Net cash payments (no tax)	
Flexible 'pot' which can be drawn on up to maximum amount specified, at the individual's discretion to cover items such as in-region rest and recreation trips, flights for 'home' leave, club memberships, etc (3)	
Housing and transport costs	
Tax-free 'inducement' payment at start and conclusion of assignment, linked to whole-assignment performance achievements	
Total net value of expatriation package (4)	
Estimated additional tax charge to employer's account (5)	
Total estimated additional cost to employer before addition of 'hidden' costs	
Estimated total cost to employer of the assignment once 'hidden' costs are included	

The above terms compare with the market-assessed total costs of employing someone on 'host country' terms to perform an equivalent role of [currency] over the equivalent period of the assignment. This comparison is intended to inform the managerial decision to approve or vary the expatriate package specified above, and to evaluate the excess cost/excess value of deploying an expatriate against 'local' employee resource options.

Approved: Line manager

Notes

1 Assessment of income tax and social insurance contributions that would be payable (on salary and any additional payments) were the post based in the 'home' country. Tax advisors to confirm figure, taking individual's fiscal circumstances into account.

2 Recommended payment method/timing will be that which is tax-efficient for employer.

3 Sum calculated based on research into circumstances/costs associated with accompanied/unaccompanied assignment. Provides scope for individual to customize budget maximum apportionment to own preferences, trading one 'standard' item value against another. Budget make-up and draw-down audit trail remains in place.

4 This value is increased once 'hidden' costs (such as pension funding, international health care and related insurance premiums, company-paid household utility charges) plus shipping and other miscellaneous cost reimbursements are included.

5 Additional tax liability is adjusted to reflect cost of assignment benefits (including any location 'mark-up' cash lump sum, for example).

'Hidden costs' = 'hidden benefits' – see note 4 above.

INTRA-REGION MOBILITY AND DIVERSITY: 'THIRD-COUNTRY NATIONAL' REWARDS

The search for talented people to oversee devolved multinational operations may give rise to a need for policies to support regionalized employee mobility, accompanied by the notion of 'continental' pay and conditions. Third-country nationals (TCNs) may be deployed by international businesses between a variety of countries close to their country of origin, but within a regional geographical setting. These intra-regionally mobile executives may either not aspire to, or not satisfy criteria for, membership of a globally mobile executive cadre. However, they may have skills that businesses find appropriate to deploy across their regional operations, and individuals may comply with this resourcing arrangement for career development reasons.

In some cases a decision may be taken to identify individuals drawn from within a particular geography in key leadership roles as part of the corporate cadre, despite an expectation that their career trajectory is likely to remain within the region. Given the intensive competition for scarce skills in a variety of environments – the 'tiger' economies of south-east Asia, for example – the price that organizations have to pay has increased significantly. In these cases, imagination and flexibility become essential ingredients. For example, Stephen experienced a situation where a high-level search had been launched to recruit a regional director to run a business development team covering the whole of the Far East sector. The search, which itself was not without difficulties – finding individuals with the right combination of 'Asian values' (and business connections) and western sense of urgency – was particularly challenging. The 'ideal' candidate displayed an impressive background of working in both an Asian and western environment, for a leading multinational US corporation, operating out of Singapore. However, it looked as though it would be impossible to make the appointment because of the difficulty in balancing the need to recruit an individual at the going market rate with the realities of a domestic business in rationalization mode, where internal relativities would be adversely affected.

In the end, a compromise solution was agreed. The individual's employment terms were set as though he was an expatriate living in his own country! The salary and incentive regime reflected the going rate for the job applicable across the organization. However, the organization was able to find other ways in which to provide additional finances – as a halfway house measure, as the organization's corporate reward arrangements began to be developed to bring them into line with the aspirations of this new internationalizing business. The individual was suitably motivated to sign his contract, while ensuring that the organization's corporate needs were not unduly compromised.

Stephen experienced a similar challenge in the course of integrating a top management team in the United States. The group of executives had been acquired as part of the business acquisition. Their reward arrangements were, to say the least, generous and imaginative. However, they were grounded in what had been a very successful start-up business operation. The organization had been formed as a subsidiary to a large American corporate starved of cash at that time, limiting investment funds available to the new enterprise. However, the subsidiary management team had none the less created an extremely lucrative additional new business and new revenues for the parent corporation. In fact, they had grown the business to the extent that it could be packaged up and sold as a going concern at a premium to an interested and willing buyer. The individual executives in the start-up had ensured that the reward arrangements negotiated early on in the organization's life meant they would have a stake in, and hence access to, a significant share of the new value they had created. The challenge here was to convince a European parent board that, as part of their North American investment programme, they should accept that the top team they had acquired might, at times, receive total reward levels above their own.

MANAGING THE EFFORT–REWARD BARGAIN FOR NON-HEADQUARTERS-SOURCED EMPLOYEES

The 10 per cent of the workforce engaged on 'expatriate' terms and conditions have tended to receive disproportionate attention in the IHRM literature. Given the scale of relative costs and complexities, to some extent, this is understandable. We too have reviewed the choices and consequences associated with compensation arrangements for 'global champions', therefore. But that leaves 90 per cent of the managerial and other multinational workforce members potentially neglected. This population represents not only a major pay bill cost, these people are also a source of 'insider' added value for multinational managements seeking to generate and network the knowledge and skills needed to compete in global markets. We therefore turn our attention now to compensation strategies for local national employees.

Sparrow (2000) argues that how multinational organization managements take account of national characteristics and contexts in reward system design is a neglected area of research. Normative literature may be interpreted as implying an inevitable convergence in the way reward systems are 'best' organized, and prescribing strategies to that end. Reference will be made below to commentary on the so-called 'new pay', a term coined by Edward E Lawler and popularized by consultants Schuster and Zingheim (Lawler, 1990, 2000; Shuster and Zingheim, 1990; Zingheim and Shuster 2000), and the underlying assumptions that may be discerned. Will there be eventual convergence, or will there be continued cross-national divergence, or perhaps some form of hybrid pattern or 'cross-vergence' (Anakwe, 2002; Sparrow, 1999, 2000)?

Geographical diversity in reward issues

By way of illustrating the potential diversity of compensation practice that managers and their advisors in the internationalizing business may encounter across business systems, consider the following three regional examples (GRO, 1996):

- **Europe:** Scandinavian countries have a relatively high level of social benefits. In the United Kingdom company cars remain a widespread contractual benefit, despite changes in fiscal practice. In German company pension plans, employees require ten years in-post for vesting purposes. In Hungary, western reward practices seem to be accelerating more quickly than in Poland.

- **Asia-Pacific:** pay levels generally remain relatively low in India, Borneo and the Philippines. Conversely, pay levels tend to be high in Hong Kong and Singapore. In some areas in India and in China, housing is provided as part of the total reward package. In Malaysia, there is a typical 48-hour week, yet Singapore is closer to 42–44 hours per week. In Japan, housing allowances may be provided to core employees, and salary progression reflects age and service.

- **Latin America:** Latin and South America tend to be described as high-inflation countries, creating pressure on employee reward levels. However, this tends to be concentrated in countries such as Brazil and Venezuela. Over the past decade, countries such as Chile, for example, have experienced relatively low levels of inflation.

Intra-regional differences of the kinds illustrated in the above vignettes add further to comparative business systems complexity. And vast geographical territories such as China can act as regions on their own with variation between coastal China, rural China, and major cities such as Beijing, Shanghai and (since 1997) Hong Kong. An internationalizing business faces business-system-influenced choices regarding the extent to which it will operate as a 'local' firm or a 'foreign controlled' business. While local, national or international legislative frameworks mandate some of the options that affect reward system outcomes, others (performance management arrangements, for example) are open to corporate control. Without strategic global philosophies to provide guidance in making these reward choices, inconsistent reward and performance management practice may result, adversely affecting the overriding managerial aim – motivating employees to work in support of organizational goals (Rehu *et al*, 2005).

At the very least, it seems appropriate to explore the extent to which 'corporate practices' initiated in the multinational organization's country of origin can be transplanted across the variety of multinational operations. Employees are rewarded based on local competitive market practices and local legislation, both of which have developed through the years, usually in a way unique to each country. What does this imply for attempts to apply practices operating in the home country, unaltered, in another country (for example applying Anglo-American-style individualized 'incentive programmes' in the Far East, in 'social market' Europe, or South America)? Internationalizing organizations' managers may be advised to study the local setting closely, to identify what is competitive and what reward systems will support the process of attracting, motivating, retaining and developing talented employees for sustained high performance. But what about an aspiration to develop and sustain 'global mindsets' across the entire workforce, as advocated by Milkovich and Bloom (1998)?

US 'new pay' consultants Zingheim and Schuster argue that '[f]ew things get the attention of people in a company as well as pay does' (2000: 4). As such they believe organizations everywhere should use extrinsic rewards strategically: 'to communicate the business value of goals such as those associated with shareholder value, financial success, customers, market share, growth, product and service innovation, speed and cost management' (2000: 4). They perceive pay as a 'change agent'. While it does not represent 'an initiative itself', they argue that compensation helps managers to put 'momentum into other business initiatives' (2000: 4). In short, the material aspects of the reward bargain represent 'a way of gaining understanding, acceptance, and commitment of what people can do to help make a company a success' (2000: 4).

Zingheim and Schuster (2000) outline six 'Reward Principles' distilled from their consultancy experience, which they hypothesize offer the basis on which managers can achieve their business goals. The underlying assumption appears to be a situation in which pay management is a unitary (management-controlled) phenomenon, rather than an effort–reward bargaining process between plural interests. The 'Principles' are summarized with an accompanying commentary in Table 5.3.

Table 5.3 Paying people right?

Principle	Comments
1 Create a positive and 'natural' reward experience	'Involve and educate' the workforce about the reasons and shared benefits for changing reward systems
2 Align rewards with business goals to create 'a win–win partnership'	Provide a clear managerial direction that individual employees must continue to 'add value', which the company will recognize with rewards
3 Extend people's 'line of sight' between effort and outcome, motivating 'smart' working over simply expending extra effort	Ensure that all members of the workforce are 'knowledgeable stakeholders': they are to be shown how their efforts impact on the work team, business unit and company, including the need to adapt to customer needs
4 Integrate rewards with strategic aims and the kinds of contribution desired	Use each 'reward tool' for what it does best, integrating each element of total reward to offer a customized 'deal'
5 Reward individual ongoing (input) value to the organization with base pay	This has three elements: employee salary is to reflect increases in competencies the firm finds useful; consistent performance over time; and the individual's value in the external labour market
6 Reward results (outputs) with variable pay	It is uncritically accepted that the firm 'must meet shareholder expectations' (whose reasonableness relative to other stakeholders is not discussed); variable pay is deemed suitable as part of the 'total reward' offer to reward these 'results', as well as enjoining employees in the corporate project

Source: after Zingheim and Schuster (2000).

Turning their attention to 'the global workforce', the same consultants cite the mantra of 'strategize globally, act locally'; but they concede that this is meaningless unless the workforce understand that the proposition by the multinational's management is a 'win–win' for them and the company. Problematically, they argue, 'global rewards' tend to lag corporate 'globalization' initiatives. The problem is that this undermines the universal goal of alignment of all people and operations wherever they are located – and means that remedial action will be necessary at a later stage (losing the early advantages that integration is supposed to bring).

Evidence offered to support the claimed universalizing trend in rewarding employees in multinationals is 'the fact that executive pay is becoming progressively more global', influencing the design of rewards for the rest of the workforce (Zingheim and Schuster, 2000: 336). The argument is that 'total reward strategies are becoming more global and less industry-specific', as 'global talent can migrate from company to company because of their success in global business, rather than industry-specific success' (2000: 336). Hence, rewards in the multinational 'must communicate what's necessary in terms of paying for individual ongoing value and for results the company needs if it's to be successful' (2000: 336).

Zingheim and Schuster conclude that this should be facilitated by the introduction of 'consistent global guidelines for total pay and other rewards [to] integrate local pay translations, while taking into account the business case for the specific location, local culture and local laws' (2000: 337). They believe there is an opportunity for MNC managements 'to have people unified around global business goals' (2000: 318). They cite with satisfaction (albeit without much detail) examples where 'companies transcend culture and local practices to make pay reflect the business and create a unified workforce of global workers' (2000: 334).

EVALUATING NORMATIVE COMMENTARY: THEORY AND PRACTICE

In theoretical terms, while at first glance a resource-based strategic orientation appears to inform the approach advocated by 'new pay' writers, an underlying agency perspective might be evident: an attempt to institutionalize universal workforce compliance with governance mechanisms privileges a particular interest orientation. 'New pay' theory is subjected to criticism by Heery (1996), who takes an ethical stance, on the basis that propositions by 'new pay' commentators do not hold out the prospect of successful outcomes for employees, who face a riskier employment contract that is disserved by the decline in third-party representation. He is also sceptical of the prospects for employers seeking unitary alignment of employee–employer interests. Heery (1996) points out that underlying 'new pay' is 'a desire to use remuneration policy to reinforce a particular, flexible form of organization' (which may be deemed to reflect a transaction-cost-economics theorization of the organizational problem).

The perception is that payment systems will reinforce responsiveness to market signals, linking pay to measures of customer satisfaction, customer retention, repeat business and revenue growth. Pay structures will be person rather than job-based. Individuals will be allocated to positions on the basis of skill or competence. 'New pay' systems are structured using a few 'broad bands', in order to discourage hierarchy and promote flexible cross-functional application of labour, with a focus on partnership and self-reliance as well as recognizing the needs of the diverse workforce. However, Heery (1996) points to contradictions between new pay prescriptions for employee involvement in compensation design and operation, and the proscribed need for 'nimble reward systems': continually evolving reward policies which contain a minimum of formal rules and which can be applied with minimum cost by line managers to business units.

In terms of employee well-being, Heery (1996) argues that the uncertainties of 'new pay' (reflecting a managerial orientation to employment relations characteristic of the US business system) grate with European notions of well-being, encouraging over-work, for example, leading to longer-term adverse health consequences (which may have negative implications for publicly funded welfare systems). And the greater the managerial discretion, the more issues of 'organizational justice' associated with effort–reward bargaining may be compromised without the institutional checks and balances that constrain managerial room for manoeuvre to determine pay outcomes unilaterally (Heery, 1996). The consequences of finance capital market discipline on top management (for example, the threat of hostile corporate takeovers) may be traced to 'contingent pay' regimes: transferring the risk to labour when distributing value created by members of the multinational enterprise, in order to prioritize shareholder interests. Heery (1996) perceives tensions with the 'new pay' partnership rhetoric, where employees are called on to make sacrifices to serve the interests of other stakeholders, especially during a period when the gap between top management pay in Anglo-American organizations and the pay of other employees has grown significantly.

While not mounting a specific critique of normative commentary on 'new pay', Bloom, Milkovich and Mitra (2003) argue that, to understand strategic approaches to international employee reward management, macro-level attention is needed to the ways in which multinational enterprises balance the competing pressures for consistency of approach in pursuit of global alignment with organizational aims and the need for local conformance. The proposition is that the 'dominant logic' for managing the reward system will influence how management in multinationals craft the terms on which the various workforce segments are employed (Bloom *et al*, 2003).

Empirical enquiry may usefully be focused on gathering evidence on the extent to which multinational reward strategic choices are in the direction of applying a 'one world, one strategy' 'export' orientation, or of reward systems localization.

In the first case, export-oriented reward strategies aim to transfer wholesale the parent firm's reward system to overseas affiliates, in pursuit of a 'common mindset', driven by headquarters thinking. Adapters, by contrast, choose practices designed to match as closely as possible the conditions of the local context. As a third alternative, evidence may be found to indicate that managers in multinationals are attempting to find ways in which to integrate their approaches to managing the reward system. While at worst such an approach may be little more than a cobbling together of a diverse array of practices, the aim may be to craft a coherent and comprehensive transnational reward management regime that recognizes the mutually interdependent nature of the multinational enterprise and its workforce members. As such, policies may flow as easily between subsidiaries and from subsidiaries to headquarters, as from headquarters 'down' and outwards to operations located worldwide.

By way of a further set of phenomena with which to capture data international organizations' reward system practice, Bloom et al (2003) identify three complementary features that may reflect or influence multinational reward strategies: responsiveness to institutionally generated pressures to conform to the conditions of local jurisdictions and markets; avoidance of or forestalling acquiescence with local conformance pressures wherever opportunities arise – where the application of regulatory and market practices is lax; and resistance to such pressures mediated through attempts to challenge or change (at least in some way to influence) factors in the local host context.

To test these theoretical propositions empirically, Perkins (2006) surveyed HR specialists in multinationals, seeking responses to the question of whether reward strategy design was polarized between the extent to which corporate priorities prevailed and a tendency for accommodation to local operating circumstances. Just over a third of respondents (34.9 per cent) argued that 'home-grown' principles (an 'ethnocentric' orientation, using Perlmutter's (1969) terminology) directed reward policy setting, while just under a third (31.7 per cent) claimed that it was necessary for their organization to accommodate local environmental differences impacting on the employment relationship (a 'polycentric' approach). However, the remaining third (33.3 per cent) stated that reward strategies evolve continuously, taking account of different regulatory and market conditions, so that neither blanket corporate nor more locally oriented approaches are feasible.

In terms of the alignment of corporate strategy and reward management, the great majority of respondents indicated a tendency to modify corporate reward practice, with 43.5 per cent of respondents stating that their organizations found that, on balance, adaptation of corporate reward management practices to match the multiplicity of local operating contexts was preferred, while 32.2 per cent said they reacted to local regulatory requirements (including matching local competitors' practices). In contrast, almost a quarter of respondents indicated that they either looked for ways to avoid local pressures to conform to local regulation, and practices they believe could inhibit organizational and HRM flexibility and the ability to align the reward system with corporate strategy (11.3 per cent), or actively resisted such local pull to compromise the integrity of corporate strategy to accommodate local operating contexts (12.9 per cent).

In spite of the majority indication in favour of adaptation, 44.5 per cent of respondents indicated adherence to the belief (7.9 per cent of them strongly) that in the event of the organization's management being unable to manage rewards in accordance with corporate strategy, they would seriously question the merits of directly employing people in a particular country. By contrast 35 per cent disagreed with this statement, a further 17.5 per cent neither agreed nor disagreed, and 9.5 per cent said the statement was not applicable.

OBSERVABLE TRANSNATIONAL PRACTICES

What does this imply for practice in the kinds of extrinsic reward practices being applied in multinational organizations across the world? A major academic consortium studying international HRM practices set out to measure the current position on various reward management approaches in 10 countries around the world (although notably excluding Europe). Reporting findings in the *Asia Pacific Journal of Human Resources*, the researchers also gathered managerial perspectives on what 'should be'. Lowe *et al* (2002) organized compensation practices into four groups: pay incentives, benefits, long-term focus in pay and seniority. Each of these is discussed below.

Pay incentives

Across the 10-country sample studied by Lowe *et al* (2002), only Japan, China and Taiwan had significant scores indicating that, on average, pay incentives were currently prevalent. At the 'should be' indicator, four countries, the United States, Taiwan, Mexico and Latin America (as a group) indicated they should ideally have a greater emphasis on incentives. For all countries surveyed the 'should be' scores were higher than the 'is now' position. The researchers concluded from this that there is an 'ideological gap' between normative preference for contingent pay and the actuality. Interestingly, scores were generally low for practices linking pay and group/organizational performance. While one might expect this in the case of 'individualist' countries (such as Canada, the United States and Australia), Asian and other 'collectivist' countries were not significantly more likely to favour pay practices likely to foster group harmony.

On the 'should be' dimension, again only a limited number of country respondents, on average, indicated their conviction that group-based reward practices should be increased: the United States, Taiwan, Mexico and Latin America. In terms of the proportion of pay represented by incentives, the evidence from around the world suggests that few organizations currently emphasize pay incentives highly. Three countries (Australia, Canada and the United States) had especially low scores, despite being labelled in the 'cross-culture' literature as predisposed to a pay-for-performance ethic. None of the countries surveyed placed a very high priority on orienting employee pay highly in the direction of incentives – from which the researchers conclude (in an interesting echo of Heery's (1996) concerns) that 'to some degree it may be a worldwide phenomenon that employees don't want to have a large portion of their pay at risk (i.e. based on incentives rather than base pay)' (Lowe et al, 2002: 63).

In the Anglo-Saxon countries, the 'should be' indicator was higher than the 'is now' statistical average score – with a large gap in the NAFTA countries and a moderate gap in Australia and Latin America. The same kind of pattern emerged in response to the proposition 'Job performance is the basis for pay raises' in the 'current position' scores. In terms of future preference, there seems to be a bias in favour of performance-based reward – but at an individual level – as long as this does not form too large a component of total cash reward.

Lowe et al's (2002) findings are consistent with those reported from another more qualitatively organized study, by Brown and Heywood (2002), who also included some European countries in their eight-country sample. They conclude that experimentation with 'paying for performance' is notable worldwide, although an expectation at the start of their project of increases in its application was not fulfilled.

Benefits

Lowe *et al* (2002) found the current state of practice in respect of benefits to be relatively high, in general. Asian countries (except for Taiwan and Indonesia) had low 'is now' scores relative to the United States and Latin American countries. And while 'should be' scores were all higher than 'is now', the trend line indicates that American countries regard benefits more highly than Asian countries. In the United States, Taiwan, Canada and Latin America, relative to other countries, the current value of benefits is relatively high – most countries indicate that increased benefits provision would be welcome, however.

Long-term emphasis in pay

The three 'individualistic' countries (Canada, the United States and Australia) had the lowest 'is now' average scores in respect of a long-term pay emphasis. With the exception of China and Taiwan, countries sampled did not appear to have a current futuristic pay orientation. Looking at preferences, Lowe *et al* (2002) concluded that managers across all 10 countries surveyed feel compensation systems should be more forward-focused.

Seniority

Previous commentary has hypothesized that 'collectivist' cultures focus much more on seniority-based reward policies. The results reported by Lowe *et al* (2002) suggest that with the notable exception of Japan, Indonesia and Taiwan, no clearly matched pattern is visible. Of the stereotypically individualistic countries, while Australia was low on seniority-based current practice, the United States scored relatively highly (surprising given the proportionately lower rate of unionization). The 'should be' scores were more in line with the normative predictions.

Overall, Lowe *et al* (2002) found managerial perceptions of the extent to which reward practices were related to the employment of high performers, satisfied employees, and an effective organization to be remarkably consistent across the 10-country sample. As the researchers conclude:

> Collectively, these findings suggest that there is a high degree of cross-cultural consistency in the perceived utility of compensation plans as a method for achieving organizational effectiveness. However, the mix of appropriate compensation practices is likely to vary across these same countries.
>
> (Lowe *et al*, 2002: 69)

The researchers were able to conclude from their data that managers surveyed had given thoughtful item-by-item responses, rather than displaying any 'within-country scale-anchor preferences' (2002: 71). With the exception of seniority, across the transregional sample managers generally expressed a bias in favour of increasing the incidence of incentives, benefits and long-term pay focus compared with the current situation. Consistent lines between the results of 'cultural programming' variances across countries and regions, and the practice and preferences of organizational managers, are not in evidence from this research. The findings are both contradictory *and* confirmatory. Drawing out 'best practice' recommendations such as Zingheim and Schuster's (2000) six universalistic 'reward principles' is rendered problematic by this empirical data, therefore.

Organizations may therefore be encouraged to conduct systematic 'due diligence' analysis in order to match their plans for reward and recognition of employees in particular countries around the world when expanding their overseas operations. The value of the study, according to Lowe *et al* (2002), is that the findings may challenge ethnocentric exportation of compensation practices by enhancing understanding of 'best practices' in other countries, and the notion that adopting the status quo in a given locale as being 'locally responsive'. Managers in multinationals are thus challenged to place greater emphasis on finding out what employees want the compensation offer to be ('human capital perspective' in our introductory model), rather than being overly concerned with 'what is' now. However, given Milkovich and Bloom's (1998) 'global mindset' imperative, it may be possible to avoid becoming trapped by a perceived need to replicate perceived cultural norms. Tailoring reward management to what employees in a given cultural situation indicate will motivate them may assist managements in pursuit of high-performance organization interventions.

DESIGNING REWARDS FOR THE INTERNATIONALIZING BUSINESS UNIT

Let us conclude the chapter as we began, by reflecting on some 'picture postcards'. The following four cameos share practical experience of the kinds of problems newly internationalizing firms have faced, in our experience, when wrestling with global/local pressures in different regional business environments.

▌ In Eastern Europe anxiety to adopt 'western', particularly North American, management techniques may be perceived. As a result, local management tend to have a prescriptive orientation. In this case, they wanted to be 'told what to do' and appeared to be unwilling to develop home-grown solutions. The difficulty for corporate management in this situation was to encourage local subsidiaries to take responsibility for designing a fit-for-purpose reward system. The historical circumstances of a political economy undergoing a radical transition may require extra sensitivity on the part of the internationalizing management team, in understanding the pace at which fundamental change can be achieved.

▌ In direct contrast, the local management attitude in an acquired US subsidiary was that they knew best. They had been successful (so they believed). They therefore looked to the new parent simply to provide funding within an overall corporate strategy, and then to 'get out of the way'. This may be not uncommon with acquisitions in developed economies. Where institutionalized reward management arrangements are particularly entrenched, the 'global mindset' aim may be additionally challenging. In this case, a corporate culture of high financial rewards was reflected in a 'scorecard' mentality: the executives appeared more concerned about their pay and status in relation to their US comparators than they were about the medium-to long-term performance requirements of the new multinational parent company.

▌ The Asian environment presented a different problem again, this time in the Indian subcontinent, where operating a plant meant the internationalizing firm acquiring a role in the community. This could be expressed as: 'you think you employ 1000 people (where operationally 200 people were judged necessary), but this effectively supports 10,000 people in the community' (allowing for extended families and so on). A multinational may need to factor into the investment strategy the cost of these responsibilities in the community, inevitably impacting on the reward system.

▌ Given the emphasis on paying for performance in the normative literature, our final example of practice focuses on attempts to export what is deemed to be best practice for (westernized) performance management and reward on a cross-cultural basis. We have reported variations in pay-for-performance practice, and criticism of the principle, but that does not mean it cannot be done. Stephen's experience of this has included a project in the south-west periphery of Europe, part of a business system change programme with the introduction of private capital to an erstwhile state-owned enterprise. The values-driven workforce and middle management preferences were recognized, and accommodated, including a more collectivist environment where, at least at a national political level, trade union activity was far more pronounced than tends to be the case in Anglo-American *laissez-faire* environments. An added twist to the project was the cocktail of nationalities involved in the management process itself. The project was a joint venture drawing inputs from the United Kingdom, France, Spain and Portugal. The challenge was to understand what would motivate each of the parties to find a common purpose, and to ensure that, in designing the reward scheme relevant for their circumstances, it was possible to respect the institutional environment. To achieve the performance-related reward system desired corporately took a significant time investment on the part of the local line management (expatriate and senior local executives) with local HR support. It was necessary to develop the necessary credibility as well as the capability to design, communicate and implement a performance-related reward management regime that did not appear to undermine the more collectivist, traditionally seniority-based setting. The emphasis was placed on team rewards, where individuals could be rewarded by the way in which they were judged to contribute to the operation of workgroup and business unit performance as a whole.

CONCLUDING REMARKS

In this chapter we have attempted to sketch ideas and report practice relevant to the choices and consequences facing managements who are attempting to manage effort–reward bargaining within a multinational theatre of operations. This is a massive area of literature and practice. In drafting the chapter, our choice was to segment the populations targeted by international reward policy, first, into those who are required to be regularly mobile across international borders. This is an area that has generated a significant literature, reflecting the complexity involved in managing technical and highly personal phenomena under competitive conditions. In our approach, we have drawn attention to the organizational angles as well as socio-political considerations that multinational managers may wish to take into account in their decision making.

Second, we devoted space to explore the interplay of normative commentary and reported empirical trends that may influence corporate managerial decision making on the design and operation of reward systems applicable to the majority of the worldwide workforce – those sourced to work beyond the parent organization country of origin. While strong views exist on both sides of the convergence–divergence debate, in practice significant experimentation is evident, and this continues to inform commentary and practice.

YOUR TURN

▌ Setting and managing rewards in an internationalizing business context matches the very process of developing international operations itself in terms of complexity. What steps might human resource professionals take to learn to manage this diversity and complexity of practice and expectations?

▌ How may choices and consequences be evaluated, when organizations attempt to balance standardization of corporate practice – in order to communicate strategic priorities to employees wherever they may be located, and to provide a sense of 'corporate glue' – and being responsive to the need for differentiation in terms of local culture, values, and market practice?

▌ If the organization aspires to adopt a 'geocentric' approach, what are the prerequisites informing an analytical approach to collect and analyse relevant information to inform strategic options, and then the sensitivity to manage what may be potentially conflicting corporate and local reward policy requirements?

▌ In consultancy surveys, organizations claim to have recognized the imperative of more effectively integrating their expatriate and local national remuneration. How do multinational managements balance the demands associated with trends in compensating globally mobile senior executives, seeking increased simplicity as well as cost and tax-effectiveness, against motivating increasingly crucial 'local national talent', needed to secure 'insider' operational advantages within a specific marketplace?

REFERENCES

Anakwe, O P (2002) Human resource management practices in Nigeria: challenges and insights, *International Journal of Human Resource Management*, **13**(7), pp 1042–59

Barney, J (1991) Firm resources and sustained competitive advantage, *Journal of Management*, **17**(1), pp 99–120

Bloom, M and Milkovich, G T (1999) A strategic human resource management perspective on international compensation and reward systems, in *Research in Personnel and Human Resource Management*, ed P M Wright, L D Dyer, J W Boudreau and G T Milkovich, Suppl 4, pp 283–304, JAI Press, Greenwich, C T

Bloom, M, Milkovich, G T and Mitra, A (2003) International compensation: learning from how managers respond to variation in local host contexts, *International Journal of Human Resource Management*, **14**(8), pp 1350–67

Bradley, P, Hendry, C and Perkins, S J (1999) Global or multi-local? The significance of international values in reward strategy, in *International HRM: Contemporary Issues in Europe*, ed C Brewster and H Harris, pp 120–42, Routledge, London

Brown, M and Heywood, J S (eds) (2002) *Paying for Performance: An international comparison*, ME Sharpe, Armonk, NY

Dowling, P J and Welch, DE (2004) *International Human Resource Management: Managing people in a multinational context*, 4th edn, Thomson Learning, London

Drucker, J and White, G (2000) The context of reward management, in *Reward Management: A critical text*, ed J Drucker and G White, pp 1–24, Routledge, London

Edelsten, M (2005) Survey – pay management programmes in multinational firms, http://www.mercerhr.com/pressrelease/details.jhtml/dynamic/idContent/1173210, released and accessed 10 March 2005

Ernst & Young/CBI (1996) *Localisation*, Ernst & Young/Confederation of British Industry (CBI) Employee Relocation Council, London

Ghoshal, S and Bartlett, C A (1998) *Managing Across Borders: The transnational solution*, Random House, London

GRO (1996) *International Total Remuneration*, American Compensation Association, Scottsdale, Ariz

Hamel, G and Prahalad, C K (1994) *Competing for the Future*, Harvard Business School Press, Boston, Mass

Heery, E (1996) Risk, representation and the new pay, *Personnel Review*, **25**(6), pp 54–65

Hofstede, G (1981) *Cultures Consequences: International differences in work-related values*, Sage, Beverly Hills, Calif

Hofstede, G (1991) *Cultures and Organisations: Software of the mind*, McGraw-Hill, Maidenhead

Kessler, I (2000) Reward system choices, in *Human Resource Management: A critical text*, 2nd edn, ed J Storey, pp 206–31, Thomson Learning, London

Kuwahara, Y (2004) Employment relations in Japan, in *International and Comparative Employment Relations*, ed G J Bamber, R D Lansbury and N Wailes, pp 277–305, Sage, London

Lawler, EE III (1990) *Strategic Pay: Aligning organizational strategies and pay*, Jossey-Bass, San Francisco, Calif

Lawler, EE III (2000) *Rewarding Excellence: Pay strategies for the new economy*, Jossey-Bass, San Francisco, Calif

Lowe, K B, Milliman, J De Cieri, H and Dowling, P J (2002) International compensation practices: a ten-country comparative analysis, *Asia Pacific Journal of Human Resources*, **40**(1), pp 55–80

Marsden, D (1999) *A Theory of Employment Systems*, Oxford University Press, Oxford

Milkovich, G T and Bloom, M (1998) Rethinking international compensation, *Compensation and Benefits Review*, **30**(1), pp 15–23

ORC (2002a) *Worldwide Survey of International Assignment Policies and Practices*, Organization Resources Counselors (ORC), London

ORC (2002b) *Dual Careers and International Assignments Survey*, ORC, London

ORC (2004) *Worldwide Survey of International Assignment Policies and Practices*, ORC, London

Perkins, S J (2006) *CIPD Guide to International Reward and Recognition*, Chartered Institute of Personnel and Development, London

Perkins, S J and Hendry, C (1999a) International compensation, in *The Global HR Manager*, ed P Joynt and B Morton, pp 115–43, Institute of Personnel and Development (IPD), London

Perkins, S J and Hendry, C (1999b) *Guide to International Reward and Recognition*, IPD, London

Perkins, S J and Hendry, C (2001) Global champions: Who's paying attention?, *Thunderbird International Business Review*, **43**(1), pp 53–75

Perlmutter, M V (1969) The tortuous evolution of the multinational corporation, *Columbia Journal of World Business*, January–February, pp 9–18

Rehu, M, Lusk, E and Wolff, B (2005) Incentive preferences of employees in Germany and the USA: an empirical investigation, *Management Revue*, **16**(1), pp 81–98

Rosenzweig, P and Nohria, N (1994) Influences on human resource management practices in multinational corporations, *Journal of International Business Studies*, Second Quarter, pp 229–51

Roth, K and O'Donnell, S (1996) Foreign subsidiary compensation strategy: an agency theory perspective, *Academy of Management Journal*, **39**, pp 678–703

Scarborough, H, Swan, J and Preston, J (1999) *Knowledge Management: A literature review*, IPD, London

Schuler, R S and Jackson, S E (2005) A quarter-century review of human resource management in the US: the growth of the international perspective, *Management Revue*, **16**(1), pp 11–35

Shortland, S (2002) Why have an international assignment policy?, *Managing Internationally Mobile Employees Briefing*, **35**, pp 2–5

Shuster, J R and Zingheim, P (1990) *The New Pay: Linking employee and organizational performance*, Jossey-Bass, San Francisco, Calif

Sparrow, P (1999) International reward systems: To converge or not converge? in *International HRM: Contemporary issues in Europe*, ed C Brewster and H Harris, pp 103–19, Routledge, London

Sparrow, P (2000) International reward management, in *Reward Management: A critical text*, ed G White and J Drucker, pp 196–214, Routledge, London

Toh, S M and DeNisi, A S (2005) A local perspective to expatriate success, *Academy of Management Executive*, **19**(1), pp 132–46

Zingheim, P and Schuster, J R (2000) *Pay People Right! Breakthrough strategies to create great companies*, Jossey-Bass, San Francisco, Calif

TECHNICAL APPENDIX

PART 1: GUIDING PRINCIPLES FOR EXPATRIATION: THE 10-STAGE JOURNEY

The principles summarized below may be used to guide organizations in expatriation policy design and its evaluation. It is specified as a 10-stage journey of assignee management. These objectives are to:

1   **Support business strategy**
    Organizations need to recognize the reasons for using expatriate staff including:

    - ensuring corporate business objectives are met;
    - providing managerial and technical expertise aimed at long-term development of local national staff to assume executive responsibilities;
    - as a part of a structured process, enhancing and developing the capabilities of the firm's international cadre of staff.

2   **Manage costs as appropriate**
    A key feature in the determination of an assignee's package should be the 'excess cost/excess value' equation. Each assignment should therefore reflect considerations of:

    - an expatriate assignment versus local recruitment;
    - a corporate philosophy of providing flexible incentives and reimbursing costs, necessarily incurred;
    - the local custom and practice;
    - the rationale behind the costs.

3   **Involve line management**
    The process should play a critical supporting role to line management, and it is important jointly to:

    - understand and clearly define the requirement to mobilize an expatriate;
    - understand any specific issues or problems relating to the assignment that could impact on the final selection of the assignee;
    - recognize and get line-HR agreement on the cost implications and justification.

4   **Communicate the value of international assignments**
The importance of any international role should be communicated:

- by clearly defining the roles and responsibilities of the posting;
- in terms of both the individual's growth and achievement of corporate objectives;
- as contributing to the development of a corporately networked 'global cadre'.

5   **Select the right expatriate**
The cost and complexities associated with international assignments combine to create a need for a high-quality identification and selection process, aimed at:

- establishing the specific competencies required for the post and matching them to potential assignees;
- ensuring that potential candidates are progressed through an appropriate development centre before any commitments or decisions are made on either side;
- ensuring that the motivational and personal/domestic aspects related to the individual are fully recognized and understood.

6   **Set realistic expectations**
The objectives of the assignment should be clearly stated at the outset:

- depending on the category of the assignment, performance objectives should be set by the appropriate manager(s);
- setting realistic requirements will also assist in the identification and selection of the optimal candidate(s);
- the personal and career development issues will be able to be more accurately defined as a result.

7   **Prepare the expatriate for the move**
Fundamental to the planning and preparation phase will be the design and implementation of a programme designed to take the individual (and family, as appropriate) through a carefully prepared series of events and discussions. This approach seeks to reduce the likelihood of assignment failure due to personal/domestic problems, to include:

- cultural, language and orientation briefings/training;
- consideration of all health/medical issues;
- arrangements for visas, work permits, residence permits, passports;

- taxation and social security advice/guidance;
- schooling, accommodation, transport, insurance (covered in pre-assignment briefings, and forming part of the assignment conditions); and
- wherever possible, provision of a comprehensive range of services to the assignee covering the above areas, 'customized' to reflect the individual circumstances.

8   Career management
The assignment should:

- be part of a structured framework within which line management should ensure that the assignment represents a valuable element of the individual's personal and career development;
- be reflected in the creation of an international development plan for the individual, aligned to the company's career management process;
- provide for early consideration of any redeployment issues to be established, recognizing both 'home' country management requirements as well as the potential for further international assignments upon successful completion;
- consider the appointment of a mentor as part of the process.

9   Communication
Effective communication will enhance the application of assignment policy with regard to:

- an understanding of the company's approach to international assignments, and the structure of the programme;
- communication links, established at the outset, to maintain the channels between the organization and the assignee while he/she is away from the 'home' country, keeping abreast of 'home' company developments and assisting in any subsequent redeployment issues (mentoring may play an important role in this regard).

10   Apply consistent policies
Consistency and coordination are prerequisites for an expatriate policy management suite, while remaining sufficiently flexible to satisfy both assignee and line management.

PART 2: INTERNATIONAL ASSIGNEE REMUNERATION APPROACHES

In what follows we look at the detail of packages comprising elements of remuneration, various allowances and benefits, plus support services typically received when assignees work abroad (Dowling and Welch, 2004). Expatriate packages vary widely from organization to organization, although they may broadly be categorized into five main approaches:

- home-based/salary build-up (balance sheet);
- host-based (or with enhancements);
- better of home or host;
- individual negotiation/ad hoc;
- global assignee.

The provision of relocation allowances and benefits depends on which of these approaches is adopted. We also refer below to a sixth category of 'commuter assignee'.

Home-based remuneration approaches

Under the home-based approach, the remuneration package is designed to preserve equity with home-country peers. The organization meets the incremental costs over and above home-country costs for goods and services, taxes and social security. This represents the traditional approach to expatriate compensation and is usually known as the 'balance sheet'. The fundamental principle is that employees should be no worse off while working abroad than they would have been had they remained at home. The intention is not to 'reward' assignees as such, but rather to compensate them for changes in lifestyle, enduring 'hardship' and so on. So, for example, allowances may be implemented to compensate for working in remote or difficult locations, to compensate for political instability or poor health provision, indeed even just for 'being mobile'.

The costs of housing and education for children are met, recognizing that the employee and family must be kept 'whole'. Differences in costs of living are also addressed. Other allowances may include home leave, relocation/shipping, spouse assistance/dual-career allowances and so on. Although the 'keep whole' principle underpinning the balance sheet is that of 'no better, no worse', in effect assignees are often better off under this methodology than they would have been at home. It is therefore, generally speaking, an expensive system of expatriate compensation, particularly when large numbers of expatriates are involved. However, it may prove to be an appropriate methodology for those on relatively short-term assignments who are going to be repatriated – although the policy elements for short-term assignees may be tailored to reflect the special circumstances of their assignments (in respect of home leave, unaccompanied status and so on).

The balance sheet is underpinned by the principle of tax equalization. Hypothetical tax the employee would have paid at home is deducted from the home base pay to arrive at a net salary. Allowances and premiums are then added to that amount, and the organization pays any tax falling due within host jurisdiction on the total of the remuneration package.

The balance sheet approach remains popular in the United States and Japan, where it is used by around 85–95 per cent of organizations. In Europe, the figure is about 70 per cent (ORC, 2002a). Its continued usage over many years reflects its perceived advantages. These may be summarized as:

▌ maintaining the link with home-country salary and thereby aiding pension calculation and repatriation;

▌ maintaining the link with home-country consumption patterns;

▌ facilitating inter-country transfers and geographic mobility;

▌ facilitating salary reviews;

▌ facilitating communication with employees;

▌ providing consistent treatment of assignees from the same home country.

Host-based remuneration approaches

Organizations facing competitive challenges internationally have been exploring ways of moving away from an approach to expatriate rewards based on 'topping up' home-based compensation without any reference to local market conditions. This is especially pronounced in 'developed' countries; in 'developing' countries, expatriates at middle and senior executive levels still tend to expect some compensation for 'hardship'. Among a newer generation of globally mobile professionals (a 'trainee executive' group), even in the latter territories a more 'bare-bones' approach may be tried. A destination-based approach, where expatriate rewards use the local assignment market context as a platform, may be judged more appropriate in some locations.

The pure 'host-based' approach to compensation treats expatriates exactly the same as their local counterparts. Although this approach may be used for permanent transfers ('localization'), on the whole the use of pure host-based remuneration systems is rare. Net-to-net comparisons need to be calculated to determine the feasibility of this approach, and the rationale for the assignment needs to be considered carefully. Even if the net-to-net calculation provides the basis for this approach to succeed (in host reward policy terms), international assignees who are expected to return home or move on to another location are likely to have issues that set them apart from locals – most notably housing and schooling. They are also likely to require some assistance with home leave to maintain home country ties and ease repatriation. International assignees may wish to retain home-country housing (assuming they are home owners), and with the exception of very young children, are most likely to wish to keep their children in either a school of their own nationality or an international school, so that the children's education is not compromised. In addition, assignees are likely to require assistance with taxation – from the very basics of completing tax returns in the foreign jurisdiction to ensuring that additional tax liabilities are met.

In a local approach, assistance given is more likely to reflect local treatment rather than expatriate conditions. Housing assistance is therefore more likely to reflect peer housing than the expatriate 'ghetto'. Education for children is likely to reflect more closely local treatment than the most expensive international schools. Organizations may therefore scale back well behind the full 'balance sheet' package.

Taxation is an aspect deserving particular attention. To facilitate mobility, employers may, as under home-based systems, tax-equalize their employees, as this means that the assignees can move from one jurisdiction to another without penalty – they remain no better, no worse off in tax terms. Alternatively, organizations may opt to tax-protect rather than tax-equalize. Under tax protection, the employee pays no more tax in the host location than he or she would have paid on company-earned income at home, but could pay less. The organization assumes responsibility for any taxes owed to the host location tax authorities in excess of the hypothetical home tax. However, if the assignee goes to a lower tax jurisdiction, he or she benefits from the windfall under tax protection. This may have implications for subsequent mobility. A further option is to provide no assistance on tax, but this may jeopardize both the inclination to be mobile (to high-tax countries and from low-tax countries) as well as inadvertently endangering the assignee in jurisdictions where tax irregularities can result in prosecution and imprisonment.

The host-based approach to assignee remuneration (in either its pure form or the modified host plus enhancements approach) offers a number of advantages:

▌ it provides equity in the host location and a consequent morale boost for locals;

▌ in assignee populations with multiple nationalities, equity is preserved;

▌ it is significantly less expensive than the home-based approach.

A host-based emphasis requires careful involvement of all the parties to the expatriate reward contract: individuals, their families, and corporate and local management. Participation in the detail in this way means a more efficient system is called for, and effective HR guidance to accompany it.

Better of home or host

This approach is self-explanatory – the assignee receives the better deal, depending on assignment location. This is probably an attractive prospect for assignees, but is likely to be a costly option for the employer.

Individual negotiation/ad hoc

This approach may result in costs being ratcheted up and introduce widespread equity concerns across the multinational's internationally mobile cadre. However, there are organizations, possibly new to international assignments, that take this approach for reasons of expediency (perhaps they have limited specialist resources). Difficulty may lie ahead as the multinational grows: it will need to implement more consistent approaches later on at a cost-effective level. A large healthcare retailer encountered just such difficulties, in our recent experience.

Global assignee systems

Under these approaches, organizations devise remuneration systems to meet the needs of their globally mobile assignees. Such systems are usually applied to international cadres, and may be tailored to the level of assignee and rationale for the assignment. For instance, 'trainee cadres' may experience terms and conditions more akin to locals but with particular tailored elements reflecting their mobility. For example, allowances tend to be focused, housing tends to be in line with peers, and incentives are limited (reflecting the developmental nature of the assignment). Senior mobile cadres' allowances and benefits may reflect the disruption that continuing mobility poses to their lifestyle and families.

The advantage of using specially tailored international remuneration approaches is that equity is preserved among the mobile population, regardless of destination location. Such arrangements may prove complex to administer and communicate, however. Pension issues are particularly complex to handle, and usually require the use of offshore or 'top-up' plans rather than maintenance of the individuals in either the home or the host-country pension plans. Tax issues too are complex, and a tax equalization approach is usually required to ensure mobility and tax compliance.

Commuter assignees

The commuter assignee (sometimes referred to as a 'flex-pat') does not really fit in with the traditional categories for assignment policy design. Commuters may service their international assignments weekly, monthly or for some other duration, leaving their family at home. Their packages therefore tend to be home-based and contain elements primarily relating to travel (air fares paid) and accommodation (bachelor apartments, that is, serviced accommodation, rather than hotels, are paid for). Particular care needs to be paid to taxation and visa issues for this group of international assignees.

PERFORMANCE MANAGEMENT ISSUES

In assessing international assignee performance, it is important to consider the variables in the host location that make the assignment different from the home country. The assignee has to contend with the new environment, job requirements and culture – both societal and organizational. In terms of reward policies, a home, host or international approach may be taken. If home-based payment systems were being applied, it would be expected that performance rewards would fall into line with the home-based systems. So if the assignee receives an excellent performance rating while abroad, the level of additional reward applicable had that rating been achieved at home would be applied – this maintains equity with home-based peers. If a host-based approach is used, it follows that local increases are applied to local salaries. International systems will use specially devised performance rewards applicable to the international nature of the payment system. (Performance management complexities are explored in more detail in Chapter 2.)

ALLOWANCES AND BENEFITS COMPONENTS

In this section, we outline some of the typical allowances and benefits that might be included in an international assignment policy, and comment on current trends in their usage. A traditional balance sheet policy may include a large number of these elements, whereas a host-based package may include very few. Assignment policies relating to different types of transfers again may contain many of these elements (for instance, for skills transfers) or relatively few (for developmental transfers, volunteers and so on). The mobility strategy adopted (short-term, commuter, regular assignment, mobile cadre) will also have an impact on the level of benefits provided, for example reflecting the assignee's accompanied or unaccompanied status. Potential elements of the package are therefore described and comments appended about when such elements may be applied.

Mobility premium/foreign service premium

A payment may be made to encourage employees to be mobile or to reflect their mobile status. There are, in effect, two approaches to the payment of such an allowance. Traditionally, a 'foreign service' premium (FSP) was paid, usually monthly with salary. Today (ORC, 2004) such premiums are generally no more than 10 per cent of salary, although this figure was higher in the past. The regular nature of the payment encourages mobility, but the main drawback is that it does not facilitate repatriation or localization. Consequently, and in order to reduce costs, FSPs are being replaced by one-off mobility premiums, generally paid at the beginning and perhaps again on completion of the assignment. In this way, the requirement to be mobile is recognized but it does not become an impediment to repatriation.

Hardship/location allowance

Using data tables constructed by organizations such as Employment Conditions Abroad (ECA) or Organization Resources Counselors (ORC), organizations can make payments to assignees based in what are termed 'hardship' locations to provide compensation to reflect such conditions as isolation or instability, harsh climates and so on. It is important to remember that 'hardship' is a subjective issue. Westerners moving to third-world countries might expect to be compensated for the difficulties associated with their new environment, but thought also needs to be given to other nationalities moving to unfamiliar climates and regimes. As such, data may be obtained in a matrix form so that it can be applied to populations of third-country nationals and developing-country nationals moving to various permutations of locations throughout the world. The term 'hardship' is also being replaced by the use of 'location' allowances – what is 'hardship' to one might not be 'hardship' to another.

Cost of living allowance (COLA)

The cost of living allowance (COLA) typically applies when the balance sheet is used. It is designed to compensate assignees for any increase in the costs of goods and services abroad. When the balance sheet is applied, cost of living adjustments, again based on data tables from organizations such as Employment Conditions Abroad (ECA) and Organization Resources Counselors (ORC), are made to the 'spendable' income element of home country salary (excluding elements of housing, savings, and tax and social security). If the cost of living in the host country is higher than at home, this will increase this element of basic remuneration. However, if the cost of living is lower in the host country, then to maintain the balance sheet principle of 'no better, no worse off', a negative cost of living differential should be applied.

In some countries, the implementation of a negative COLA is relatively normal practice (for instance the Scandinavian countries and Switzerland) whereas in others (such as the United Kingdom) the implementation of negative COLA is fraught with difficulties, as it is a highly emotive assignee issue.

COLAs may take many forms. Standard indices reflect home-country consumption patterns very closely. Efficient purchaser indices are designed to reflect the fact that assignees will change their consumption patterns and shop more cost-effectively while abroad. Other indices include catalogue-style data to reflect the fact that assignees in remote locations cannot buy goods locally. Custom-designed indices are gaining in popularity. These exclude items that the company provides directly to the employee via policy. Much can be saved through the use of more efficient purchaser indices, although again this can be an emotive issue for assignees.

Housing allowances

Other than for pure local terms assignee policies, the provision of housing allowances or company housing is a given. The balance sheet works on the principle that the employer ensures that the assignee's housing costs are met. If it is applied in a pure sense, then any income that the assignee receives from letting out a home-country property is set against the cost of the host-country housing in the form of a home housing deduction. American organizations usually apply this principle, but in so doing undertake to provide significant help to the assignee in the form of home management assistance via relocation agencies. British companies, by comparison, take a 'hands-off' approach to housing. They tend to provide the housing abroad – either in the form of company housing or as an allowance – and leave the employee to make his or her own arrangements regarding letting out and managing the home-country property.

The two main areas of current interest in housing concern the savings that can be made on this highly expensive part of the package via tax-efficient delivery and the use of peer housing. The provision of company housing rather than an allowance may prove to be more tax-efficient, and thus can lead to great savings for the organization. The use of peer-style housing rather than expatriate-style properties can also result in significant cost reductions for companies. The main difficulty in encouraging the use of peer housing, though, tends to be linked into schooling issues, in that assignees may need to live in the expatriate 'ghetto' area in order to have access to the most appropriate school for their children.

Education allowances

Another expensive element of the package, which like housing tends to be almost universally applied, is the provision of education assistance. Assignees are unlikely to accept a posting if it jeopardizes their children's education. The options are to provide continuity in education provision either in a home-country school (via boarding) or a local school (if one is available) or international school. The cost of all of these is, however, significant. Local schools may be appropriate for younger children and some others, but are unlikely to be acceptable when children reach critical stages in their education. In an effort to reduce costs, companies are beginning to tighten up on the choice of company-funded schools available to parents. Alternatively, only a contribution may be made towards costs. Some organizations are applying an education deduction following the same principle as home-housing deduction – if employees met the costs of private education at home, they are expected to meet equivalent costs abroad. Again this is an emotive issue, but in the drive to reduce costs, this approach is gaining in favour (ORC, 2004).

Car allowances

If an expatriate received a company car at home, it is usual practice to supply either a car or an allowance while abroad, if the employee remains on a home-based package. Custom and practice sensitivity is important here – if it is not usual practice for locals to drive company cars, an allowance may be given rather than the car itself, to reduce the visibility of such benefits and consequent effect on local morale.

Vacation allowances

Depending on whether a home or host-country approach is taken, vacation entitlement may reflect the home country or the local entitlement. It is in this aspect of the package that companies sometimes follow a better of home or host approach. There may be a special vacation scheme designed for mobile cadres. Clearly there can be issues when an employee from Europe is used to receiving five or more weeks' leave and finds the entitlement reduced to two or three weeks, say, in the United States. Strict adherence to local terms would mean that the lesser entitlement applies – but again this can prove to be an emotive issue, particularly if the employee is encouraged to maintain home-country ties in preparation for repatriation via home leave.

Home leave allowances

If the employee is to repatriate, home leave should be used to renew ties at home and keep up to date with home country developments and changes. In the past, home leave became a perk that was effectively used by assignees to travel the world at their employer's expense. Although this does serve to broaden horizons, it undermines the purpose of the benefit, which is to renew home-country attachments. Organizations are therefore increasingly stating that home leave must be used for its stated purpose. Home leave allowances may not apply in the case of short-term assignments – particularly if the assignment is less than around six months' duration, and especially if the distance home is significant, or for longer periods abroad if the assignee is accompanied by the family.

Sickness and medical issues

Depending on whether a home or host approach is taken, sick leave will follow home or host-country practice. Medical insurance and emergency evacuation cover is usually provided for the assignee and family – most certainly in the case of home-based approaches and for mobile cadres. Help may be given with medical insurance under host-based policies too, for example in the United States. Medical issues can become particularly problematic in remote regions.

Relocation and freight expenses

Organizations usually meet or pay an allowance towards the costs of ship ping personal effects to the new location. Whether the accommodation at the receiving location is furnished or not will affect the policy on shipment of furniture and other large household items. The current trend is to reduce costs by providing furnishing allowances or furnished property in the destination location. A relocation or disturbance allowance may also be given to meet the costs of new electrical items, for example. The cost of transporting pets is increasingly not being met by organizations.

Rest and relaxation trips

In hardship locations, the cost of flying out for periods of rest and relaxation is typically met, along with accommodation and subsistence costs (see Chapter 2).

Tax/tax assistance

The package should include tax assistance (equalization or protection) and the costs of using a specialist tax provider to deal with local tax returns as discussed earlier in this chapter.

Preparation and training assistance

As discussed in Chapter 4, the policy should include meeting the costs of orientation/briefing, language training, cultural training and so on, for all assignees and preferably for spouses/partners and accompanying family members as appropriate.

Pre-assignment trips

The costs of hotels, subsistence and travel are usually met for up to a week for the employee, spouse and possibly accompanying family members as part of the selection/preparation process (see Chapter 4). The costs of using specialist advice to find housing and schools are also usually met.

Dual careers

Some 80 per cent of organizational policies now include provision for dual-career assistance (ORC, 2002b). Assistance includes both financial and practical support. Financial help may include provision of allowances to further education or set up business ventures while abroad. It is uncommon to provide compensation simply for loss of earnings. Practical support may include CV preparation, career counselling, interview training and visa assistance.

Retirement benefits

The options concerning retirement fall into three main categories: to remain in the home-country scheme, to join the local scheme, to join some form of top up or offshore plan, or a combination of these. Home-based assignee remuneration plans are most likely to maintain their employees in the home-based scheme for retirement purposes. Permanent transfers and localized employees may well join the local provision. Mobile employees are more likely to become part of an offshore arrangement. Pension provision is a complex area, and specialist advice is necessary at an early stage.

Social security

Social security is another complex area – one that is an emotive issue for employees and again an area where professional advice should be sought. There are reciprocal agreements in place between many nations, and it is crucial that legal requirements are followed.

PART 3: INTERNATIONAL CONTRACTS AND THE GLOBAL EMPLOYMENT COMPANY

In order to tackle the issues surrounding employment terms for a truly international cadre of expatriated professionals, some organizations are considering whether to form a global employment company (GEC), which could become the legal employer of managers and professional staff during periods of international secondment. There are a number of implications associated with employing expatriates via a GEC. Key aspects are summarized below.

STANDARDIZATION OF CONTRACTS

It is important to determine to what extent contracts of employment should be standardized for all employees. Factors to consider are:

▌ Where the company will be registered and what law will govern in the event of a dispute?

▌ What contractual rights will apply?

▌ What existing 'home' contractual rights will be preserved?

▌ Where existing contracts of employment must be terminated, how will variation of rights be handled? What action, such as compensatory measures, will be taken to avoid disadvantaging employees as a result of a change of employer?

▌ Will employees be granted continuity of service, and what will the effect be on service-related benefits such as pensions, holidays and redundancy entitlements?

RELATIONSHIP OF GEC WITH THE HOME FIRM

Factors to consider include:

▌ Who will have the right to hire and fire?

▌ Who will be responsible for handling disciplinary and grievance matters?

▮ How will appeals be handled?

▮ What support services will be available, such as employee assistance programmes?

STATUTORY RIGHTS

A key issue is determination of what statutory or mandatory rights should apply, so as to guarantee employees a certain level of protection regardless of where they are assigned.

EMPLOYEE POPULATION

It will be necessary to agree the target employee population at the outset. For example:

▮ Will the GEC employ only the 'brightest and best'?

▮ If so, what will be the relationship of this 'elite' global cadre with the rest of the organization?

PENSION IMPLICATIONS

This is perhaps the most complex area, and includes such questions as:

▮ What pension arrangements will apply? Is it possible and practicable to establish a pension scheme, provident fund, or other deferred compensation arrangement, which transcends country-specific legislation?

▮ How portable will such a scheme be?

▮ What will be the effect upon home-country pension schemes: for instance, what will happen to accrued pension rights in the home country?

▮ What will be the tax implications on contributions, and what will be the effect on any tax-free elements of the pension?

MEDICAL COVER AND LIFE ASSURANCE

Key issues to consider include:

▌ Will it be feasible to establish a global provider?

▌ If so, what standard and level of medical cover will apply?

▌ How will variations of medical cover be handled?

PERFORMANCE MANAGEMENT

Core issues to consider include:

▌ How will performance be monitored?

▌ How will performance be rewarded?

▌ Who will determine the capability and readiness of an individual to take on new assignments?

▌ How will the GEC ensure that the reward structure is competitive?

TAX AND SOCIAL SECURITY

Tax and social security provisions will be major issues. The key considerations from an employee's perspective include:

▌ What tax regulations will apply?

▌ Will employees always be required to pay host-country tax or will 'hypothetical tax' be applied?

▌ Will employees receive 'equalization' treatment if the host-country tax liability is greater than a figure agreed at the outset, and if so, how will this be determined?

▌ Who will be responsible for tax planning activities?

▌ What will be the impact on home-country social security benefits?

▌ What will be the contribution requirements on the part of the employer and employee, and how will these be made?

ADMINISTRATION

This covers such matters as:

▌ How will employees be paid, for example via an international bank account?

▌ In what currency will employees be paid?

▌ Will employees receive protection for exchange rate fluctuations: for instance, should a rate be agreed at the beginning of each year and any differences reconciled at year-end?

▌ How will the payroll be administered: who will resolve issues such as missing and/or late transfers?

POTENTIAL BARRIERS

Certain issues have been identified by international organizations, reviewing policy options in this area, as potential barriers to the harmonization of expatriate remuneration policies and packages. Issues may be summarized as follows:

▌ The present diversity of expatriate remuneration policies and practices used among a group's strategic business units (SBUs) means that a harmonized approach may be more difficult for certain organizations to implement initially than for others. A phased approach to implementation may be required.

▌ A lack of effective administrative and HRM systems may well hinder the implementation of a successful international secondment programme for the 'brightest and best'. Senior management commitment to support the programme is therefore essential.

▌ The potential costs associated with harmonizing expatriate remuneration packages, and the allocation of these costs, may seem prohibitive to some SBUs. Group-wide funding may therefore need to be considered, to pump-prime GEC initiatives.

6

Choices and consequences in international employment relations

---

CHAPTER AIMS

This chapter sets out to do the following:

▌ introduce you to the nature of 'employment relations' and the parties to 'employment systems';

▌ consider ideological and practical influences on the choices and consequences open to the management of multinational organizations in establishing employment relationships in respect of the 'international workforce';

▌ outline prevailing employment relations trends in a multinational context, particularly experimentation around the 'flexibility agenda' and 'employee voice'.

INTRODUCTION

In Chapter 1, we explained that attempts by multinational managements to diffuse HRM (in its idealized form – cf Guest, 1987) might be perceived as associated with the uncritical acceptance of a westernized 'neo-liberal' corporate governance regime, setting the stage for a particular approach to relationships around employment. However, at various stages in the book we have also given reasons why an impulse to conclude that some form of 'normative convergence' is inevitable should perhaps be resisted: diverse traditions and institutional factors appear to drive equally diverse empirical practice. An alternative to the notion of centre-driven homogenization of HRM is the countervailing diversity in experimentation and hybridization in substance and process across transnational sites of workforce–management interaction. In any case, the pressure to emulate business and employment systems practices identified in 'exemplar economies' is not a new phenomenon: over the final third of the 20th century it was the turn of Germany in the 1970s, Japan in the 1980s, before the United States was held out as the source of 'world's best practice' in the 1990s and into the early 21st century.

Conceptualizing organization and management in purely technical terms, downgrading the 'political', and pursuing an aspiration to achieve 'transnational' and/or 'geocentric status' (Ghoshal and Bartlett, 1998; Perlmutter, 1969), may nonetheless encourage multinational managers to search for universal solutions to the problem of regulating employment relations. Townley (1994) argues that the focus of attention is on what may be 'enclosed' (to avoid non-managerially-determined influences); on workforce segmentation (into 'core' and 'peripheral' groups); and on 'ranking'. An example of the latter is contrasting organization approaches to accent the 'modern' (that is, 'objective', managerially led) over the 'under-developed' – say, 'ubuntu' (the more subjective notion that 'I exist because of others'), used to characterize the managerial paradigm in African contexts (Kamoche et al, 2004).

The combined logic of corporate governance discipline via globally integrated capitalist markets, and the 'networking' of organizational knowledge, irrespective of its source, as the source of sustainable competitive advantage, implies that foreign direct investment units must be integrated in the corporate project. To that end, their direction must emphasize 'catching up' with 'world-class' practice, as this is defined by currently prevailing (westernized) ideology. Those unwilling or unable to 'add value' within time frames determined by the capital investment market risk permanent marginalization.

How do we make sense of these tendencies? Critics such as Townley (1998: 206) are unconvinced of the merits of starting from an idealized, universal model (of HRM and concomitant 'employment relations management') and seeking to test its empirical correspondence as the preferred route to comprehend what is really occurring. Instead, Townley advocates analysis of organizational practices to see how they structure social relations around production.

In this chapter, we enter the debates surrounding employment and work relations, and the ways in which these socio-economic relations may be situated within the various employment systems in different parts of the world. We reflect on material and ideological influences brought to bear in seeking to manage the interface between business strategy and its resourcing, comparative environments in which multinational management seeks to pursue productive activities, as well as the orientation and 'voice' of human capital (whether individually or through collective institutions). In particular, we examine notions of 'deregulation' and 'flexibility', prescribed in influential circles as prerequisites for sustained competitive advantage in 'globalized' markets.

REGULATING EMPLOYMENT RELATIONS

Let us begin with some basics. How can we begin to understand 'employment relations', as something giving rise to choices and consequences facing multinational managers? As the name implies, 'employment relations' (sometimes the terms 'employee relations' or 'industrial relations' are used) is concerned with the socio-economic relationships that form and evolve around a contract between parties to perform work in return for employment benefits, such as remuneration (see Chapter 5). Regulation of the substance and process of the contract between the parties (that is, what is involved in the employment relationship and how it may be determined, and redetermined while the relationship exists) provides a distinctive analytical focus.

As a discipline with a long heritage, employment relations commentary has tended to concentrate on the formation and application of 'rules' between 'the parties' to 'systems' of employment relations (Clegg, 1970; Dunlop (1993 [1958]). Is that regulation unitarily determined, or is a plurality of interests in play, implying scope for a political dimension? The presence of 'parties' to employment contracts and systems suggests that another significant area of enquiry concerns those who are involved in the regulatory process and their relative capacity to influence outcomes. Here we may look at the involvement of employers and employees, but also at a more macro, economy-wide level, the state and its various agencies; employers' associations at industry-wide and national level; and trade unions (who may seek to represent employee interest groups at a micro level and industry level, as well as through efforts to have an influence on the national political context).

Socio-political relations around employment are not static: it is pertinent to ask about the future for 'bipartite' and/or 'tripartite' employment systems contexts for determining employment relations outcomes. Are 'rules and processes' to be directed exclusively along unitary lines? Or is there scope for more pluralistic (multi-party) employment relations intermediation? Is regulation of the employment relationship to be disaggregated and devolved, with an emphasis on the individual? Or will managerial policies need to encourage (or at least accommodate) higher levels of engagement between the 'social partners' to industry and commerce? The disaggregated or 'liberal' market variety of capitalism, idealized as the neo-American approach to economic regulation, may be juxtaposed with the integrated or 'social market' variety idealized in the 'Rhenish' model typified by Germany, to help address these questions – see Albert (1993) or Hall and Soskice (2001) for a fuller discussion.

While at the most basic level, the parties are of course employer and employee, sophisticated rules-based employment relations systems have been recorded as developing alongside industrialization, involving employers (sometimes acting across industrial sectors); employees represented by member-based associations such as trade unions (in organization-specific or sector-wide formations); and the state as the economy and employment system-wide regulator – the source of 'employment law' and its enforcement.

Such considerations lead us to the next question: given the variety of actor configurations in different employment systems, how can we make sense of the scope for variation in employment relations regulation? A tradition of comparing and contrasting the features of employment systems, and the social relations nested within each one, has led to a significant cross-national employment relations literature (eg Bean, 1994; Bamber, Lansbury and Wailes, 2004; Poole, 1986; Traxler, Blaschka and Kittel, 2001).

In order to conduct comparisons systematically, it is helpful to draw on a common set of features, similarities and differences which can be catalogued and interpreted across the business and employment systems under scrutiny. Table 6.1, building on earlier work by the comparative economist Alan Blinder, offers a set of possible comparators that we have found helpful in seeking to understand how employment relations systems may be specified to inform empirical analysis and explanation.

Table 6.1   Indicators for a two-system comparison

	Employment system A	Employment system B
Basic principles		
Dominant factor of production		
'Public tradition'		
Centralization		
Reliance on price-mediated markets		
Supply relations		
Industrial groups		
Extent privatized		
Financial system		
Market structure		
Banking system		
Stock market		
Required returns (ROI)		
Labour market		
Job security		
Labour mobility		
Labour/management		
Pay differentials		
Turnover		
Skills		
Union structure(s)		
Strength of TU/pressure groups		
The firm		
Governing objective		
Role of top management		
Social overheads		
Welfare system		
Basic principle		
Universal transfers		
Means-testing		
Degree educated – tiered by class		
Private welfare		
State policies		
Role of government		
Openness to trade		
Industrial policy		
Top income tax rate(s)		

Source: adapted from an adaptation by Blinder (1975).

MANAGERIAL STRATEGIES:
GLOBAL RULES – MULTI-LOCAL PROCESSES?

Much of the normative (that is, the 'should do') commentary from writers over the past half-century has advocated the transplantation of western approaches, unitarist or pluralist.[1] The Japanese 'best practice' movement altered the focus somewhat, shifting the emphasis away from naturally forming (often competing) employee representative institutions to 'enterprise unions' and work teams focused on quality improvement, where managerial imperatives were delegated to the point of production (Eaton, 2000).

However, empirical observation has indicated problems in attempts to transfuse work organization and employment practices forged in one political economy into another with different traditions (eg Itagaki, 1991). With the latest phase of isomorphism – where 'one-best-way' commentary has privileged an Americanized 'market-liberalizing' model, governed by overriding attention to the interests of the shareholder – attempts may be perceived not only to transplant managerial practices, but to alter the structural and ideological context as well (Harvey, 2003). The accent among state policy makers, wishing to appear 'business-friendly' to major multinationals engaged in 'regime shopping' (Edwards and Ferner, 2002), has been on deregulating the employment system so that a more managerially (that is, unitarily) determined agenda may be followed. (This is more a change in who sets the rules than abandoning rule-making as such, then.) Again, in practice the relative capacity of actors in an employment system to interpret the dominant trends in ideas and practice appears to offer room for the 'dominant logic' to be tempered to varying degrees. We discuss the state's role in regulating the context for employment relations below.

Let us shift the discussion from abstract to concrete, with a simple but telling 'postcard' from Germany. Until recently, pressures to deregulate the 'Rhenish' employment system have been less pronounced than in some other advanced industrial economies. An underlying tradition of seeking to realize human potential (*Personalführung/PF*), regarding apprenticeships and training (*Personalentwicklung/PE*) as an investment, has been central to German employment relations stability. Economic market 'liberalism' has been balanced against the principle of social justice: 'joint economic growth' and 'common wealth'. Participation and concerted action between employer and workforce as *Sozialpartner* (social partners) are each enshrined in the legislative framework. The *Mitbestimmungsgesetz* (code of co-determination) as well as the *Betriebsverfassungsgesetz* (corporate constitutional law) mandate the holding of regular meetings between management and elected employee works council representatives, to enable bipartite participation and joint decision making in company affairs. Workplace representation, as indirect participation, and co-determination as a form of direct participation are rooted in three laws, established after 1945 and strengthened over time: the Act on Co-determination in the iron, steel and mining industry (1951), the Works Constitution Acts (1951/1972/1989), and the Co-determination Act (1979).

A large publicly quoted, UK-parented diversified services company developed German business interests, and so acquired a workforce of around 700 people, mainly located in southern Germany. Two years following the acquisition, a rationalization programme was initiated which involved plans to reduce the workforce by some 50 per cent. Our correspondent, Volker Rennert (working in the United Kingdom at the time as an 'employee communications' consultant) received a telephone call from the plc's UK-based group human resources director. According to Volker, 'she was confused about "a very polite letter" that had been received from the head of the German works council', addressed to the European managing director (who happened to be an American national, based in Wokingham, UK). The essence of the letter was that the German workforce was 'completely frustrated' over the planned regime change. The letter concluded: 'We therefore kindly invite you to our next works council meeting which will take place at [date and time]'. The European Managing Director had sent a courteous, but one-line, reply stating that he was too busy to attend a meeting, and that (to paraphrase) the works council should 'sort itself out and let him know the position'.

The parent company had subsequently received notification from legal counsel to the effect that the organization was in breach of German works council regulations. These regulations required senior company representatives, on request and with due notice, to attend works council meetings. The works council was entitled to summon the managing director, as the person responsible corporately for the rationalization initiative, to a meeting involving employee representatives, to justify managerial decision making, and to enable the works council to seek clarification directly from him.

The 2002 European Commission Directive on Informing and Consulting Employees, premised on the notion of seeking to maximize production efficiency through 'concerted action' collectively between the parties, has recently been diffused across the region. Following the publicity that has accompanied the extended regulatory framework, future human resource directors in this position might be expected to make a less naïve response. But the case vignette still serves to illustrate that multinational managers cannot simply assume that they can sustain a corporately formed orientation to managerial priorities – with employment relations consequences – in their relationships with the global workforce.

Let us return to analysis with a more general question. How can we interpret the 'renewed American challenge' in managerial strategies, compared with alternative employment relations models? Edwards and Ferner (2002) draw attention to three perspectives and four 'influences' that may help. Taken together, these may be interpreted as summarized in Table 6.2, and discussed below.

Table 6.2   Influences and viewpoints on employment relations strategies

Influence/ viewpoint	Rational	Culturalist	Political
Country of origin	Corporate-led knowledge transfer while exploiting local adaptive potential	Culturally trained sensitivity in applying home-grown policies	Pressure on host regulators to conform to corporate norms
Dominant	'World's best practice' distinguishes 'best from rest'	'Educating' recipients of transplant practices albeit with attention to subjectivity	Supranational institutional norms privilege adaptation to one-best-way processes
Integration	Globally networked technology transfers	Technology used to facilitate practice diversity	Trade-offs: technology and work processes
Host country	Micro-adaptation to serve meta-level managerial aims	Local context conditions policy interpretation	Multinational will adapt to secure place in market

Rational view

There is a common assumption that this is what makes multinational corporations significant. The 'transnational' enterprise depends on networking sources of knowledge: Ghoshal and Bartlett (1998) argue that this will be the prerequisite for international competitive survival in future. The problem Edwards and Ferner (2002) identify is that the approach is seen in wholly technical terms. The resource-based view of strategy that underpins this perspective amplifies the need for an 'appropriate management mentality'. But what if research reveals a tendency for the issues to be intensely political?

Culturalist view

Hofstede (1981, 1991) and other cross-cultural management researchers argue that the prospects for transferring employment relations and work practices between economies are influenced not so much by the forces of competition as by the legacy of national practices. The emphasis is on, first, adapting practices to the host culture, and second, the need for awareness of the way 'corporate' culture is informed by traces of the culture of the firm's country of origin. Edwards and Ferner (2002) observe that this view helps to bring to the surface the scope for tensions when top management embark on a transfer of practice initiative.

In a study of Japanese-owned manufacturing plants in the United States, Itagaki (1991) highlights the problem of the extent to which parent company managements have to adapt to the American business environment, on the one hand, and the extent to which they may transfer their own production system, on the other. Itagaki (1991) illustrates the problem with the culturalist explanation of this: that it may overlook the influence of tradition and politics on dominant 'values', to which institutional theory draws attention, and which represent more than 'culture' – they are a feature of the whole society.

Political view

This viewpoint indicates the ways in which multinational managements may try to 'manage' processes for the transfer of practices in ways that enhance their legitimacy. The 'good corporate citizen' may be a favoured headquarters strategy, as well as attracting business locally from less 'aware' multinational competitors. And this may flow down to the ways in which employees (and their representatives) may be persuaded to accept corporate practices when the alternative might threaten investment continuity (as illustrated under the propositions of transaction cost theory). The utility of the approach is to bring to the surface the impact of actor motivations. But Edwards and Ferner (2002) point out that it does not really open up understanding of wider business systems issues.

To help add depth, the three 'viewpoints' may usefully be observed and applied analytically in tandem with a framework of 'influences' (Edwards and Ferner, 2002) on the ways employment relations strategies pursued by multinational managements may be interpreted across different national settings, and the ways in which these in turn influence outcomes.

Influences framework

Country of origin effect

As is implied in the Japanese example above, the embedded influence of home country experience on management orientation and nature of employment practices, while evolving over time, has a lasting effect on managerial style. An example from Malaysia later in the chapter shows how foreign capital investors may engage in forms of 'regime shopping' to require local policy makers to adapt their employment regulatory regime to legitimize and enable transplantation of the multinational's preferred (or instinctive) managerial practice.

Dominant effect

Multinational managements' attempts to exploit the opportunities across different geographies may be strongly shaped by the relative strength of a particular economy in the international hierarchy of countries. As we noted earlier, a number of countries in recent memory have been 'top nation of the day', and the fact that the status changes over time implies the hollowness of universal prescription as if there were no other way. However, analytically, from post-war US reconstruction to so-called 'after Japan' programmes in the 1980s, there are traces to be found that make it useful to use this notion to interpret what is observable. In employment relations terms, local workforce candidates, including sometimes trade unions which submit themselves to 'beauty parades', may be screened for their enthusiasm and capacity to follow the lead of the inward investor and its managerial style. Incentives for compliance may include employment terms offering a premium over local employment market competitors.

Integration effect

A worldwide trend towards economic deregulation, and the degree of access to technologies to facilitate communication and transport links, might bring pressure to bear on the non-managerial parties while also facilitating synergistic initiatives across subsidiaries on the part of multinationals. In employment relations terms, the effort may be to de-link workforce segments from a sense of solidarity with local–national counterparts, and cause them instead to form bonds with functional specialist entities across business-wide lines. Human resources management functions may themselves be established in parallel with the transnationally integrated structure.

Host country effect

Local statutory regulation and the managerial culture of a host country (for example, the co-determination requirements referred to in the German 'picture postcard') may leave employment systems less open to significant adaptation to meet the demands of inward investors. Multinational managements then have the choice of either moderating their 'corporate' approach, where the ability to influence policy makers to effect change is limited, or not investing. The question for multinational managements here is whether or not they can afford to leave a market open to the competition, or to accept the possible impact on their worldwide presence.

If we consider each of these influences as they might interact with one another in particular settings, it might help to build a more sophisticated understanding. For example, the dominant effect could be reinforced by a specific country of origin effect (Edwards and Ferner, 2002). The framework adds employment relations detail complementary to our tripartite strategy–business systems–human capital model for examining influences on multi-national managements' choices in approaching employment relations strategy and practice, taking account of a variety of constraints, opportunities and pressures.

EXTRA-MANAGERIAL ROLES IN REGULATING EMPLOYMENT RELATIONS SYSTEMS

So what about locating (single-party) managerial strategic choices in a comparative business systems context populated by other employment relations actors? Let us begin by addressing the roles that states (governments and their agencies) may play in regulating the employment system in interaction with the other main parties.

Theory on the role and impact of the state on employee relations systems is contested. Applying a neo-classical economist's worldview to employee relations systems is likely to result in the conclusion that outcomes will be the result of more or less third-party 'interference' in the operation of free markets (see Friedman, 1982 [1962]). Under this theorization, regulatory interventions by the state, say by legislation specifying minimum wage levels, or placing limitations on employers' ability to hire and fire, or providing welfare benefits that allow workers to become less reliant on selling their labour at any price in the employment market, are economically inefficient. Effective market functioning depends exclusively on supply and demand governing commodity prices – for example, wages (assuming that employee labour is a production commodity). The inference is that economic market norms offer the most efficient way to regulate employment relations. Other approaches are dismissed as irrational.

An alternative view argues that a more deeply textured orientation is needed to help understand what regulates employment practices (including valuing employees) and their context. Business systems theory (see Whitley, 1992, 1999) postulates that, rather than expecting the universal spread of Anglo-American liberal market economies, comparative practice can be explained only by reference to the ways in which different social elites vie with one another for dominance, in particular times and places, in dictating which ideas and institutions should be regarded as legitimate. The logic underpinning one institutionally embedded interpretation of socio-economic organization is not suitable as a basis for validating or critiquing alternative business systems, without reference to the social context in each case.

Factors such as the dispositional advantage (Edwards, 1986, 2003) enjoyed by certain actors to capture the trappings of authority to impose their views more generally, and the socialization of the participants as to what is or is not held to be legitimate, need to be included in the analytical equation. And in the case of sophisticated production systems such as those applicable to Japanese electronics and automotive manufacture, it may be argued that competitive advantage depends on 'a unique method of skill formation ... sustained by a sense of participation at various operational levels, from shop-floor to engineering and marketing divisions' (Itagaki, 1991: 118). One conclusion that may be drawn from business systems theorizing is that, if the state comes to be dominated by free market economists (or their agents), then it is to be expected that the state's role in the regulation of employee relations will be downplayed.

The notion of strategic choice (Child, 1972), influenced by the wider economic, political, social and technological context, and the advantage these phenomena may give to some groups over others over time, may be introduced to build further on the institutionally orientated approach to evaluating comparative employee relations systems. Strategic choices exercised by the parties – such as state intervention, or not, in employee relations – become an important explanatory factor (Poole, 1986). Of course, especially in developing countries that are attempting to develop the means to become competitive in markets for goods and services in the global economy, the state's choices may be limited. If the country is relatively poor, it may become dependent on multinational companies and/or supra-governmental institutions (such as the International Monetary Fund (IMF) or the World Bank) to provide investment to put in place the basic infrastructure on which industrial production depends (electricity and other forms of power, modern transport systems, and so on).

Dependency theory has been developed by analysts such as Valenzuela (1992), who argues that dominant views of the way an economy and its employment relations should be organized (currently the Anglo-American variety) come to prevail as a price for gaining external capital. An example is the 'strategic adjustment programmes' that are imposed on developing economies by the IMF. Thus, the state may introduce policies to repress or incorporate employee interest groupings such as trade unions (so as to neutralize them), so that market regulation prevails unimpeded.

As with other aspects of socio-economic relations, the position remains dynamic: the basis on which employment systems operate, and the implications for the parties, are not petrified. They shift with prevailing currents of structurally derived advantage and disadvantage and mainstream ideological thinking, as interpreted by the parties.

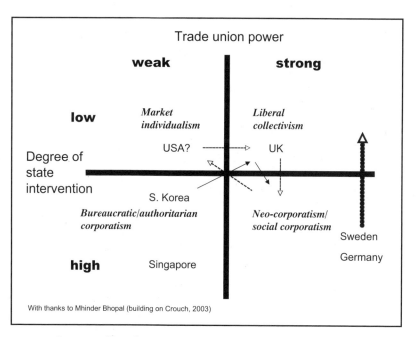

Figure 6.1 State and trade union interactions in employment systems

What are the implications of strategic choices by state regulators for the third major actor in employment relations – the representatives of organized labour? Figure 6.1 illustrates the ways in which the incidence of state intervention in employment systems has consequences for trade unions. To inform systematic comparison, four idealized forms of political economic systems and associated employment subsystems may be classified as 'market- individualistic', 'liberal collectivist', 'state corporatist' and 'social corporatist'. Focusing on relative dispositional advantage, we can weigh the incidence of interventions by the state and its agencies against the strength of trade unions. (Trade union 'strength' can be judged either by 'density' – membership levels as a proportion of the total workforce – or by access to state policy making.)

Let us discuss the interpretation summarized visually in Figure 6.1 in a little more detail, before offering a 'picture postcard' to illustrate the case of the 'dependent' state and its interactions with multinational managements and domestic trade unions.

The market individualist state is characterized by limited regulatory mechanisms beyond the economic market. Business managements tend to predominate, and the substance and process of employment relations tend to be unitarily determined. The United States may be located as an exemplar employment system within this quadrant – although the question mark indicates that even in this current bastion of market liberalism, there exists a legacy of significant collectivism. This is the very model of industrial relations that influenced Dunlop's classic study almost five decades ago (see note 1). Trade union power has become increasingly weakened as neo-liberal political forces have dominated thought and action, impacting on the employment system over the last three decades, and the economy has restructured away from traditional large-scale labour intensive manufacturing. The public sector remains less developed than in (for example) European counterparts. In countries such as the United States, where the contemporary institutional shareholder-aligned governance system was developed, the dynamics of the socio-economic system sanction large wage/income differentials.

The liberal collectivist employment system has long been seen as the British model, although many of the same 'deregulating' and industrial restructuring forces attributed to the United States apply to the British context as well. However, grass-roots 'labourism' and a still significant public services sector (though shrunken compared with its equivalent three decades earlier) continue to afford trade unions residual influence in political economic affairs, and the ability to surprise government administrations with the capacity to mobilize in pursuit of employment grievances. There has been a dynamic conflict between two different tendencies since the late 1990s. One is exemplified by formal integration into the Social Charter and neo-corporatist partnership rhetoric, while the other consists of deregulating forces in government and management, which sustain at least an ideological preference for market individualism in the employment system. We are unlikely to see a reappearance of tripartite labour relations management of the form experienced in the 1970s, with 'quangos' comprising employers' associations sitting alongside national trade union officials, coordinated by state officials, and setting national incomes and prices policy.

Forms of 'concertation' have been a recent experience for employment systems of countries on the periphery of Europe, such as Portugal, in pursuit of a settlement to achieve the convergence criteria for membership of the European single currency. Even here there are post-convergence pressures, as long-standing grievances have resurfaced between the protagonists (employers wanting more labour market flexibility, and unions wanting enhanced commitment to wealth-sharing and human capital investment) (Ferreira *et al*, 2004).

By contrast with each of the first two quadrants in Figure 6.1, the corporatist state exemplified by South Korea and Singapore has an interventionist state regime, in pursuit of rapid economic growth, where people resources are to the fore, given the limited supply of natural resources, and industrialization has been effected as a 'nation-building' project. In South Korea, for a decade beginning in the late 1980s, trade unions appeared to be breaking out of a repressive state-sponsored model of export-oriented industrialization. In the post-1997 financial crisis era, there appears to have been a retreat in the face of employment system reforms initiated by government and management parties – although some commentators argue that the Korean unions are preparing for a 'second leap' (Lee, 2000: 146). In Singapore, close relations between the trade unions and the ruling political party have not prevented restraints on trade union power, attributed to 'a framework of laws' (Bean, 1994: 214).

The model positions countries such as Sweden along the same categorical latitude, but they might be characterized as social corporatist employment systems: they have relatively high levels of unionization even in the face of a global decline in organized labour institutions. Welfare-oriented state policy may rely on trade unions to act as a pseudo-state arm, administering social insurance benefits, for example. In Germany, as the 'postcard' case vignette illustrated earlier, a highly regulated employment system has been perceived as the basis for employment system stability and a high-skill economy, founded on principles of social justice, while remaining unequivocally capitalist. The directional arrows on the figure show how Sweden and Germany have been undergoing changes which affect the fortunes of their economic and employment systems. The trends may indicate a preference by the state to downgrade intervention, leading trade unions towards a more liberalized view of their future options.

In short, Figure 6.1 offers a useful basis for examining how the interaction between state and trade union agency affects the characteristics of a comparative employment system and the context in which multinational managerial strategies may be evaluated. However, the situation remains highly fluid and any generalization needs to be recognized as provisional. To illustrate the ways in which, for example, state–labour relations are likely to be affected significantly by a range of ideological and practical phenomena accompanying foreign direct investment (FDI) channelled through multinational corporations, let us look at another story from one of our 'postcard correspondents'.

THE DEPENDENT STATE AND DIVERSITY IN EMPLOYMENT RELATIONS CONSEQUENCES

A colleague of ours, Mhinder Bhopal, told us this story on return from one of a series of visits to conduct research in Malaysia.[2] He was exploring the fortunes of trade unions, and learnt of the ways in which the employment relations priorities transplanted with multinationals vary according to ideological and institutional experiences imported by managers from the home business system. Their corporate governance orientation also translates into a preferred employment relations strategy.

Mhinder studied evidence associated with three multinationals: one Australian, a second from Japan, and a third from the United States. To put the example into context, Malaysia is looking for further industrial development in pursuit of competitive engagement in worldwide consumer markets, but this requires capital investment, in particular the physical infrastructure of plant and equipment to support production. The state of the economy is such that the finance is not available locally, so the country is in need of foreign direct investment. Malaysia depends on the willingness of foreign investors to bring their capital to develop production facilities, and with it the prospect of employment and related skills development in using contemporary technology for the Malaysian workforce.

Of course, this is something of the highest significance to state policy makers. State legislators in this position (nominally entrusted with oversight of economic management, with aspirations to win a share of global market opportunities, but lacking the capacity to guarantee the infrastructure needed to do so) inevitably find themselves seeking outside intervention. This might be through development resources such as the World Bank or IMF, supranational institutions which are likely to impose a 'reconstruction' agenda which severely limits local legislators' capacity to regulate the business system. An alternative route is to open special economic zones and/or 'development areas' (which might even cover the whole country) that offer favourable terms to foreign direct investors willing to place funds – and accompanying managerial expertise – to support economic development on a piecemeal basis. Local elites within the business system with influence in government circles may, in turn, seek opportunities to partner with foreign capital investors for mutual advantage.

Thus multinational companies, as vehicles for FDI, may anticipate opportunities to secure advantageous terms from the 'dependent state' (Valenzuela, 1992), whether they are proposing a sole project or a local–international joint venture. Such special treatment might include a tacit or explicit understanding that state regulators will take action to ensure that they obtain the cooperation they want not only from local business elites but also from institutions representing the interests of working people. Outside investors want to be able to handle management–labour relations in their preferred style, and this could mean excluding third-party labour institutions from the scene.

So Mhinder's story is about employment relations in a situation where the capital interests have the upper hand (the 'dispositional advantage', in Edwards' (1986) phrase), and the Malaysian government functions as a dependent state. But there are still various options for how the multinational chooses to strike the terms for its FDI bargain, so there is not necessarily a single universally applicable outcome.

The Australian multinational had a capital interest, and had transplanted senior managers to oversee operations, in various locations where the presence of trade unions was regarded as unexceptional. The Australian investors were used to pluralistic employment relations within a statutory regulatory framework in which disputes were subject to state-administered resolution mechanisms, and had no specific qualms about the likely presence of third-party representatives.

The Japanese investors and expatriate management team were socialized by experience in the Japanese employment system, and here too trade unions are a normal feature of employment relations. However, institutional practice in the Japanese system differs from that experienced by the Australians. The Australians were used to multiple unions that operate wholly independently of management, and external resolution of disputes by reference to state agencies; the Japanese to an internal focus, and managerial expectations of a different role for, and outlook among, third parties. Senior managers in Japanese organizations expect to play a part in selecting the trade union judged appropriate to represent the workforce (possibly on 'greenfield' sites, prior to the recruitment of a workforce/union membership). They also expect the entire unionized segment of the workforce to be represented by a single trade union, as a precondition for affording the union bargaining rights. Recognition as a 'company union' carries with it tacit understandings about how the union will operate. It has a role similar to the Australian union role in representing members individually in disputes concerning the employment contract, which are regarded as an inevitable feature of workplace relations, but it has a different role in block negotiation. The officers of the union are expected ultimately to have regard to managerial priorities, and to work to ensure organizational efficiency in the utilization of labour resources to achieve corporate goals.

While the relationship between the parties in the Australian multinational was one of mutual tolerance, the assumption was that management and union interests would coincide only in the course of bargained outcomes, with imposed solutions where internal resolution of differences proved elusive. There are moves underway by more business-leaning Australian state administrations to drive through reforms, so the traditional *modus operandi* is changing. But the fundamental management and union objectives, and the sense of accountability in corporate governance terms, tend to be arms' length, at best, under Australian employment relations. In contrast, after a post-war era of conflictual employment relations, Japanese practice changed.[3] Japanese practice since the reforms presupposes at root a partnership orientation, where management and trade unions are joined in a problem-solving agenda. It is the means to the ends (rather than the ends in themselves) that may be subject to pluralistic interactions and possible dispute.

In both the Australian and Japanese cases, the Malaysian state's role was limited to ensuring that indigenous labour institutions understood these ground rules. If they accepted them, their presence would be tolerated by the multinational employers.

The American multinational demanded a more 'disciplinary' role for Malaysian state regulators. In recent years in the US employment system, it has become commonplace to exclude trade unions from workplace relations. The investor and management team required the Malaysian state to ensure a 'union-free' environment for their operations as a precondition to making a capital investment in the economy. Any conflict that might arise was to be redirected away from the managerial party to state regulators, to allow those leading the business to transplant a unitarily oriented system for regulating relations between management and workforce, individually and collectively.

The US stance is inspired by a hands-off attitude among contemporary federal and state administrations in the United States, which condones a variety of union avoidance strategies. Privately organized action to enforce a ban on unionization employs a variety of means including rooting out suspected dissident groups. In effect, in the Malaysian situation, the state was given the task of removing scope for what the American investors regarded as third-party interference in the management of their organization.

The point of the story is that, while the host nation may be faced with a common problem in securing FDI, the employment relations implications cannot simply be read off a 'standard' template. Embedded knowledge plays a part in the ways in which multinational managerial strategies are formulated, and this is associated with attempts to reduce the level of risk to the investment and production system integrity. What is familiar is likely to be preferred to the unknown. Learning to manage within a particular business system affects the likely employment relations orientation in international development projects. Institutional practice in the investors' home employment system influences the approach to managing the workforce in the local environment.

Several consequences for state regulators and their agencies follow, depending on the multinational managerial stance. There may be an expectation that their role will be fairly 'hands-off', at least to the point at which local management–union bargaining becomes incapable of dispute resolution. There is no question but that trade unions remain independent actors, and managements used to this situation may simply factor in a trade union presence to managerial policy and tactics. As a second alternative, the state's role may be to create conditions locally that are conducive to the incorporation of third-party employee representatives, as 'company union' officials. And as a third possibility, state regulators may be required to engage in strategies designed to 'disable' trade unions from accessing foreign plants to recruit and represent workforce members.

Mhinder's story does not imply that any one of these outcomes is likely to be reached without challenge by collective employee interests. However, it does require attention to the ways in which employment relations strategic choices by foreign investors give rise to a variety of consequences for both the state and trade unions. The common requirement may be for national-level 'deals' to be reached between sources of foreign capital and dependent states, but their application may involve a variety of local-level interventions.

REGULATORY NORMS UNDER PRESSURE?

So where does this leave us in reflecting on comparative international employment relations and how to analyse them? We have considered the parties and their respective roles, and the context in which the relations around production in different employment systems are played out – including issues when multinational managements attempt to transfer cherished ways of getting things done involving people contracted as employees. We have introduced some ways to think about the dynamics of employment relations, and tools for systematic comparison and interpretation of observable trends. And we have maintained a focus on the notion of regulation, although the details depend on both prevailing ideology and the relative dispositional advantage between the parties to influence what is done, and have it seen as legitimate. Awareness of this 'contested terrain' (Edwards, 1979) leads to the question of the extent to which there are calls to downgrade or remove third-party interventions (either state or trade-union sponsored) in contemporary employment systems, and the implications for 'employee voice' within the employment relationship. While this is not the place to attempt definitive answers to this question, we can sketch some of the arguments and their implications.

Irrespective of the transplantation issues associated with managerial strategies, some commentators moving into the early years of the 21st century have questioned whether traditional (pluralistic) rules-based employment relations systems can continue to survive. The perceived and actual restructuring of the industrial-commercial landscape has different impacts on the major parties. Writers focus particular attention on the weakening power of employee collectives to face management interest groupings, the growth in non-union employment, and the declining influence of the voice of labour in the formation of state policy. This has been highlighted for Asia, Africa and Latin America (Thomas, 1995), as well as the United States (Katz and Wheeler, 2004; Kochan, Katz and McKersie, 1986). In the case of Western Europe, evidence has been presented of change as well as continuity (Ferner and Hyman, 1998). Does this suggest a universal sounding of the death knell for collectively organized labour and tripartitism? On the level of generalizations, the trends to de-unionization and deregulation (that is, shifting from pluralist to unitarist employment relations) have been largely unquestioned. However, many national studies indicate considerable diversity within regions.

For example, an Austrian research team 'comprehensively dispense' with what Vernon (2002: 90) terms 'vague culturalism', to concentrate their attention on 'the cross-national variation in the IR [industrial relations] infrastructure, or "institutions"... in 20 advanced industrialized (OECD) countries', as these have developed over the last third of the 20th century (Vernon, 2002). Traxler *et al* (2001) enquire whether, and how, 'globalization' has translated into economic performance patterns (such as wage restraint and productivity growth) or into national IR systems themselves. The researchers' interest is in quantifying the outcomes of rational choices, rather than in focusing on qualitative influences such as identity or ideology, to establish whether there is 'an alternative, or functional equivalent, to... "market-driven opportunism" – the neo-liberal vision of employment relations' (Vernon, 2002: 91).

Neo-liberal discourse has positioned collective 'interest organizations' (employers' and employees' associations) as 'part of the problem', inhibiting rather than contributing to economic growth and social progress. They have been held responsible, at least in part, for 'high (minimum) wages and the attendant high level of unemployment, for (excessively) short and inflexible working hours and for unnecessary delays in introducing technological, social and organizational innovation' (Van Ruysseveldt, Huiskamp and van Hoof, 1995: 11). But other viewpoints (such as Hutton, 2002) argue that it is the institutional heritage of regions such as mainland Europe that forms part of the solution to present-day, far-reaching economic restructuring. Specifically, Traxler *et al* (2001) attempt to evaluate the ('neo') 'corporatist' approach that is 'very influential in Austria' (Vernon, 2002).

In seeking to understand transnational employment relations by attending to issues of context and practice, account needs to be taken of the prevailing institutional climate, particularly the form of 'organized' (for example, corporatist) capitalism compared with the 'disorganized' *(laissez faire)* variety. In the latter, multinational managements governed along 'exit-based' lines, as discussed in Chapter 1, have to consider how to satisfy their 'owners', whose interest may be limited to an expectation of maximum investment returns, while adapting their people management practices to accommodate a more 'voice-based' institutional climate.[4] State and supranational regulation may reinforce a new variant of pluralism (such as statutory recognition for trade unions, works councils, and EU directives on employee information and consultation).

Managements face decisions about the level of importance attached to their firm's locating operations in a particular country (which might bring access to indigenous skills, or perceived benefits of 'insider' status in trading terms). Alternatively, they might choose to locate production in a country more 'dependent' on foreign direct investment, and hence more willing to accept deregulation. For example, this might be agreed as part of a 'developmental' initiative sponsored by a government willing and able to control labour interests through trade union accommodation (or at least peak level 'incorporation'),[5] or through decentralization and fragmentation of the IR system, as illustrated in the Malaysian story. The latter approach is designed to weaken the market power of labour versus capital interests, by constraining and limiting the capacity of workers to mobilize against 'alien' practices such as western HRM (see Valenzuela (1992), cited by Bhopal, 2001).

The emphasis on dismantling the institutional frameworks long regarded as fundamental to the operation of employment relations systems around the world has had consequences for the focus of the HR function. From the United Kingdom, new research concludes that 'organizations are internationalizing their HRM as they endeavour to survive against global competition' (Brewster, Harris and Sparrow, 2002: 33). Data from the study indicates that such activity signals 'a significant shift in the nature of HR from the traditional concerns of international HRM functions (managing an internationally mobile workforce)' (2002: 33). Instead, attention is being directed to 'the need to manage international HRM activities through the application of a global set of rules to HRM processes'. The researchers regard these as 'the concern of a *global* HR function' (2002: 33, emphasis added), in which cross-country and cross-function business issues are to the fore. Brewster *et al* suggest that international HR managers are in effect becoming 'guardians of national culture' (Brewster *et al*, 2002). Their role is to help organizations in identifying the boundaries between globally standardized and localized employment practices. This suggests shifting sands and experimentation rather than blanket deregulation effected by an ascendant financially governed managerial interest.

GIVING VOICE TO HUMAN RESOURCES *AND* RESOURCEFUL HUMANS?

If you read the normative literature, you will frequently find HRM divided into 'hard' and 'soft' variants. Adopting a more critical stance, Keenoy (1997: 837) regards this tendency as setting up 'a series of binary "oppositional" conceptual-theoretic constructs' (which he finds rather artificial). 'Hard' HRM emphasizes the demand for effective human resourcing (maximum value creation from labour for minimum cost) – a depersonalization of people to the status of a market commodity: 'human resources'. 'Soft' HRM instead calls for 'resourceful humans' (Legge, 1995: 67), able and committed to work flexibly in the interest of organizational effectiveness under hyper-competitive conditions. Keenoy (1997) draws attention to the implication that each component of the dyad implies the necessary, or potential, presence of the other.

What choices face the nominally ascendant managerial party in providing channels for the 'voice' of the employee in an apparently deregulating and decollectivizing world of work and employment? Summarizing a collection of research articles by authors drawn from all the world's continents, Gollan and Markey (2001) argue that attempts by multinational managements to increase workforce efficiency and productivity, in response to globalization pressures, may be linked by with a greater managerial focus on 'the link between employee participation policies and corporate business strategy' (2001: 322). This conclusion chimes with Tayeb's (1998) argument (cited by Halsema and Benschop, 2000: 3) that managers in 'global' organizations must solve a paradox that involves, on the one hand, development of controlling and coordination mechanisms consistent with efficient global operations. On the other hand, they must remain responsive to national interests that may impede the achievement of corporate goals worldwide.

Some researchers argue that 'employee participation and empowerment are progressive management practices which have universal benefits to performance management, as opposed to most other HRM practices whose success is contingent upon the organizational context' (Markey, 2001: 3). Knudsen (2002: 559) adds that, if it occurs 'in an industrial relations climate marked by trust and cooperation between the parties [, employee participation] promotes organizational efficiency'. The transnational research evidence summarized by Gollan and Markey (2001) is that participatory practices are growing in general, as is the variety in the forms of participation. Markey (2001) distinguishes between financial, direct and indirect employee participation, and relates these variants to the 'hard' versus 'soft' HRM dichotomy. While 'hard' HRM attempts to undermine or bypass forms of indirect/representative participation, especially if the participation is based on trade union representatives, 'soft' HRM practices are found in general to be implemented in cooperation with trade unions and/or works councils. Both HRM styles tend to favour direct participation (group work and other forms of delegation of control or influence to employees). There is evidence that works councils, for example, can either complement or be a substitute for trade unions, therefore.

However, Musa (2001) draws attention to the fragility of participation structures in certain circumstances, in particular in 'transitional' economies. He describes an illustrative case study from a Ghanaian state-owned enterprise, where participation arrangements were introduced originally to boost support for a military government, and are now threatened by World Bank and IMF-induced privatization. Another problem area for participation appears to be the situation of small and medium-sized firms (Monat, 2001). The source of the reported difficulty in this sector is the weakly institutionalized participation through trade unions as well as works councils.

Similarities and differences in patterns of management–labour participation over time and across societies may be sought using a conceptual framework, referred to as the 'favourable conjuncture' approach. Poole, Lansbury and Wailes (2001) substitute this way of thinking for universalistic conceptualizations reliant on either utopian expectations (industrial democracy as part of the 'inevitable' evolution of social 'progress') or cyclical patterns (waves of relative market advantage, associated with the acceptance of more or less employee involvement in the determination of capital–labour relations). Poole *et al* (2001) use four sets of variables to operationalize the model: macro-conditions external to the organization, strategic choices of the actors, the power of the actors, and organizational structures and processes at firm level. It may be at this latter point that HR specialists, as interpreters of corporate (global) requirements, matched to 'situated' local practice (Brewster *et al,* 2002; cf Clegg, 1990), influence the nature of contemporary social relations around production (Townley, 1998).

EXPERIMENTATION: THE (NEW) NORM IN EMPLOYMENT RELATIONS PRACTICE?

For Teague (2002), analysing European employment relations systems (but other regional formations may be viewed similarly), the debate has become increasingly complex. Comparative perspectives vary between Streeck's (1997) pessimism and other commentators' optimism (such as Hutton, 2002; Simons and Min, 2002) regarding European social policy. The emphasis is now on ambiguities. For example, European banks might be interpreted as continuing their traditional role as sources of long-term corporate finance, in corporatist configurations (a characteristic of the Rhenish model we referred to earlier in the chapter), or they might be seen as instrumental in driving through flexibility and wage restraint (supporting a more market liberal orientation). Alternatively, some combination between these extremes may be occurring. The effects are rooted in developments in employee relations practices – such as team working, where a convergence may be observed between 'Fordism' (limiting scope for worker intervention in mechanized production) and 'Toyotism' (decision making on detailed quality management delegated to production line work groups).

Teague (2002) argues that it would be erroneous to suggest either that a blanket US-style employment relations 'flexiblization' is occurring, or that the restraint of traditional labour market institutions remains intact in contemporary Europe. To set a context for his discussion, he looks back to the work of American commentator Lloyd Ulman in the 1950s, to suggest that employment relations institutions and rules follow developments in economic markets. Teague (2002) observes that Ulman attributed the rise of the specifically national trade union to the economic conditions created by the emergence of the US national corporation. The changes in economic context may thus be releasing tensions for future employment relations activity. As just one example, the traditional role of German works councils to co-determine organizational factors in a centralized fashion grinds against the new production logic of decentralization to front-line team decision making.

But the exact nature of current developments is as yet unclear. On the one hand, it may be inaccurate to say that European firms are unanimously moving away from governance by co-determination to shareholder value-based management (SHV). But on the other hand, the growth of SHV is not the sole factor behind the fragmentation of employment relations institutions. Instead SHV is acting to accelerate existing pressures that have the effect of constraining discretion in co-determination. Issues in observed experiments in employee relations include an increasing focus among works councils on developing enterprise-level business plans to assure market competitiveness, rather than acting as guardians of employment relations procedural rights. This may be interpreted as a trend away from works councils acting as social institutions to 'mediums of collusion with management'. However, tensions remain between management strategies of 'responsive behaviours', in tune with competitive product market dynamics, and the time-consuming nature of works council decision making.

Not unlike Teague (2002), but this time based on research across seven advanced industrial economies including Australia, Japan and the United States, as well as European countries, Katz and Darbishire (2000) observe a multiplicity of practice not only between employment systems, but also across different sectors and geographies in the same economy. Table 6.3 summarizes the observable patterns, where bundles of employment relations and work system practices may be grouped under the rubric of a unitarily focused 'low-road' managerial strategy, or one that, while still reliant on a managerialist orientation, follows more 'high-road' principles. The two alternative forms fall under a managerial orientation that, while accepting the plurality of interests in the employment system, invests in processes intended to secure a managerial upper hand for core workforce segments (with less critical labour sources outsourced to the periphery). A codetermination approach remains in line with the social market model attributed to Germany, at least prior to the changes that appear to be in train since reunification (Lane, 2000). The table may usefully be used as a cross-reference to help interpret the 'picture postcard' stories presented in this chapter.

While it is difficult yet to judge likely definitive outcomes, Teague's (2002) thesis is that the dynamics of employment relations are being shaped as much by 'social partnership' logic as by SHV. If social partnership is concerned with process building, then, if carefully enacted by managements, it may have a substitution potential for traditional 'trench warfare' in those employment relations systems based on a tradition of 'free collective bargaining'. Equally, it may be replacing the traditional role of the employee representative under co-determination systems (refer back to Figure 6.1). And what of the human capital perspective when asked for a view on contemporary management–workforce strategies? Commentators such as Guest

Table 6.3 Trends in employment relations

	Unitary 'low road'	Unitary 'high road'	Managed 'core' pluralism	Co-determination
Decision-making and procedural emphasis	Managerial discretion – informal procedures	Emphasis on communication and corporate culture	Standardization in procedures	Joint decision making
Managerial stratification	Hierarchy in work relations	Managerially directed work groups	Problem solving delegated to work teams	Semi-autonomous work groups
Basis of reward management	Low (piece rate) wages	Above-average contingent rewards using managerial discretion	Seniority and performance appraisal linked with high pay	Pay for 'know-how' (high relative to external market)
Employment tenure and development	'Hire and fire'	Individualized internal labour market	Tenure stabilization for functional flexibility	Apprenticeships and career management
Stance towards third-party employee representation	Anti-union orientation	Managerial 'compact' in substitution for trade unions	Enterprise-oriented third-party representation	Works council-style union and employee involvement

Source: after Katz and Darbishire (2000).

(1999) argue that the workers' verdict on (normative) HRM is a positive one, where it is being comprehensively applied. The attraction may come from the opportunity for employees to feel more engaged in complex problem solving, rather than holding the status of 'degraded' mass production labour.[6] And the trade unions, with their traditional manufacturing industry and public-service sector concentrations, and non-politically-correct orientations ('male, pale and stale...') may be less attractive to the new generation of workers in atomized employment, in whose social customs union membership may be absent or at least dormant (Visser, 2002). (The ubiquitous call centre workplace, found in both the developed and developing world, may be an important exception.) The practical downside is that comprehensive HRM application is observable in just 14 per cent of workplaces according to UK data (WERS 98: Cully *et al*, 1999: 291), with similar findings reported in the United States.[7]

CONCLUDING REMARKS

Over the last three decades, employers in industrialized market economies have faced new challenges and opportunities. Many industries have had to restructure in the face of increasingly fierce competition. The outcome has been greater managerial emphasis on labour efficiency and cost control. Bamber and Lansbury (1998: 301–2) add that governments saw that industries' struggle for survival precluded adding to their cost burden, and sought to 'lighten the load'. At the same time growing unemployment sapped the strength of workers and their unions. Thus, a tougher employers' stance and the introduction, at least in part, of HRM practices may be observed, albeit with continuing interesting differences between and within countries.

> [However] the link between industrial relations and macroeconomic outcomes is complex [and] we should be wary of prescribing any particular set of institutional arrangements within the spectrum of institutional arrangements and strategic choices available, as the simple key to success.
>
> (Bean, 1994: 242)

Over the course of this chapter we have tried, albeit briefly, to explore recent debates in the international and comparative employment relations and HRM literature, keeping a two-part question specifically in mind to guide our exploration of the literature:

▌ To what extent is it open to the management of multinational enterprises unitarily to choose to regulate the employment relationship in accordance with 'global' managerial priorities?

▌ Is the inevitable consequence of western governed multinational employment relations strategy the pursuit of a strategy of disorganization and disintermediation?

We have adopted this question to connect with the wider 'globalization' problem discussed in Chapter 1, and the concomitant strategy options open to those who seek to lead and manage multinational organizations competing for capital investment to fund growth aspirations. It invites consideration of universalistic prescriptions for employment relations management, weighed against the merits of adopting a more contextual analysis of cross-national and cross-organizational practice, for understanding social relations around production. We acknowledge the perceived imperative for international business managers to maximize the efficiency of their operations, in order to satisfy the disciplinary infrastructure of contemporary market capitalism. HR specialists are presented with the challenge of 'adding value' on terms dictated by the dominant corporate governance mindset. Delving into metaphor, as 'people-pilots' of multinational FDI management 'supertankers', it helps HR practitioners close to 'harbour' to reflect on the macro-level 'oceanic' policy context dictating micro-level practices, influenced by the globalization of financial markets. However, given the potential for micro-level employment relations structures and processes to influence the outcomes consequent on strategic choices exercised by the parties, HRM policy advisers may have scope to channel 'organizational effectiveness' programmes sensitive to the vagaries of multi-domestic 'reefs and shoals' around continental and national shorelines.

The environment is dynamic, and 'the espoused shift from a pluralist/ collectivist to a unitary individualist conception of the employment relationship has been widely recognized' (Keenoy, 1997: 836). But, in our view, the case is not proven that multinationals are universally in the grip of a bipolar idealized employment relations rationale. The evidence reviewed above points to a dyad of 'flexible' or efficiency-focused 'human resourcing' being pursued *in combination* with participative models that may create a climate for voluntary 'employee resourcefulness' to emerge. Academic commentary is indicative of a convergence in corporate-level policy around managerial orientations to the employment relationship led by cost-effectiveness, combined with divergence of practice in its execution in different cross-national units of the enterprise.

In sum, when approaching international employment relations management, at least one analyst is able to conclude that 'unitarist, hard HRM approaches are not an inevitable global future' (Knudsen, 2002). More pluralistic people management, involving cooperation with unions and works councils, as well as individualized and direct forms of employee participation in the enterprise, remains a viable alternative choice. While 'conjunctures' may favour differences in degree, a case seems to exist for (re) envisioning the scope for joint regulation of capital–labour relations, rather than token or enforced acquiescence in a zero-sum game. Multinational managers and their advisors may wish to reflect on these findings in policy-making deliberations.

YOUR TURN

| To what extent may multinational enterprises expect to regulate the employment relationship in accordance with 'global' managerial priorities?

| Does success in regulating employment relations imply pursuit of a strategy of disorganization and disintermediation?

| If employment relations is essentially concerned with 'regulation', then are novel frameworks required to evaluate the debates about a shift from pluralistic (bilateral and trilateral regulation) to unilateral or non-union 'partnership' working?

| A dominant logic, from American multinational sources, has challenged the status quo, in particular advocating the transfer of US-style employment relations practices. How do we place this in its ideological context? And how do we evaluate the consequences, bearing in mind the 'converging divergences' observable in the substance and process of transnational employment relations?

NOTES

1 The line of reasoning was first associated with an expectation that the formalized collective employment relations regulation would be diffused to industrializing countries around the world (Dunlop, 1993 [1958]). Neo-liberal 'disorganized' and 'unitarist' employment relations commentary was a latter-day phenomenon.

2 The research, in collaboration with an Australian colleague, Patricia Todd, is published in Bhopal and Todd (2000).

3 For a description of the dispute-ridden character of Japanese employment relations in the 1940s and 1950s, see the chapter by Yasuo Kuwahara in the international and comparative employment relations reader edited by Bamber, Lansbury and Wailes (2004). Lansbury and Wailes' chapter in the same text may be consulted for coverage of the Australian conciliation and arbitration-based employment relations tradition.

4 'Exit-based' corporate governance (Grahl, 2002) tends to be characterized by active stock markets with widely dispersed capital investment holdings in firms. The term 'active' is intended to imply that shares frequently change hands, as shareowners liquidate their assets at will, and firms that are perceived to perform poorly relative to their sector (in terms of total returns on investment – dividends and growth in share price) are at risk to the ever-present threat of hostile takeover. The major alternative form of corporate governance is 'voice-based' (Grahl, 2002), where investment holdings tend to be more concentrated and owners adopt a more long-term orientation in appraising returns on their capital. Rather than equity finance, long-term bank lending is the preferred source of capital to support corporate growth strategies. Whereas

under the equity-based variant of capitalism, 'owners' are prohibited from actively engaging in strategy formation within their ownership portfolio, sources of long-term debt funding frequently play an active role in supervising their debtor firms' operational management – a 'voice' through a seat on the board.

5 Bhopal (2001) argues that the state can adopt policies that balance a perceived need to create employment relations conditions favourable to capital, while accounting for labour and political considerations reflective of the richness of local context. States can sponsor, so as to incorporate, organized labour in an attempt to create a cooperative and populist movement accepted by workers. Such a strategy may become unstable where concession making is undermined by the contradictions between capital, labour and the state. That is, there are conflicts of interest between (often absentee) investors intent on maximizing capital accumulation potential, workers seeking to raise the level of economic surplus distributed to labour over capital, and the state's interest in employment creation and macroeconomic growth nationally.

If the state is unable to accommodate unions, but lacks the material and/or ideological predisposition to attack organized labour, it may seek instead to control autonomous action by unions through peak-level incorporation – for instance, establishing 'concertation' arrangements wherein national trade union officials bargain over incomes and productivity levels, and set the pattern to be jointly enforced at industry sector and workplace level. The risk here is that disgruntled local workers may mount a challenge to the 'official' labour movement. This was the finding of the Donovan Commission (1968), set up to investigate the disorderly state of the industrial relations environment in Britain in the 1960s. The report found a two-tier system operating, where the national 'rules-based' system, endorsed by national union officials, was ignored by lay representatives at workplace level. What was labelled 'wild cat' industrial action led by 'militant' shop stewards, to secure local management concessions, undermined government macroeconomic 'prices and incomes' policy.

6 Low-skill, poorly rewarded work may now have been exported to nations beyond the triad.

7 See Milkman (1998), cited by Cully *et al* (1999: 291).

REFERENCES

Albert, M (1993) *Capitalism against Capitalism*, Whurr, London

Bamber, G and Lansbury, R (1998) *International and Comparative Employment Relations*, Sage, London

Bamber, G J, Lansbury, R D and Wailes, N (eds) (2004) *International and Comparative Employment Relations*, Sage, London

Bean, R (1994) *Comparative Industrial Relations: An introduction to cross-national perspectives*, 2nd edn, Thompson Business Press, London

Bhopal, M (2001) Malaysian unions in political crisis: assessing the impact of the Asian contagion, Asia *Pacific Business Review*, 8(2), pp 73–100

Bhopal, M and Todd, P (2000) Multinational corporations and trade union development in Malaysia, Asia *Pacific Business Review*, 6(3 & 4), pp 193–213

Blinder, A S (1975) *Toward an Economic Theory of Income Distribution*, MIT Press, Cambridge, Mass

Brewster, C, Harris, H and Sparrow, P (2002) *Globalising HR*, Chartered Institute of Personnel and Development (CIPD), London

Child, J (1972) Organizational structure, environment and performance: the role of strategic choice, *Sociology*, **6**(1), pp 1–22

Clegg, H A (1970) *The System of Industrial Relations in Great Britain*, Blackwell, Oxford

Clegg, S R (1990) *Modern Organizations: Organization studies in the postmodern world*, Sage, London

Crouch, C (2003) The state: economic management and incomes policy, in *Industrial Relations: Theory and practice*, ed P L Edwards, pp 105–23, Blackwell, Oxford

Cully, M, Woodland, S, O'Reilly, A and Dix, G (1999) *Britain at Work: As depicted by the 1998 Workplace Employee Relations Survey*, Routledge, London

Donovan, Lord (1968) *Report of the Royal Commission on Trade Unions and Employers Associations*, HMSO, London

Dunlop, J (1993 [1958]) *Industrial Relations Systems*, Harvard University Press, Boston, Mass

Eaton, J (2000) *Comparative Employment Relations*, Polity Press, Cambridge, UK

Edwards, P K (1986) *Conflict at Work: A materialist analysis*, Blackwell, Oxford

Edwards, P (2003) The employment relationship and the field of industrial relations, in Edwards, P (ed.) *Industrial Relations: Theory and Practice*, 2nd edition, ed P Edwards, pp 1–36, Blackwell, Oxford

Edwards, R (1979) *Contested Terrain: The transformation of industry in the twentieth century*, Heinemann, London

Edwards, T and Ferner, A (2002) The renewed 'American challenge': a review of employment practice in US multinationals, *Industrial Relations Journal*, **33**(2), pp 94–111

Ferner, A and Hyman, R (1998) *Changing Industrial Relations in Europe*, Blackwell, Oxford

Ferreira, A C, Cristovam, M L, Lima, M P and Lino, M S (2004) *Annual Review for Portugal*, European Industrial Relations Observatory [Online] www.eiro.eurofound.eu.int, accessed 29 August 2005

Friedman, M (1982 [1962]) *Capitalism and Freedom*, University of Chicago Press, Chicago

Ghoshal, S and Bartlett, C (1998) *Managing across Borders: The transnational solution*, Random House, London

Gollan, P and Markey, R (2001) Conclusions: models of diversity and interaction, in *Models of Employee Participation in a Changing Global Environment*, ed R Markey, P Gollan, A Hodgkinson, A Chouraqui and U Veersma, pp 322–43, Ashgate, London

Grahl, J (2002) Finance and flexibility: recent evidence, paper presented at Seminar on European Labour Markets, London Metropolitan University, 20 September

Guest, D E (1987) Human resource management and industrial relations, *Journal of Management Studies*, **24**(5), pp 503–21

Guest, D E (1999) Human resource management: the workers' verdict, *Human Resource Management Journal*, **9**(3), pp 5–25

Hall, P A and Soskice, D (2001) *Varieties of Capitalism: The institutional foundations of comparative advantage*, Oxford University Press, Oxford

Halsema, L and Benschop, Y (2000) Vive la difference? Diversity in international HRM, TVA-WESWA Congress, Amsterdam, Sessie 4: Effectiviteit van en diversieit in personeelbeleid

Harvey, D (2003) *The New Imperialism*, Oxford University Press, Oxford

Hofstede, G (1981) *Cultures Consequences: International differences in work-related values*, Sage, Beverly Hills, Calif

Hofstede, G (1991) *Cultures and Organisations: Software of the mind*, McGraw-Hill, Maidenhead

Hutton, W (2002) *The World We're In*, Little, Brown, London

Itagaki, H (1991) Application–adaptation problems in Japanese automobile and electronics plants in the USA, in *Japanese and European Management: Their international adaptability*, ed K Shibagaki, M Trevor and T Abo, pp 118–31, University of Tokyo Press, Tokyo

Kamoche, K, Yaw, D, Horwitz, F and Muuka, G N (eds) (2004) *Managing Human Resources in Africa*, Routledge, London

Katz, H C and Darbishire, O (2000) *Converging Divergences: Worldwide changes in employment systems*, Cornell University Press, Ithaca

Katz, H C and Wheeler, H N (2004) Employment relations in the United States of America, in *International and Comparative Employment Relations*, ed G J Bamber, R D Lansbury and N Wailes, pp 67–90, Sage, London

Keenoy, T (1997) Review article: HRMism and the language of re-presentation, *Journal of Management Studies*, **34**(5), pp 825–41

Knudsen, H (2002) Book review: *Models of Employee Participation in a Changing Global Environment, Work, Employment and Society*, **16**(3), pp 557–72

Kochan, T, Katz, H and McKersie, R B (1986) *The Transformation of American Industrial Relations*, Basic Books, New York

Lane, C (2000) Globalization and the German model of capitalism – erosion or survival? *British Journal of Sociology*, **51**(2), pp 207–34

Lee, C (2000) Challenges facing unions in South Korea, in *Employment Relations in the Asia-Pacific*, ed G J Bamber, F Park, C Lee, P K Ross and K Broadbent, pp 145–158, Business Press/Thomson Learning, London

Legge, K (1995) *Human Resource Management: Rhetorics and realities*, Macmillan, Basingstoke

Markey, R (2001) Introduction: Global patterns of participation, in *Models of Employee Participation in a Changing Global Environment*, ed R Markey, P Gollan, A Hodgkinson, A Chouraqui and U Veersma, pp 3–22, Ashgate, London

Milkman, R (1998) The new American workplace: high road or low road?, in *Workplaces of the Future*, ed P Thompson and C Warhurst, Macmillan, Basingstoke

Monat, J (2001) Small and medium-sized enterprises, employee participation and trade union action, in *Models of Employee Participation in a Changing Global Environment*, ed R Markey, P Gollan, A Hodgkinson, A Chouraqui and U Veersma, pp 284–305, Ashgate, London

Musa, E A (2001) Workers' participation in Ghana: a case study of a state-owned enterprise in transition to privatisation, in *Models of Employee Participation in a Changing Global Environment*, ed R Markey, P Gollan, A Hodgkinson, A Chouraqui and U Veersma, pp 232–46, Ashgate, London

Perlmutter, M V (1969) The tortuous evolution of the multinational company, *Columbia Journal of World Business*, Jan–Feb, pp 9–18

Poole, M (1986) *Industrial Relations: Origins and patterns of national diversity*, Routledge, London

Poole, M, Lansbury, R, and Wailes, N (2001) Participation and industrial democracy revisited: a theoretical perspective, in *Models of Employee Participation in a Changing Global Environment*, ed R Markey, P Gollan, A Hodgkinson, A Chouraqui and U Veersma, pp 23–34, Ashgate, London

Simons, G F and Min, D (2002) *Euro Diversity: A business guide to managing differences,* Butterworth-Heinemann, London

Streeck, W (1997) German capitalism: does it exist? Can it survive? in *Political Economy of Modern Capitalism,* ed C Crouch and W Streeck, pp 33–54, Sage, London

Teague, P (2002) Financial integration and employment relations in the EU, paper presented at Seminar on European Labour Markets, London Metropolitan University, 20 September

Thomas, H (1995) Challenges trade unions must respond to, in *Globalisation and Third World Trade Unions: The challenge of rapid economic change,* ed H Thomas, pp 235–46, Zed Books, London

Townley, B (1994) *Reframing Human Resource Management: Power, ethics and the subject at work,* Sage, London

Townley, B (1998) Beyond good and evil: depth and division in the management of human resources, in *Foucault, Management and Organization Theory,* ed A McKinlay and K Starkey, pp 191–210, Sage, London

Traxler, F, Blaschka, S, and Kittel, B (2001) *National Labour Relations in Internationalised Markets: A comparative study of institutions, change and performance,* Oxford University Press, Oxford

Valenzuela, J (1992) Labour movements and political systems: some variations, in *The Future of Labour Movements,* ed M Regini, Sage, London

Van Ruysseveldt, J, Huiskamp, R and van Hoof, J (1995) *Comparative Industrial and Employment Relations,* Sage, London

Vernon, G (2002) Book review: *National Labour Relations in Internationalised Markets: A comparative study of institutions, change and performance, Human Resource Management Journal,* **12**(4), pp 90–93

Visser, J (2002) Why fewer workers join unions in Europe, *British Journal of Industrial Relations,* **40**(3), pp 403–30

Whitley, R (1992) *European Business Systems: Firms and Markets in their National Contexts,* Sage, London

Whitley, R (1999) *Divergent Capitalisms: The social structuring and change of business systems,* Oxford University Press, Oxford

7

Choices and consequences: SIHRM trends and priorities?

CHAPTER AIMS

This chapter sets out to do the following:

▌ examine priorities presently being highlighted for future-focused attention by the human resource function;

▌ locate these attributed imperatives, conceptually and empirically, using the frameworks that have guided discussion throughout the book;

▌ comment on likely choices and consequences for SIHRM in the future.

GLOBAL CONSENSUS ON TOP HR ISSUES

Over the preceding pages, we have attempted to direct reflexive attention to the range of choices open to multinational managers and their advisors in approaching the people dimension of organization across international boundaries. We have organized our own sense-making using a framework that locates the aspirations for organizational effectiveness (founded on sustained employee performance) within the interacting dynamics of corporate strategy, business systems contexts, and the perspectives of human capital. We have drawn on a set of competing 'strategy ideologies' (transaction cost theory, agency theory, resource-based theory and institutional theory) to bring to the surface the assumptions underpinning the variety of prescriptions on offer to motivate appraisal of choices and consequences.

What are the underlying continuities for attention on the part of the practitioner and student approaching IHRM strategically? It may have lost its 'war for talent' fashion label, but it remains fundamental to success to have the capacity to resource the multinational in such a way that the talents of its people cohere with the organizational plans and processes set in place by the leadership. Creating and sustaining a context in which that people capability will be developed both over the immediate and longer term, informed by a sophisticated understanding of how people learn and apply learning, complements an effective resource foundation. And, in turn, ensuring that performance requirements and their assessment, reward and recognition facilitate the mobilization of knowledge and efforts relevant to the organization's purpose, functionally and geographically, cannot wisely be neglected.

Ultimately, the basis of the indeterminate employment relationship, whether it is approached with the accent on individually or collectively oriented regulation, requires an ability to evaluate the options from a corporate and multi-domestic perspective, where the demands arising from changing governance and consumer pressures are continuous. In facilitating organizational effectiveness, and being evaluated against this criterion, an HR function faces a significant challenge. On the one hand, there is a need for functional specialists to think in corporate organizational terms beyond narrow silos, working with other 'global champions' to identify and act on strategic priorities. Simultaneously, the function requires the capacity to remain in touch with, and to convincingly synthesize intelligence to managerial colleagues regarding, opportunities and threats emerging from shifting business system environments, and the patterns of needs and demands of the talent pool from which the organization seeks its human resource capability. In other words, HR must find ways of resolving the 'smart basics' at a multiplicity of micro-levels while bringing credible influence to bear on corporate-wide strategic choice making.

Many of these underlying continuities feature implicitly if not explicitly in practitioner surveys of 'global priorities', while the more discerning reader attends to what might be downplayed as 'national and regional variations' – offering important detail beneath the headlines on the surface of the currently fashionable. For example, just three issues – change management, leadership development and measuring HR effectiveness – were highlighted repeatedly as 'the greatest challenges facing the function', in a survey of some 200 HR specialists in companies located in more than 35 countries in Africa, the Asia Pacific, Europe, North America and South America.[1] Interviewed for his reaction, the current president of the World Federation of Personnel Management Associations, Geoff Armstrong, was unsurprised by the findings. 'Globalization is having a major impact on how quickly common practices are adopted in people management', he said (Griffiths, 2005: 10). Armstrong's reported attribution to the findings of a 'global recognition' that good HR practices are at the centre of 'good business', while clichéd, may be more to the point than the labels currently affixed to elements.

But the message from human resource specialists who have been questioned in situ around the world is not all in the direction of global convergence. Reports of the issues that affect the prospects for organizations to embrace 'good HR practices' vary across national and regional settings, and bring out the challenges faced by multinational managements who wish to create the conditions in which 'global mindsets' will be nurtured, networking organizational structures and know-how for a purposeful end:

- Africa: changing an authoritarian culture towards personal responsibility and reducing bureaucracy;

- Asia Pacific: developing supervisors from technical experts to people managers;

- Europe: young workers leaving Eastern Europe for jobs in other European countries;

- North America: leadership development to combat early retirement and an ageing workforce;

- South America: availability of skilled local labour; outsourcing.

As often happens, the 'global headlines' contain only part of the real story. Without discounting the significance of global 'hot topics', a holistic approach is needed to avoid losing sight of the underlying subtleties that may leave corporate managements disappointed when their chosen strategies turn out to be afforded lower priority than they anticipated, when delegated to management in subsidiary operations across different settings. Alternatively they might perhaps be interpreted in unanticipated ways – ways that are even perverse, when viewed from the home country headquarters.

In what follows, we briefly interrogate the three 'consensus' issues, taking each in turn – bearing in mind that these labels may themselves be conceptually limiting. The wording of questions to survey respondents around the world may be, more than a little, a reflection of a westernized expression of perceived global issues. They may limit the narrative open to respondents, inhibiting their facility to express concerns in terms that are contingent on local and regional ways of expressing them in their potentially diverse richness. (This is a perennial problem when administering closed-form or forced-choice survey questions.) We also explore how the issues may be unpacked, to permit them to be thought about from a variety of angles, informed by the various theoretical constructs and systems contexts signalled throughout the book, although we do so sparingly, given considerations of space in this final chapter. We also use some short picture postcard stories to illuminate what lies behind the regional variation signalled in the list above.

We open the way to more questions than answers at this future-glancing point in our narrative, with some specific issues for you to reflect on when we invite you to take your turn and set your priorities, following the concluding remarks. It is our intention to leave you with some material to stimulate focused reflection, when considering choices open to multinational managements in deciding how to act on the encouragement in the literature to build transnational organizations and global mindsets among those employed to populate them.

CHANGE MANAGEMENT

To return to the top of the list of perceived 'consensus imperatives', it is no surprise that 'management of change' remains firmly at the top of the agenda of those involved in managing organizations in the 'restless' world, where 'only the paranoid survive' according to former Intel Corporation chairman, Andy Grove (Grove, 1997). The change imperative is not new. Hendry (1995) looks back to the pattern of continuous change in organizations over the 1980s and early 1990s, and then draws attention to the implications for the HR function (which have, it appears, continued to dominate 'anxiety listings' over the succeeding decade). These changes were brought on by ongoing changes in technology – and accompanying rationalization among core production activities – as well as continuing changes in markets for goods and services.

These 'strategic shifts' (Hendry 1995: 18) have levered the focus of HR specialists from exclusively servicing stable day-to-day organizations – although as Ulrich (1997) argues, the 'HR champion' will still have to ensure processes are in place for quality and efficient administration of, for example, job evaluation, employee hiring and firing, training and development, and the host of related procedures, even if these are largely devolved for day-to-day oversight by 'line' functions. More strategically, HR specialists' role is directed towards managing change and replacing stable systems with those to ensure flexibility in production to meet consumer demands while restraining operational costs (Hendry, 1995).

'Improving productivity has been, and is likely to remain, a constant preoccupation' (Hendry 1995: 29). Change is thus presented as a process open to purposeful management, where HR value added may come from designing and advising on ways to limit the hurdles to achieving the change goals as planned. This is not only fundamental change, but also the recurring adjustment of work system cultures (Stanford, 2005), and the culture applicable to the organization as a whole. (This is further complicated in the multinational organization setting when account is taken of 'home–host culture' factors across geographies.)

'Flexibility' here means individualizing work systems (Hendry, 1995): delegating management to the point of production and/or customer interface, having enshrined a climate of trust to support such initiatives, where the entire workforce at all levels and in all locations shares a sense of commitment to the corporate aims and objectives set by management. This imperative clearly interfaces with the leadership issue also singled out globally for priority attention. The qualifier in the above definition of change – focusing on productivity issues, where the managerial aim is to do more with the same, generally fewer, people working more flexibly and effectively – adds a particularly problematic twist to the change imperative. People are not only likely to experience disturbance to their sense of equilibrium, they are also threatened actually or vicariously with the potential loss of livelihood.

Thus, the human consequences of change may invite careful reflection by those who aspire to set and guide multinational managements' approach to human resource strategy. Although our socialization into a community may equip us to accommodate change as a natural part of human life, it becomes an issue of concern when change is unexpected, imposed and fast-paced – whether it stems from acts of nature, or from a hierarchy of investors and management interests, organizing their interests as part of the restless flight of capital. How people – managers and other employees alike – think about change and institute coping mechanisms to deal with it and make it manageable (and thus reduce stress), deserves special attention on the part of those whose choices to introduce and 'manage' change drive the process along, anticipating the various consequences that may flow from the action.

LEADERSHIP DEVELOPMENT

Leadership development is another hardy perennial in management circles, and the strategically inclined HR specialist has an interest in demonstrating concern for it and facilitating holistically focused insights into it. Bearing in mind the regional emphasis on leadership development linked with demographics concerns, an emphasis on 'followers' as much as 'leaders' is noteworthy in recent commentary coming out of the United States. Howell and Shamir (2005) recommend increased attention to the traits that characterize relations between 'charismatic' leaders and their followers. Conviction-based, 'strong' leadership has been widely lauded in academic and popular literature alike alongside the US economic challenge to other economies to follow in the wake of 'liberalizing' initiatives in both economic and political spheres at the turn of the 20th and 21st centuries. Given perceived resource pressures, one approach open to organizational choice takers may be to transform 'followers' into leaders themselves, reflecting the crucial roles to be played at the multiplicity of nodes linking 'network society' (Castells, 1996).

Under the 'transnational' model, organizational effectiveness is dependent on the transfer of knowledge in circumstances where cultural differences complicate the multi-faceted direction, enhancement and redirection of knowledge across borders (Javidan *et al*, 2005). Moreover, commentators in the United States, in particular, may be feeling chastened by the still-recent cases of leadership notoriety, where myopic preoccupation with an overly simplistic (self-serving?) view of business organization may bring disastrous results affecting a wider community of interests. Conger (2004, in Von Glinow and Nord, 2005) cites Enron and WorldCom in challenging the notion of 'the unquestionable CEO' as leader. Checks and balances are crucial: Von Glinow and Nord (2005) argue for redefining leadership accountability, holding corporate boards of directors accountable for failure to take a strong leadership role in ensuring that the necessary governance framework exists to avoid over-reliance on the leader (charismatic or otherwise) at the pinnacle of the enterprise.

In Chapter 5 we reported evidence suggesting that reward management had become the focus of strategic initiatives at the global level across a wide sample of multinationals. And yet, when asked for their views on pressing concerns in a more general context, reward is not at the top of the list in the current survey of HR professionals around the world, as reported by Griffiths (2005). More holistic reflection, looking deeper than surface responses to pre-formed lists of questions, tells us that there are key 'reward' questions arising from the leadership development priority, however. The Motorola reward specialist we quoted in Chapter 5 as saying he wanted reward to become a non-issue was genuine, on the one hand, but expressing a touch of irony on the other. Reward, and its actual and perceived relationship to effort and the justice with which rewards are distributed, is never truly off the agenda, as public consciousness influences perceptions about likely resources for the organization, and the aspirations of those who set out to collectively organize labour interest representation. The apparent excesses of executive compensation – with the veritable industry that has arisen to regulate it and secure compliance – involve significant amounts of time where HR specialists, with their company secretary/legal counterparts, must draft ever lengthier remuneration committee reports for corporate annual reports and accounts.

Reward in its various forms is also a likely driver for the movement of young workers away from central and eastern Europe, leading to local anxieties about a drain on human capital to support economic transformation projects and a workforce age imbalance. In our experience, there are differences between students who come to study business from countries to the east and west of Europe (such as the People's Republic of China and Latin America, where the regional picture stresses skilled labour shortage and outsourcing issues) and those from eastern European countries such as Bulgaria, Poland and Romania. In the former case, once suitably credentialed, individuals are set on returning to pursue their careers in the home economy. In the latter cases, there is a great motivation to remain in western Europe to secure professional employment, on terms which are unlikely to be matched should they repatriate to their countries of origin.

Before moving on to the third consensus issue – measuring HR functional effectiveness – let us pause to consider briefly how choice makers may interpret these first two 'global priorities', given the inter-linkages we have suggested, and using the theoretical alternatives we have discussed throughout the book.

Transactional approaches to leadership and management of people are premised on continual change: new transactions are negotiated between managers and those engaged to work under their direction. The contract *as specified* is the key, and much attention is required to ensure its fitness for purpose. Where the labour force is divided into core and periphery groups, transactional relations for the non-core workers may facilitate change – on the basis that the relationship is designed (nominally voluntarily between equal parties) to facilitate mutual exchange on a limited commitment basis. For wider groups of workers in business systems (such as the United States) where the employment relationship norm is 'at will', then managers and employees may share a common view that this is the 'deal' and will position themselves accordingly. However, as critics of transaction cost theory have indicated, the transaction costs may rise significantly if the core relationships that the enterprise needs to remain viable are inefficient or provisional, and subject to unexpected breakdown. The costs of hiring and socializing replacements and training them to perform – with tacit knowledge of how things are done inside the organization – may be severe.

For this reason the resource-based view has come to prominence in certain circles, at least for application to core competence groups, blending people and other firm resources, whose ways of working together (evolved over time) and shared experience make them rare, valuable, inimitable and non-substitutable. Hence the focus must surely remain on the roles of resourcing, training and development within change management, regardless of whether change is adaptive or transformational, innovative or involving the reworking of current initiatives. The threat of change to competitive advantage is real. Desired ends must be achieved without harming the very fabric that secures viability. Ensuring the preservation of the organization as 'a going concern' is something board directors are expected to signify – setting an underlying focal point for understanding the essence of leadership.

Human capital perspectives require consideration in employment systems where consensus building is deemed the norm, as well as where workers expect authoritarian management to tell them what to do, with little onus on the individual to manage the process of work organization. In situations where people are reaching out for change – in transforming economies where people wish to break free of perceived bonds of the past – people may self-select to work for organizations they may perceive as more dynamic.

To illustrate this issue with a regional focus, we can give an example of cultural change among multinational organizations operating in Africa in the report we received from a correspondent in Nigeria, where large oil exploration businesses are apparently making moves to replace country heads and their senior teams, traditionally resourced from the expatriate community, with locals. Organization managements may recognize the importance of institution building with a local face if global–local dilemmas are effectively to be addressed – characterizing the hybrid forms of HRM strategy observed in Anakwe's (2002) investigation.

An 'enfolding' (Japanese-inspired?) leadership approach towards institutional frameworks (and their attendant costs) may be adopted, where managements seek to create the conditions in which people's sense of common experience will lead them to the judgement that behavioural factors may be sufficiently similar between situations – even in situations of change – that there is no advantage in operating as free riders. Rather they will agree to cooperate for mutual gain – including gain for management in securing their organizational objectives.

Considerations of space constrain further discussion of the change management and leadership imperatives. Entire libraries have been written on these subjects, and we cannot begin to synthesize or evaluate all the issues here. That is not our intention. While international surveys may record anxiety and interest among the HR community surrounding change management and the leadership development imperative – and by implication reward issues – questions immediately arise once more than a superficial glance is directed towards the topic. So we want to include in this final chapter some questions that we hope will motivate careful reflection on what the underlying issues really are, from a variety of perspectives. (They are given at the end of this chapter.) Let us now turn to the third 'global imperative' listed above.

MEASURING HR EFFECTIVENESS

Measuring their own self-worth has become another regular concern among members of the 'Cinderella function'. Measurement sounds suitably businesslike – 'fact-based' approaches appealing to production and finance-oriented senior management, getting management attention for what may be derided as 'soft' HR issues. Asia-Pacific respondents had a regional variation to the global 'hot topics' concerned with getting supervisors to shift from being technical experts to 'people managers'. This might apply to the HR function itself. To illustrate the point, we know of two HR practitioners whose experiences working in the investment banking and financial services sector in Hong Kong, almost a decade apart, suggest that much remains to be done to educate management 'up and down the line' in this regard. Our first correspondent told us about an encounter she had recently had that had left her feeling demoralized.

> Seeing HR in practice in Hong Kong and the comments I get about the role of HR has given rise to many doubts. In a conversation with a senior executive we challenged each other to find a company in HK that practises strategic HRM. We arrived at the conclusion that there is none. Here people are a resource to be exploited and dispensed with in as efficient a manner as possible. I am not sure I want to do that.

She expressed doubts about whether being in HR is the place to change things. The account is echoed exactly by another correspondent, whose role in HR almost 10 years earlier was a hire and fire one rather than one requiring a holist approach to people management. Our correspondent moved from a corporate job in Hong Kong to a recruitment agency there on the grounds that, if the job was delimited to 'hire and fire', she might as well go at least where the pay was better!

We empathize with both correspondents – but only to the extent that to change HR's role a more transformational outlook and greater vigour in harnessing top management attention are needed. A self-imposed navel-gazing orientation raises the danger of contradicting the imperative of nimbleness by tying the function down to measures in a world where these may quickly become outdated. And it raises questions about understanding the issues and opportunities for more qualitatively focused interventions, where the measure of success can only be assessed in terms of a committed workforce (working at top performance over time), low unplanned employee turnover/loss of core talent, contented loyal customers, and value-added organizational outcomes. So a more confident function may be better directed to setting standards against which those ultimately managing the international human resource need to demonstrate achievement. The corporate HR function, ably supported by a network of HR specialists in line units, should 'sign off' on behalf of top management only when the standards have been satisfactorily attained.

CONCLUDING REMARKS

We began our review of SIHRM, drawing on a range of theoretical and empirical observations, by focusing on the simple question, what does our current state of knowledge imply for future choices and consequences in the identification, development and management of people in multinational organizations? It is nearly 10 years since Ulrich (1997) popularized the view that if they are to become regarded as 'champions' for organizational effectiveness, HR specialists need to retain a balance between a 'strategic' focus on the future and attention to day-to-day operations, not forgetting the balance to be struck between processes (which become ever more sophisticated) and people (who need to be convinced that their interests are not being neglected). Management of strategic HRM complements transformation and change management. (There is nothing new here, then.) And operationally, 'firm infrastructure' management complements management of 'employee contribution'.

You can dress it up in all sorts of ways, but getting and keeping people, and motivating them to do 'productive' work to a corporate purpose, remain managements' trinity of employment priorities. Choices and consequences flow from how each aspect is defined, and the policies and practices that are designed and implemented to achieve managerial intentions, however.

These may change depending on the ideas that managements choose to embrace – implicitly if not explicitly – and the changing context (converging and diverging) and how it is interpreted and acted on. Consequences flow from whether the 'trinity' problem is theorized in terms of transaction costs, agency problems, resource-based mobilization, institutionally embedded enablers and inhibitors of cooperation, or some combination of these approaches.

Similarly, account needs to be taken of whether local or global factors are privileged: whether choices should be made to vary across the region, sector, or on some other intra-spatial or temporal basis. It is also necessary to be sensitive to learning from the developing world, rather than to assume inevitable continuities with the developed/mature economies. And of course, in locating SIHRM in the context of potentially competing economic and social interest streams, choices are necessary as to whether shareholder, customer, state, employee or the wider environment/community interests are placed to the fore, or balanced across interdependent stakeholders.

We conclude by citing the mantra attributed to students of the celebrated Chicago school of social science, when dealing with all difficult conceptual questions: 'it all depends how you define your terms' (Becker, 1998).

YOUR TURN... YOUR PRIORITIES

Whether you are a practitioner or student (or combine these roles), reflection on the issues identified as forming a contemporary global HR consensus may help you in moving beyond the headlines to grasp subtleties, more holistically theorized, which are applicable to the details encountered by multinational managements in 'real world' situations. It may also assist you in determining where your own priorities lie, and the consequences likely to flow from making a choice.

Managing change

▌ Under what circumstances might adaptive change override transformational aims? And when might innovation – doing something completely different – be more appropriate than simply a form of repackaging (being more efficient or appearing to give the appearance of being altered – such as relabelling a product while being sensitive to sustaining continuities around the 'brand', as a valuable resource)?

▌ How can a transformational change programme achieve desired ends without harming the institutional fabric for sustainable organizational effectiveness? Is this the Japanese model of core lifetime workers and a periphery of non-key labour that enables nimbleness (although the ability for functional flexibility is a part of the nimbleness internally among the core too)?

▌ Does the perception of fundamental change undermine resource-based trusting relations, where management time does not have to be spent transacting the specifics of tasks (tacit knowledge being used by self-managed groups)? Does it instead create wary agency relations? Is it possible for change initiatives to be devised in such a way that time does not appear overly short, and that those concerned are empowered to find the change solution for themselves?

▌ How can multinational managements harness energies in one location, actively seeking out change in an attempt to break free of past bonds, while (in integrated production chains across geographies) not demotivating those whose experience of perpetual managerial and organization change has instilled a more cynical view?

Leadership development and reward

▌ What is leadership, and what sort is effective in particular circumstances?

▌ What do leaders want? How do they measure and sense their recognition?

▌ Does leadership differ across business systems? Or are cosmopolitans, sought with global mindsets to lead multinationals, socialized to seek the same recognition for their contribution?

▌ How far has the agency-based preoccupation with reward management addressed or created problems in managing the effort–reward bargain? Organized labour groups may attempt to rebalance perceived shifts in the distribution of value created, away from labour and to capital. How do HR strategies measure up here?

Measuring HR effectiveness

▌ Is it possible to characterize a more self-confident HR function as not unlike that of management accountancy: paving the way for external audit, provided in human capital terms by the human capital reporting requirements, by ILO conventions, compliance with regional supranational directives and corporate governance reporting?

█ Under this transformed *modus operandi*, might corporate HR's effectiveness be subject to evaluation by the chief executive and board of directors (and only that constituency)?

█ In return, might HR rightly demand a statement of what that effectiveness is expected to look like – 'hard-wired' to the assessment and accompanied by unequivocal top management support to drive the process down the line?

█ Does this pave the way for HR to assume a place as a main board function (whether or not represented there by a specialist), acting as an agency of the corporate governing body of executives with a warrant that is not open to spurious challenge at other levels within the multinational organizational network?

NOTE

1   The survey, administered by consultancy firm PricewaterhouseCoopers, was commissioned by the World Federation of Personnel Management Associations (WFPMA) to monitor problems facing the HR function today, three years ago and in three years' time. The full survey was published in October 2005: see www.wfpma.com

REFERENCES

Anakwe, O P (2002) Human resource management practices in Nigeria: challenges and insights, *International Journal of Human Resource Management*, 13(7), pp 1042–59

Becker, H S (1998) *Tricks of the Trade: How to think about your research while you're doing it*, University of Chicago Press, Chicago

Castells, M (1996) *The Rise of the Network Society*, Blackwell, Oxford

Griffiths, J (2005) Global consensus on top HR issues, *People Management*, 11 August, p 10

Grove, A S (1997) *Only the Paranoid Survive: How to identify and exploit the crisis points that challenge every business*, HarperCollins, London

Hendry, C (1995) Human Resource Management: A strategic approach to employment, Butterworth-Heinemann, London

Howell, J M and Shamir, B (2005) The role of followers in the charismatic leadership process: relationships and their consequences, *Academy of Management Review*, **30**(1), pp 96–112

Javidan, M, Stahl, G K, Brodbeck, F and Wilderom, C P M (2005) Cross-border transfer of knowledge: cultural lessons from Project GLOBE, *Academy of Management Executive*, **19**(2), pp 59–76

Stanford, N (2005) *Organization Design: The collaborative approach*, Elsevier Butterworth-Heinemann, Oxford

Ulrich, D (1997) *Human Resource Champions: The next agenda for adding value and delivering results*, Harvard Business School Press, Boston, Mass

Von Glinow, M A and Nord, W R (2005) Review: *The CCL Guide to Leadership in Action: how managers and organizations can improve the practice of leadership*, *Academy of Management Review*, **30**(2), pp 440–42

Index

NB: page numbers in *italic* indicate figures or tables

Adler, N   99, 105
agency theory   13–14, 15
Albert, M   204, 230
Altman, Y   99, 100, 105, 125–26, 127, 135
    model   125–26, 127
America   *see* United States of America
Anakwe, O P   12, 21, 167, 179, 236, 242,
    247
Argyris, C   121, 135
Armstrong, G   237
Asia Pacific Journal of Human Resources   173
assignees, international   100–02, 185–95
        see also repatriation
    and language training   71, 112–14
assignees, localized   80, 102–03, 159
Australia   27, 59, 116, 174, 175, 216–18, 225
    and investment in Malaysia   216–18
    Department of Foreign Affairs and
        Trade   28, 35
    Human Resource Institute Annual
        Convention   27
    low context culture   61

Bamber, G   204, 227, 229, 230
Barney, J   13, 14, 21, 154, 179
Barsoux, J   4, 22
Bartlett, C A   69, 77, 123, 134, 135, 145, 148,
    149, 150, 153, 154, 180, 202, 208, 231
Bauman, Z   25, 31, 44
Bean, R   204, 215, 227, 230

Beaty, E   110, 135
Becker, H S   245, 247
Benschop, Y   223, 231
Bhopal, M   11, 21, 221, 229, 230
Blaschka, S   204, 233
Blinder, A S   204, 230
Bloom, M   12, 22, 138, 143, 144, 145, 146,
    154, 168, 171, 172, 176, 179
Boxall, P   5, 22
Boydell, T   108, 122, 135
Bradley, P   143, 144, 146, 179
Brewster, C   4, 12, 22, 26, 45, 222,
    224, 231
Brown, M 174, 180
Budhwar, P S   26, 46

Canada   116, 174, 175
capitalism, varieties of   16
career counselling   101
career development   125–28, 153
careers, international
        see international development
Castells, M   36, 45, 240, 247
change management   238–39
chapter outlines   18–21
Cheng, J L   26, 45
Child, J   41, 45, 212, 231
children and education   113, 192
China   91, 167, 173, 241
    and culture measurement   61

choices and consequences (in)
see international employee
compensation; international
employment relations; resourcing
global business operations;
SIHRM: choices and consequence(s)
and SIHRM trends and
priorities
Clegg, H A 203, 224, 231
communication: national
differences 61–62
compensation and benefits policies 144
compensation management
approaches 146
compensation/reward systems 138–39
competencies, international 92–95
competencies and capabilities 95–96
Cooper, C 68, 77
Cooper, D 26, 45
corporate governance 19, 38, 202
models/attitudes 16, 58
Coyle, W 101, 105
cross-cultural
approach to performance 62–63
differences 82
management 54–55, 209
cross-cultural awareness training 114–20
coping strategies 116
Cully, M 226, 230, 231
cultural baggage 54
cultural differences 82, 98
in language 114
research study: China and Taiwan
117–20
and reward management 143–45
culture, influence of 53–64
cross-cultural management 54–55
in national, industry and corporate
contexts 143–45
national culture: displays and
events 53–54
on business operations 80
culture and welfare 51–73
see also culture, influence of and
definition(s)
communication 61
cross-cultural approach to
performance 62–63
culture measurement (Hofstede)
see main entry
culture measurement in different
countries 60–61

culture measurement (Trompenaars
and Hampden Turner)
see main entry
culture shock 64–66
see also main entry
differing cultures: conceptions and
assumptions 58–59
economic and cultural profiles 59–60
references 77
repatriation/reverse culture shock
72–73 see also repatriation and
reverse culture shock
stress: international assignments
66–72 see also international
assignments and stress
culture measurement (Hofstede)
55–56, 57–58, 60–61
individualism/collectivism 56, 61
long-term/short-term orientation 56
masculinity/femininity 56, 61
power distance 56, 60
uncertainty avoidance 56, 60
culture measurement (Trompenaars and
Hampden Turner) 56–57
environment domain 57
inner-directed/outer-directed 57
relationships and rules domain 56
achievement/ascription 56
individualism/communitarianism 56
neutral/affective 56
specific/diffuse 56
universalism/particularism 56
time domain 57
past and present/future 57
sequential/synchronic 57
culture shock 64–66
ambiguity 64
cross-cultural communication skills 64
environmental readjustment: U-curve
theory 65
expatriate stressors 64–65
reverse 121
timetable of cycle 65–66, 121
culture shock training 120–22
and incidental learning theory 121
Cultures Consequences 55

Dall'Alba, G 110, 135
Darbishire, O 43, 45, 225, 226, 232
debriefing: operational, personal and
critical incident 72–73

definition(s) of
  career 125
  change 239
  choice 7–8
  consequence 8
  critical incident debriefing 73
  culture 55, 143
  developed world 80
  development 122
  employee reward/compensation 140
  globalization 27, 28–29, 35, 41
  life events 95
  localization 102–03, 159
  multinational employees 147
  operational debriefing 72–73
  personal debriefing 73
  strategy 12
  stress 66, 68
de Geus, A 8, 22
De Haan 40
DeNisi, A S 139, 181
Dowling, P J 4, 22, 111, 114–15, 121, 135, 162, 180, 185
Drucker, J 141, 142, 180
Dunbar, E 115 , 135
Dunlop, J 203, 214, 229, 231

Earnshaw, J 68, 77
Eaton, J 206, 231
Eby, L 126, 135
Economic Co-operation and Development, Organisation for (OECD) 7, 8, 29, 41, 46, 220
Edelsten, M 138, 144, 180
Edwards, P K 6, 12, 22, 36, 45, 212, 217, 231
Edwards, R 220, 231
Edwards, T 206, 208, 209, 211, 231
employee(s) 104–05 see also repatriation and reward management
  assistance programmes 72
  compensation see international employee compensation
  local national 132–33, 166–70
  multinational 147
  participation and empowerment 223
  resourcing 19
  welfare 19
Employment Conditions Abroad 190, 191
employment relations, regulating 203–04
  two-system comparison indicators 205

employment relations, trends in 226
employment relations and communications 142
employment relations: managerial strategies 206–08, 208, 209–11
  culturalist 209
  German system 206–08
  influences framework 210–11
    country of origin effect 210
    dominant effect 210
    host country effect 211
    integration effect 210
  political view 209
  rational view 208
employment relations: research in Malaysia 216–19
  capital interests and dispositional advantage 217
employment relations systems: extra-managerial roles 211–16
  dependency theory 213
  role and impact of state on 211–12
  state and trade union interactions 213, 214–16
  strategic choices 212–14
equal opportunities and legislative requirements 98
Ernst & Young/CBI 103, 105, 160, 180
ethnocentric global development stage 123
ethnocentrism 64, 88–89, 145
European Industrial Training Journal 44
European Social Contract 214
European social policy 224
Evans, P 4, 22
ex-host-country nationals 139
expatriate see also culture shock and repatriation
  compensation 151–52
  effort-reward bargaining 159
  ghettos 152–53
  myopia 146
  pay and benefits packages 139–40
  remuneration systems 163, 163–64, 164
  staff 145, 166
  women 99–100
experiential learning theory 123

Ferner, A 206, 208, 209, 211, 220, 231
Ferreira, A C 215, 231
Florkowski, G W 26, 46
Floyd, D 28–29, 45

foreign direct investment/investors
    (FDI)   10, 52, 216–19
France   35, 178
    and culture measurement   60, 61
Franklin, T   16, 22
Friedman, M   68, 77, 211, 231
Fry, J   152

Germany   35, 102, 224, 225
    and culture measurement   60
    legislation   207
Ghoshal, S   69, 77, 123, 124, 135, 145, 148,
    149, 150, 153, 154, 180, 202, 208, 231
Giddens, A   25, 27, 45
global business operations *see* resourcing
    global business operations
global growth models   123–25
global reward strategies   146
global workforce   169
globalization and international HRM
    orientations   19, 25–47
    criticism   28
    disciplinary definitions and
        regionalization tendency   28–29
    globalization: conceptual and
        operational definitions   41
    globalization: 'Jones corporation'
        example   36–39 *see also main entry*
    globalization and HRM trends   42–43
    governance and SIHRM
        implications   32–35, *35*
        corporate regulation and IHRM   32
        exit-based governance   34
        polycentric adaptation   33
        voice-based governance   34
    impact of globalization on
        organizations   41
    implications for employment and
        IHRM   42
    inexorable or 'bargained' globalization
        35–36
        generic labour   36
        knowledge management   36
        scientific management   36
        variable pay systems   36
    notes   44
    optimism   27
    references   44–47
    research findings: employment system
        flexibility   40–41
        flexibilization of labour markets   40

innovative and non-innovative
    firms   40
    wage restraint   40
theorizing globalization and corporate
    consquences   29–30, *30*, 31–32
    first phase (1970s)   30
    second phase (1980s)   30–31
    third phase (1990s–)   31–32
globalization: 'Jones corporation'
    example   36–39
    international knowledge/skills
        transfer – organization and HRM
        calibration   37–39
    questions for analysis   39
Globalization: The people dimension   x, xi
Gollan, P   222, 223, 231
Goodernham, P N   82, 105
Grahl, J   29–30, *30*, 34, *35*, 35, 41, 45, 229,
    231
Granell, E   27, 33, 39, 45
greenfield startups   81, 88
Griffiths, J   237, 240, 247
Grove, A S   238, 247
Guest, D E   42, 45, 74, 77, 202,
    225–26, 231
Guth, S   26, 45

Hall, E T   61, 77
Hall, M R   61, 77
Hall, P A   19, 22, 204, 231
Halsema, L   223, 231
Hamel, G   108, 135, 152, 180
Hammonds, K H   12, 22
Hampden-Turner, C   55, 56, 62, 77, 98,
    106, 114, 136
Harris, H   4, 22, 26, 45, 100, 105,
    222, 231
Harvey, D   31, 32, 36, 45, 206, 231
Harzing, A   4, 22
Heenan, D A   88, 105
Heery, E   170–71, 174, 180
Heise, A   32, 46
Hendry, C   16, 22, 143, 148, *149*, 152, 153,
    162, 179, 180, 238, 239, 247
Heywood, J S   174, 180
Hobsbawm, E   32, 45
Hofer, C W   84, 105
Hofstede, G   55–56, 57–58, 60, 77, 98, 102,
    105, 110, 135, 143, 180, 209, 231
    dimensions of culture   56, 60
Holmes, T H   67, 77

Howell, J M   240, 247
Hughes, C W   29, 45
Huiscamp, R   221, 233
Hull, R   36, 45
human resource management (HRM)
    hard   222–23, 228
    practices   237
    soft   222–23
Hutton, W   31–32, 35, 224, 232
Hyman, R   220, 231

Incomes Data Servces (IDS)   32, 45
India   81, 91, 98
Informing and Consulting Employees: EC
    Directive (2002)   207
institutional theory   14
international assignee remuneration
        approaches   185–95
    allowances and benefits *see* international
        assignees: allowances and
        benefits
    better deal for assignees   188
    commuter/flex-pat   189
    global assignee systems   188–89
    home-based   185–86
    host-based   186–88
    individual negotiation/ad hoc   188
    pension issues   189
    performance management issues   189
    taxation   187
international assignees: allowances and
        benefits   190–95
    car allowances   192–93
    cost of living allowance (COLA)   191
    dual careers   194–95
    education allowances   192
    hardship/location allowance   190–91
    home leave allowances   193
    housing allowances   191–92
    mobility premium/foreign service
        premium   190
    pre-assignment trips   194
    preparation and training
        assistance   194
    relocation and freight expenses   194
    rest and relaxation trips   194
    retirement benefits   195
    sickness and medical issues   193
    social security   195
    tax/tax assistance   194
    vacation allowances   193

international assignment policies   156–58,
        160–61
    development principles   156–57
    documentation and detail   157–58
international assignments and stress   66–72
    behavioural symptoms   67
    crisis/emergency planning   70
    environment and security   69–70
    in working environment   68
    language training as coping
        mechanism   71
    reactions to   66–67
    repatriation   71–72 *see also* repatriation
        and reverse culture shock
    social readjustment rating scale   67–68
    stressors   68–69, 70–72
international competencies   92–95
international contracts/the global
        employment company (GEC)   196–99
    administration   199
    employee population   197
    medical cover and life assurance   198
    pension implications   197
    performance management   198
    potential barriers   199
    relationship of GEC with the home
        firm   196–97
    standardization of contracts   196
    statutory rights   197
    tax and social security   198
international development   122–31
    capabilities development via
        development centres   128–30
    careers/career models   125–28
    experiential learning theory   123
    global growth models   123–25
    opportunity, action learning and virtual
        HRD networks   131
    project team capabilities   130–31
    talent and executives   125
international employee
        compensation   137–99 *see also*
        technical appendices
    conclusion   178
    defining multinational employees   147
    intra-region mobility/diversity: third-
        country national rewards
        165–66
    local national employees: reward/
        compensation strategies
        166–70 *see also main entry*

national, industry and corporate
        contexts 143–45 *see also* cultural
        differences
newly internationalizing units,
        designing rewards for 176–78
normative commentary: theory and
        practice 170–73
    new pay systems 170–71
    references 179–81
reward management, substance and
        process in *see* reward
        management
reward strategies: internationally
        mobile executives 155–64
    see also main entry
reward systems 145–47
reward systems, international 145–47
strategic choices 147–48, *149*, 150–55
    centralized hubs 153–54
    classic multinationals/family
        ownerships 150, 151
    coordinated federation
        150–52
    expatriate ghettos 152–53
    multinationals 148, *149*, 150
transnational practices 173–76
    see also reward practices,
        transnational
international employment relations 201–33
    conclusion 227–28
    employment relations: research in
        Malaysia 216–19 *see also main
        entry*
    employment relations systems: extra-
        managerial roles 211–16
        see also main entry
    experimentation 224–26
    hard and soft HRM: human resources
        and resourceful humans 222–24
    managerial strategies 206–22 *see also*
        employment relations: managerial
        strategies
    notes 229–30
    references 230–33
    regulating 203–04, *205*
    regulatory norms under pressure 219–22
    two-system comparison indicators *205*
international mobility and the
        psychological contract 19, 74–76
International Monetary Fund (IMF)
        x, 11, 216, 223
international reward systems 145–47

international training 108–22
    briefing 109–10
    cross-cultural awareness training 114–17
    language training 112–14
    pre-assignment visits 110–12
internationally capable executives
        93–94
Itagaki, H 206, 209, 212, 232

Jackson, S E 143, 181
Jackson, T 4, 22
Japan 27, 80, 173, 175, 186, 209,
        216–18, 225, 242
    and communication 61
    and investment in Malaysia
        216–18
Javidan, M 240, 248
Jensen, M C 13, 22

Kaldor, M 29, 45
Kamoche, K 202, 232
Katz, H C 43, 45, 220, 225, *226*, 232
Keenoy, T 222, 228, 232
Kessler, I 140, 141, 180
Kittel, B 204, 233
Kleinknecht, A 40, 46
Knudsen, H 223, 228, 232
Kochan, T 220, 232
Kolb, D 123, 135
Kuwahara, Y 154, 180

labour as human capital 15
Lane, C 225, 232
Lansbury, R 204, 223, 227, 229, 230, 232
language training 71, 112–14
    as coping mechanism 71
    assignees' children and local
        schools 113
    business language 114
    cultural differences 114
Lawler, E E 167, 180
leadership development 240–43
    enfolding approach 242
    redefining accountability 240
    transactional approaches 241
Lee, C 215, 232
Legge, K 26, 46, 222, 232
life events/adaptation skills 95–96
    personality factors 96
    predominant coping styles 96
local national employees: reward/
        compensation strategies 166–70

geographical diversity in reward
    issues 167
local training and development 131–33
    of local nationals 132–33
    of third-country nationals (TCNs) 133
    off-shoring 132
Lovell-Hawker, D 72–73, 77
Lowe, K B 145, 146, 173, 174, 175, 176, 180
Lusk, E 140, 181

McDonald, F 32, 46
McKenna, B 28, 31, 35, 46
McKersie, R B 220, 232
Mackie, B 16, 22
McSweeney, B 57, 77
Mahony 138, 143
Makin, P 74, 77
March, J G 13, 22
Markey, R 222, 223, 231, 232
Marsden, D 10, 22, 142, 180
Marton, F 110, 115, 120, 135
Maund, L 66, 77
Meckling, W H 13, 22
Mendenhall, M 115, 120, 135
Milkman, R 230, 232
Milkovich, G T 12, 22, 138, 143, 144, 145,
    146, 154, 168, 171, 176, 179
Min, D 224, 233
Mitra, A 13, 22, 171, 179
Monat, J 223, 232
Moore, M J 99, 105
Musa, E A 223, 232

networked knowledge management 145
Ng, C H 33, 46
Nielsen, J 26, 46
Nohri, N 144, 181
Nord, W R 240, 248
Nordhaug, O 82, 105

Oberg, K 64, 65, 77
Oddou, G 115, 135
O'Donnell, S 146, 181
offshoring 81, 132
Olsen, J P 13, 22
Organization Resources Counselors
    (ORC) 112, 135, 158, 180, 186, 190,
    191, 192, 194
organization theorists 29
organizational resource
    internationalization 81

Ozbilgin, M 4, 22

Parkinson, J 34, 46
pensions 189, 197
performance-based employment
    relationship 16
Perkins, S J 6, 9, 10, 16, 22, 44, 143, 148,
    149, 152, 153, 162, 172, 179, 180, 181
Perlmutter, H V 33, 46, 88, 89, 105, 106,
    123, 135, 172, 181, 202, 232
Personnel Management Associations,
    World Federation of 237
polycentric stage: global development 124
Poole, M 204, 212, 223, 224, 232
Porter, M 12
Prahalad, C K 108, 135, 152, 180
Preston, J 145, 181
psychological contract and international
    mobility 74–76
public finance, globalization of 31
Pucik, V 4, 22
Purcell, J 5, 17, 18, 22, 26, 46

questions for reflection/discussion
    (on) 20–21
    cultural issues 76
    employment relations 229
    globalization 43
    international employee resourcing
        104–05
    leadership development and
        reward 246
    managing change 245–46
    measuring HR effectiveness 246–47
    reward management 179
    training and development: global and
        local 134

Rahe, E M 67, 77
Ramsden, P 110, 120, 135
references 21–23, 44–47, 77,
    105–06, 135–36, 179–81,
    230–33, 247–48
regiocentric development model 124
Rehu, M 140, 168, 181
repatriation 71–73, 91, 99, 100–02, 121, 128
    see also definitions
    briefing prior to 110
    and cultural factors 102
    debriefing: operational, personal and
        critical incident 72–73

employee assistance programmes
  (EAPs) 72
and job security 99
and localization of international
  assignees 80
of international assignees 100–02
  career counselling 101
  support on assignment 101–02
and pre-repatriation visits 112
and reverse culture shock 72–73, 121
research (into/on)
  culture (IBM) 55–56
  global pay strategy 138
  reward systems management 146
  selection process for internationally
    mobile employment 96–99
  stress (UCL/CBI) 67, 68–69, 70
  women and international
    assignments 99–100
resourcing global business operations
  79–106
  conclusion 103–04
  employee resource internationalization/
    organization process 81–83
    cultural/cross-cultural
      differences 82
    foreign takeover 81–82
    greenfield startup 81
    joint ventures 82
  international competencies,
    specifying 92–95
  international executive capabilities,
    identifying 92
  increasing pace of
    internationalization 81
  international executive
    recruitment 90–91
    cross-cultural sensitivity 91
    dual careers/family issues 91
    graduate recruitment
      programmes 91
  international leadership resourcing:
    the international cadre 87–90
    defining multinational career
      paths 88
    ethnocentric approach 88–89
    frameworks and models 88
    parent country nationals (PCNs) 89
    transnationals 87
  internationally mobile employment
    selection process 96–99

recommendations 96–97
selection tools 97–99
localization of assignees 102–03
psychological research on international
  adaptation 95–96
  life events/adaptation skills
    95–96 *see also main entry*
references 105–06
repatriation of internationally assigned
  employees 100–02 *see also*
  repatriation
strategic international investments,
  managing 83–86
  strategic themes 84, *85*
women and international
  assignments 99–100
resource-based theory 13, 14
reverse culture shock 72–73, 101, 121
reward management 140–43,
  154–55, 176, 240 *see also* international
  reward systems
  choices and consequences 140
  delivery format 141–43
  and multinational employees 147
  national values and reward
    systems 144–45
  team pay, gainsharing, profit-sharing 141
  theory 140
reward practices, transnational 173–76
  benefits 175
  best practices 176
  long-term emphasis in pay 175
  pay incentives 173–74
  seniority 175–76
reward strategies: internationally mobile
  executives 155–62, *162*, 163–64
  assignment policies: development
    principles 156–57
  assignment policies: documentation and
    detail 157–58
  designing/redesigning policy 161
  expatriate effort-reward bargaining:
    socio-political context 159
  expatriation remuneration systems in
    practice 163, *163–64*, 164
  international policy objectives 160–61
reward systems 144–47, 166–70
  geographical diversity in
    167–69, *169*, 170
    Asia-Pacific 167
    Europe 167
    Latin America 167

international 145–47
local national employees 166–70
multinational employees 154–55
third-country nationals (TCNs) 165
reward–effort bargain 20
Richardson, K 112, 135
Rigby, S 16, 22
Riusala, K 125, 135
Rosebaum, R 68, 77
Rosenzweig, P 144, 181
Roth, K 146, 181
Rousseau 126
Rowley, C 27, 46
rules-based employment relations
systems 220

Scarborough, H 145, 181
Schein, E H 121, 135
Schendel, D E 84, 105
Schön, D A 121, 135
Schrecker, C 26, 45
Schuler, R S 26, 46, 111, 135, 48, 181
Scullion, H 4, 23
selection methods: internationally mobile
employment 97–99
Selmer, J 125, 135
Seyle, 66
Shamir, B 240, 247
shareholder value-based management
(SHV) 225
Shortland, S 71, 77, 99, 100, 102, 105, 106,
115, 117, 121, 122, 135, 159, 181
Shuster, J R 167, 168, 169, 170, 176, 181
SIHRM: choices and consequence(s) 3–23
competing international managerial
streams 9–12
conceptualizing strategic choice making
and its consequences 12–16
agency theory 13–14, 15
governance strategy 15–16
institutional theory 14
resource-based theory 13, 14,
strategy, interpretations of 12–13
transactional cost theory 13, 15
workforce 15
defining 6–9 see also definitions
material influences 16, 17, 17
boundary tensions 16
corporate governance 16–17
performance-based employment
relationship 16
systems theory 16

note 21
references 21–23
summary 17–18
SIHRM policy making 11
SIHRM trends and priorities 235–48
change management 238–39, 245
conclusion 244–45
global consensus on top HR
issues 235–38
leadership development 240–43, 246
measuring HR effectiveness 243–44,
246–47
note 247
references 247–48
Silverman, D 4, 23
Simons, G F 224, 233
Siu, N Y M 33, 46
social security 195, 198
socialization 10–11
Soskice, D 19, 22, 204, 231
Sparrow, P 4, 22, 26, 45, 90, 106, 143, 166,
167, 181, 222, 231
Stanford, N 239, 248
Stoll, K 66, 77
strategic HRD: local training and
development see local training and
development
strategic international human resource
management see SIHRM
Streek, W 224, 233
stress 95–96, 101, 112 see also culture and
welfare and international
assignments and stress
subjectivities, individual 11
Suutari, V 125, 135
Swan, J 145, 181
Sweden and culture measurement 60, 61
systems theory 16

tax 187, 194, 198
Teague, P 224, 225, 233
technical appendices 182–99
guiding principles for expatriation: the
10-stage journey 182–84
international assignee remuneration
approaches see main entry
international contracts/the global
employment company (GEC)
see main entry
Teulings, A 6, 9, 23
theorizing globalization and HRM 20

third-country nationals (TCNs)
133, 139
rewards for   165–66
Thomas, H   220, 233
Todd, P   11, 21, 229, 230
Toh, S M   139, 181
Torbiörn, I   65, 77
Townley, B   203, 224, 233
trade unions   213, 214–215, 217, 219, 223,
226, 227
training and development, global   19,
107–36
conclusion   133–34
cross-cultural awareness training   114
culture shock training   120–22
international development
122–31 see also main entry
international training   108–22
see also main entry
language training   112–14
see also main entry
local training and development   131–33
see also main entry
pre-assignment visits   110–12
references   135–36
transaction cost management   13
transactional cost theory   13, 15
transnational employment relations   221
transplantation issues   220
Traxler, F   204, 220, 221, 233
Triandis, H C   57, 58, 77
Trompenaars, F   55, 56, 62, 77, 98, 106,
114, 136
Tung, R L   115, 120, 125, 136
Tüselmann, H-J   32, 46

Ulman, L   224
Ulrich, D   238, 244, 248
United Kingdom   35, 59, 98, 116, 178, 191,
221–22
culture measurement   60

low context culture   61
market equity system   35
United States of America   27, 59, 98, 116,
173, 174, 175, 177, 186, 193, 209,214,
216, 218, 225, 241
culture measurement   56, 61
employment relations style   224
hegemony   32
imperialism   31
investment in Malaysia   216–18
management style   42
unilateralism   32, 41

Valenzuela, J   213, 217, 221, 233
van Hoof, J   221, 233
Van Ruitenbeek, D   74, 77
Van Ruysseveldt, J   4, 22, 221, 233
Vernon, G   220, 221, 233
Visser, J   226, 233
Von Glinow, M A   240, 248

Wailes, N   204, 223, 229, 230, 232
Wallerstein, I   81, 106
Walton, J   124, 131, 136
Watson, M   5, 7, 11, 23, 27, 47
Welch, D E   4, 22, 111, 135, 162, 180, 185
Wheeler, H N   220, 232
White, G   141, 142, 180
Whitley, R   16, 23, 212, 233
Whittington, R   12, 23
Williamson, O E   13, 23
Wolff, B   140, 181
women expatriates/international
assignees   99–100
World Bank   x, 11, 216, 223
Wright, M   6, 13, 23

Yu, P W   116–17, 118–19, 136

Zingheim, P   167, 168, 169, 170 176, 181
Zuleta, L   138–39